Library of
Davidson College

"ANTIKE ROMAN"

"ANTIKE ROMAN"

POWER SYMBOLOGY AND
THE ROMAN PLAY IN
EARLY MODERN ENGLAND,
1585–1635

Clifford Ronan

The University of Georgia Press   Athens and London

© 1995 by the University of Georgia Press
Athens, Georgia 30602
All rights reserved
Designed by Erin Kirk New
Set in ten on fourteen Galliard by Tseng Information Systems, Inc.
Printed and bound by Thomson-Shore, Inc.
The paper in this book meets the guidelines for
permanence and durability of the Committee on
Production Guidelines for Book Longevity of the
Council on Library Resources.

Printed in the United States of America

99 98 97 96 95 C 5 4 3 2 1

Library of Congress Cataloging in Publication Data

Ronan, Clifford.
"Antike Roman" : power symbology and the Roman play in early
modern England, 1585–1635 / Clifford Ronan.
p. cm.
Includes bibliographical references (p.) and index.
ISBN 0-8203-1672-5 (alk. paper)
1. English drama—Roman influences.   2. English drama—Early
modern and Elizabethan, 1500–1600—History and criticism.
3. Politics and literature—England—History—17th century.
4. Politics and literature—England—History—16th century.
5. English drama—17th century—History and criticism.
6. Historical drama, English—History and criticism.   7. Political
plays, English—History and criticism.   8. Shakespeare, William,
1564–1616—Knowledge—Rome.   9. Power (Social sciences) in
literature.   10. Rome—In literature.
PR127.R66   1995
822'.051409003—dc20   94-7604

British Library Cataloging in Publication Data available

for Denise

I am more an Antike Roman than a Dane.

SHAKESPEARE
Hamlet Folio

CONTENTS

Preface   xi

Introduction: "Antike" Rome and the Renascent *Fabula Praetexta*   1

Part 1. Anachronism, Politics, and the Antike

Chapter 1. Anachronism and Stage Roman Times   11

Chapter 2. *Rhomé:* Power, Place, Politics   36

Part 2. Playing Stoics and Tyrant-Kings

Chapter 3. *Nobilitas* and *Majestas:* Munificence, Clemency, and Sensitivity to Slight   65

Chapter 4. Suicide and the Dynamics of Stoical *Constantia*   87

Chapter 5. *Superbia:* Insulting, Aquiline, Overmounting Pride   108

Chapter 6. *Saevitia:* Wolves, Demons, Parricides, and Self-Corrosion   125

Afterword: Stage Rome and the Romanized Plays   151

Appendix A. Short-title Descriptive List of Extant Secular Roman Plays in English, 1497–1651   165

Appendix B. The Tudor-Stuart Roman Play: A Survey   171

Tables   175

Notes   187

Works Consulted   197

Index   223

PREFACE

This book could never have been written without the patience and help of my loving wife, Denise, and our children, David and Michelle. For a leave of absence and material resources, I wish to add thanks to my professional family at Southwest Texas State University: to the Faculty Senate, the administration, the Alkek Library, and in particular my supportive colleagues in the Department of English. I am grateful too to the National Endowment for the Humanities for a summer seminar at the University of California, Berkeley, and to the gracious library staff there, at my own institution, and at others where I have worked, especially the Bibliothèque Nationale, Bodleian Library, British Library, Harvard University, Jagiellonian University, Shakespeare Institute, University of London, and University of Texas at Austin.

I am thankful for the processes of review and discussion that are fostered by scholarly conferences, journals, and presses. For kind permission to reiterate in these pages arguments broached by me in previously published essays, I wish to thank the AMS Press, the University Press of America, and the editors of *Classical and Modern Literature, Comparative Drama, Hamlet Studies, Medieval and Renaissance Drama in England,* and *Shakespeare Studies*. I am especially grateful also to the University of Georgia Press: to my indefatigable copy editor Ellen Harris, and project editor Kelly Caudle; to Nancy Grayson Holmes, Liz Makowski, Karen Orchard; and to the most helpful of Press referees, the anonymous readers of my manuscript.

It is impossible to specify correctly the precise nature and degree of one's scholarly debts. But I can never forget the written models and sustained encouragement of Norman Rabkin, Jonas Barish, Willard Farnham, and, later, John Velz, R. J. Kaufmann, Robert Miola, and Jean MacIntyre;

nor the fascinating discussions of anachronism and allied subjects with Matthew Wikander, Stephen Orgel, David Kranz, and Phyllis Rackin. To make the survey of Renaissance *Romanitas* in the pages following, I have obviously had to examine and profit from scholarship to which I have not expressly referred. Doubtless, too, I have not sufficiently meditated upon or reflected prior scholars' opinions and findings, and have therefore fallen into errors that another author could well have escaped. For such errors of negligence and simple ignorance, I can only ask the reader's forbearance.

All dates and authors for works discussed in this book fall within the options presented in the Harbage and Schoenbaum *Annals of English Drama, 975–1700*. In order to roughly separate primary from secondary sources (except where secondary editorial comment is attached to a primary source), I have chosen to divide the bibliography into pre- and post-1800 items. For textual citation I have employed the most recent MLA suggestions with a few exceptions. I specify "F" or "Q" where I choose a variant reading different from the textual editor's choice. I follow the *Chicago Manual of Style* in silently adjusting the capitalization of the first word in quotations to fit the syntax of the sentence as a whole; any alterations in internal punctuation are enclosed in brackets. Another exception is my omitting of distinctions among lines, sections, and pages when the mode of citation is easily inferred from the edition used. For example, "I.i, 3–8" indicates either lines 3–8 or pages 3–8 that happen to be in I.i; similarly, "42, 100" would indicate line 100 of a continuously calibrated sequence of lines, this one happening to fall within stanza or section 42. In citing standard authors the subdivisions of whose works have a generic notation, I have tried to supply such notation. In citing classical authors, I have usually tried to cite the generic numbering of the Loeb Classical Library, whose Heinemann and Harvard University Press imprints are obvious in my list of chief works consulted.

When a translation is enclosed in single quotation marks, the phraseology is mine. My renderings are loose but normally designed to reflect etymological affinities and English cognates: for instance, *regium* and *munificum* could have been rendered "princely" and "handsome," but here they are characteristically translated "*king*like" and "*munific*ent."

Titles are recorded with normalized typography, punctuation, and capitalization; and abbreviated titles of the chief Roman plays discussed are provided in Appendix A. All italics except those for titles or foreign terms are mine and have been provided for emphasis. Greek type has been transliterated, and archaic Renaissance typography has been silently expanded or otherwise normalized to eliminate ligatures, diphthongs, sub- and superscript letters, the thorn and long *s, vv* for *w,* and abbreviations like ";" for *que* and "-" for *n*.

INTRODUCTION

"Antike" Rome and the Renascent *Fabula Praetexta*

> To put an Anticke disposition on.
>
> SHAKESPEARE
> *Hamlet* Folio

Every epoch has its favorite mythic kingdoms of the mind—the Saturnian Age, the Homeric Age, Camelot, Norse or Celtic twilights, America's Hollywood West. Scholars like T. J. B. Spencer, G. K. Hunter, and J. Leeds Barroll correctly emphasize that paradox-filled classical Rome loomed larger in the imagination of Early Modern Europeans than it does for us today. Herbert Lindenberger, student of the European history play, concludes that "among nonnational subjects, only Roman history could convince Elizabethans or French seventeenth century audiences of its essential continuity with their civilization" (9). Indeed, it is astonishing to calculate the sheer number and prestige of the authors who provided sixteenth- and seventeenth-century France and England with Ancient Roman characters and dramatic settings: Muret, Grévin, Garnier, Hardy, Corneille, Racine, Lodge, Dekker, Kyd, E. Campion, Shakespeare, Jonson, Chapman, Marston, W. Rowley, T. Heywood, Middleton, Drayton, Daniel, Greville, Munday, Alexander, May, Fletcher, Massinger, Dryden, Otway, Lee, Denham, Crowne, T. Killigrew, Rochester, Ravenscroft, Tate, several anonymous playwrights, and (if Aeneas be a "Roman") Marlowe and Nashe. In England the popularity of the Roman play continued unabated until Addison's *Cato* in 1713 (Nicoll 1: 85). After that, though demand for new "pseudoclassical" drama somewhat declined, revivals of several Roman plays were frequent. Modern works with Roman characters continued to be offered in England and abroad by such distinguished pens as those of Ibsen, Strindberg, Grillparzer, Shaw, Bridges, Masefield, Yeats, Dürrenmatt, Brecht.

Out of huge numbers of Medieval, Renaissance, and Neoclassical plays (titles of which are listed in table 4, at the back of this volume), some forty-three extant vernacular Roman plays date from the England of 1585–1635 (see Appendix A, also at the back). Most of this select group are serious works, as the rich earlier criticism has often surmised.[1] Two similarities of genre noted by Maurice Charney (207) in Shakespeare's three Plutarchan Roman tragedies extend in fact to most Roman plays: use of conventionalized upper-class (scarlet/purple) "Roman" costume, and use of episodes of pagan suicide, approached with a measure of sympathy. To Charney's genre characteristics of the Roman play, I would add that such works generally display tyrannical rage, war, public quarrels, and political debates. For these dramas are oriented toward a public male world, where martial, political, and forensic arts customarily predominate over sexuality and the tenderer, more stereotypically female concerns of affection and family. Though stage Romans are generally characterized by a proud inflexibility, Wilson Knight (*Imperial Theme* 63–95) shows that Shakepeare's Romans are associated with sparks and the warm blood of both impassioned friendship and lethal emulation. Charney too stresses the link between Rome and the harsh and inorganic, a proclivity for the cold, the stony, the metallic, and the man-made.

Many of the same motifs evident in the Roman plays are also to be found in the neighboring and overlapping genre of European Senecan tragedy, the career and Stoical roots of which Gordon Braden studies. Braden properly finds that the life of the Stoic is conceived in terms of theater, statuary, or military and athletic struggle. After tracing the blasphemous pride of the illeistic self-crowning Stoic man, Braden sketches his view of how the self-mastery and *apatheia* of the Stoic relate to tempestuous Roman politics, with its paradoxically paired emphasis on clemency and self-destruction. The Stoic sage delineated in Seneca's essays and the monomaniacal madman in Seneca's tragedies "can be seen as limiting versions of a single style of selfhood" (Braden 85): prideful, self-willed, and (despite linguistic anachronism) imperialistic—ready to conquer and lay waste kingdoms without and within. Other issues in Stoic moral casuistry (on which Braden is less useful) are the teaching mission in Stoic individualism and the attitude toward sadism.

The propensities of the whole civilized/barbaric Roman nation are symbolized in ambivalence and dichotomy: the mighty Roman is a system of testy fire and stony or metallic restraint; and the national totems include not just the marauding—and nurturing—wolf but also the predatory eagle and Mars's horse, ambivalently symbolizing war, command, and unbridled lust. Revealingly, many of the Romans in the surviving three or so dozen English Roman noncomedies express their mad self-determination in conventional displays of verbal and physical "insul[t]ment" (*Cymbeline* III.v.140), a custom that many stage triumphers hope will propel them *ad sidera* but that instead often drags them toward the demonic.

Rome was the essence of power, yet troubled by powerlessness. When Renaissance writers dissected the *dignitas, integritas,* and *constantia* of the stereotypical Roman, they more than once found the famous national *virtus* coming up deficient. Anne Barton correctly writes that Jonson's Sejanus seems "as hollow as his own statue in the theatre of Pompey, unreal, and despite the carnage he wreaks, always verging on the absurd" (*Jonson* 97). And there are many greater and more tragic stage Romans who convey analogous voids—a danger to which public figures in any society seem particularly subject. The hero of *Coriolanus* reveals an extraordinary emotional emptiness as he plans the death of his country and compatriots over a trivial "chance," "some trick not worth an egg" (IV.iv.20–21). So too, in Shakespeare's *Caesar* it is not just Cassius who is one of the histrionic "hollow men," employing the "*tricks*" and "gallant show" of "enforced ceremony" (IV.ii.20–23; Ronan, "Incised"). Almost all the cast is susceptible to the empty, the merely theatrical, and the unintentionally antic.

Several Roman plays press, as *Hamlet* does, questions about the double problem of *acting*. What defines us? Are we inevitably (as one dramatist put it) the deed's creatures? What faces must we put on in order to act well? Truth and heroism many times coexist unstably, and soldierly and Stoical self-restraint seem empty if engaged in largely for its own sake—as, say, the self-mutilation of Shakespeare's Portia seems to have been.

In 1553 the political writer and emblematist Guillaume de La Perrière dedicated to the prince-consort of the Huguenot court of Navarre a volume of prudential advice. In the sixty-fifth emblem, (fig. 1), the author urges judicious silence by depicting a dancing jester and a dying viper. To the side of the pictura is the edge of a handsome city, containing an obelisk or spire and, apparently, an amphitheater with Roman arcade. The Latin and French verses of the emblem emphasize that 'he who talks too much arranges for his own death' ("Qui parle trop se prepare à la mort").[2]

Silence would certainly be a self-preserving virtue for Protestants in mid-sixteenth-century France. The jester represents someone with relatively great freedom of speech, but his proximity to the viper and to the admonitory verses suggests that dignity, safety, and free speech can never for long coexist.

The female pit viper of legend is an oversexed female who dies as her children eat their way out of her belly. Quite frequently, as we shall see in a later chapter, she becomes a traditional icon of civil war. Juxtaposition of the city and the viper together in the same emblem suggests a stress on the social and political dimension of speech. Talking is not simply something that can put one in jail or make one lose his life, but is a more basic part of the fabric of family and communal life. Perhaps the Roman-looking cityscape hints at a problem in Roman society as a whole: the excessive desire to speak, which ultimately encouraged factionalism and a disruption of the life of the maternal *corpus politicum*.

If indeed these are among the implications of this emblem, it is appropriate that the seemingly anachronistic Renaissance jester, busy about his antics, should appear in this ancient context. For there were several reasons why early modern Europe would associate old Rome with jesters. Recent discovery of Nero's house, submerged beside the Colosseum, had popularized antic/antique designs (figs. 1, 2): "fantastic representations of human, animal, and floral forms, incongruously running into one another" (*OED*, s.v. "Antic"). And so a whole new sense developed of what came to be known as the "grotesque": that is, the sort of design buried in an antique grotto like Nero's.

We moderns often overlook the playfulness and garishness of Antiquity, thinking instead of weather-bleached white marble Doric columns, gleaming in the noonday Mediterranean sun. But to the Renaissance, Antiquity is also grotesquely comic, whether the morose and mordant humor of a Tacitus; the flamboyant sexual reportage of a Suetonius, Juvenal, or Catullus; the sniggling sadism of Lucan; or the mannerist wit of another Renaissance mainstream favorite, Ovid. The *Metamorphoses,* a modern classicist writes, reveals an author who "quite obviously delighted in the cruel, the macabre, and the gory"; the work is pervaded with "amused detachment, irony, parody, travesty, grotesque exaggeration, over-explicit visual detail, literary wit and allusiveness, incongruities jarring and subtle, bathos, and burlesque" (Galinsky 153). According to Ovid's account of Philomel's rape, the violator repeatedly ravishes the girl (his sister-in-law) even after he has torn out her tongue—an organ that flops about all during the rape, twitching at her feet like an injured snake and trying still to call out 'the name Father' ("nomen patris," *Metamorphoses* 6.558). We today are heirs of the eighteenth century, with its simplification of the *dignitas* of Antiquity and its decorums. Hence we seldom associate the classical with this sort of black comedy—nor with black magic, or the carnivalesque. But the Renaissance did.

Few moments in history have had a wider comic range than obtained on the Tudor-Stuart stage, and the favorite examples of Roman antics will be quite different for each modern reader or spectator. In Shakespeare, say, some will enjoy the placing of a Sextus Pompeius or General Lucius in a false position. Others will think of the droll Casca in *Caesar,* or jesting Enobarbus and Menenius, or the drunken Lepidus. In another register, there are the Roman crowds of *Caesar,* who rip out the heart of a man for not being married and having the wrong name. Then too, there are the satirical villains who regale audiences in *Welshman, False One,* and *Valentinian* with a Machiavellian history of politics. The first reaction of Lodge's Scilla (Sulla) to Young Marius's suicide is laughter, as it is also to the heavenly prayers of his other noble and virtuous enemies. Many stage-Roman heroes have undignified moments. Great Antony comes close to turning "strumpet's fool" when he forfeits his sword, clothes, and gender to his woman, or portrays himself running into death prematurely, like a sexually inexpert young bridegroom. Coriolanus mutely holds his mother's hand while the gods laugh. There is often an easy slide from integrity to pathetic absurdity, as when Shakespeare's Portia and Cassius lose heart, or Brutus needs to find someone with just the right academic and social background to hold the sword on which the general will impale himself. As Shakespeare well understood, in and out of the theater there were aspects of suicide that could transform it into "play[ing] the Roman *fool*" (*Macbeth* V.viii.1).

Critics make allowances for the antics of a mad Titus Andronicus or the grotesque creatures in Jonson's *Poetaster* but often balk at the supposed indecorum of Jonson's black-comic "ladies," who show equal concern with crime, power, sex, and cosmetics in *Sejanus* and *Catiline*. Practically all the imitations of Jonson's Roman plays also have their wildly undignified Roman royals: for instance, Richards's Messallina, Massinger's Domitian (and his ladies), various of May's and the anonymous author of *Nero*'s Romans— not to mention the demotic Emperor Maximinus of William Rowley. And much to the dismay of at least one distinguished modern critic (Lucas, *Webster* 1: 136), Thomas Heywood's noble Roman peer Valerius repeatedly sings bawdy songs during the rape of the heroine of *Lucrece*.

For us, *antic* and *antique* are no longer as they were for Spenser (Glasser, Evett) and Shakespeare (*Hamlet,* ed. Jenkins, 265): homonyms in search of a pun. Spenser, in his translation of du Bellay, yokes an architecturally serene "antique" Rome with some garishly dressed modern witch or resurrected corpse ("Ruines" 27, 365–78). Editors of *Hamlet* must confront the question of the "anticke" weapon of old Priam (Q2F II.ii.469, which Pope emended with "antique"). Is this sword, which impotently wags from his hand, antic or antique in the modern sense of these terms? And is it right to excise semantically significant ambiguity from original texts? Is there Antiquishness in Hamlet's wish to put an "Anticke disposition" on (F I.v.172)? Or does Hamlet see an anticness in suicide when he condemns Horatio's wish to play the "Antike Roman" (F V.ii.341)? Might not orthographic ambiguity have once pointed readers and actors to that paradoxical mixture of passion and restraint needed by both Hamlet and Horatio as they try to play, respectively (and sequentially), the madman and the suicide?

As the hero of *Coriolanus* notes, the supernatural backdrop and numinous atmosphere of Rome feels full of divine laughter at the "unnatural scene" that men play. Commencing at least with Lodge's characters and continuing with those of Shakespeare, Chapman, Jonson, and many more, we see a fruitless insistence that there are gods and that they communicate their displeasure with man through thunderstorms. The heavens rumble, but no human or god stops Scilla from dethroning a sitting consul, even though Scilla admits that his own is a fraudulent, "pretended [office of] state" (*Wounds* V.ii.119). It is sometimes hard to tell whether it is the Romans who are the gods' antics, or the gods who are the fools of the Romans.³

As an age of colonization and empire was launched, England found in Rome a glass where the island could behold its own image simultaneously civilized and barbarous, powerful and hollow. But English Roman plays are usually concerned too with the effect of time, fate, Providence, and Roman cultural traits on England's own development. Though most Roman dramas are anachronistic, intentionally or not, they also simultaneously strive to seem historical, sober, and serious. Thus they must have been felt to belong within a prestigious classical genre: the drama of Roman national history (MacCallum 11), the *fabula praetexta:* literally, 'story of the fringe [-robed upper-class Romans].' Of this genre there are eleven fragmentary Latin examples (Seneca, *Tragedies* 2: 401–5). The one complete survivor, the pseudo-Senecan *Octavia,* depicts Nero's selfishly discarding one wife for another and was very well known in the sixteenth and seventeenth centuries (Monteverdi's *L'incoronazione di Poppea* is a musical version).

To write a Roman history play must have been a central humanist endeavor: a re-representing of the genre in which Rome itself re-presents its history. Indeed, such plays often constitute an important effort to compete with, surpass, and otherwise evaluate a civilization that many people in Early Modern Europe believed could experience a renaissance. To challenge the *fabulae praetextae* in one's own modern theatrical language, and linguistic and poetic tongue, was to confront the basic Renaissance issues of continuity, discontinuity, and mutability. More specifically, it was to problematize the topicality of anachronism, the inertness in archaeological fact, and the very possibility of cultural death and resurrection.

PART ONE

ANACHRONISM, POLITICS, AND THE ANTIKE

It hath pleased God to ordaine and illustrate two exemplar States of the worlde, for Armes, learning, Morall Vertue, Policie, and Lawes. The State of Grecia, and the State of Rome.

BACON
Advancement of Learning

CHAPTER ONE

Anachronism and Stage Roman Times

> All things that now are, have been heretofore
> much after the same sort, and after the same fashion
> that now they are: and so to think of those things
> which shall be hereafter also. Moreover, whole dramata,
> and uniform scenes . . . are all but after one sort and
> fashion: only . . . the actors were others.
>
> MARCUS AURELIUS
> *Meditations*

The ending of a fictional tragedy, tragicomedy, or comedy is more thoroughly determined by internal considerations like genre than are the ends of history plays. Because "real" history has continued after the denouement of historical plays, such dramas are suffused with a special kind of irony. The better to understand how this works, it is useful to turn to a French painter's treatment of Roman history.

Caron and Simultaneity

Caron's *Massacres of the Triumvirate* (fig. 3) displays the magnificent city of Rome, with some of its most famous statues and splendid monuments in full view. But the city itself is partially in flames, and small figures suicidally plunge from a building and a bridge, while numerous soldiers kill and mutilate the population. The picture is a triptych, the far edges held down by sorrowing females who futilely pray to the Powers on high. The three divisions of the painting are demarcated by the famous Apollo Belvedere and the Hercules (actually Commodus as Hercules) nurturing the infant Telephon. Yet neither Apollonian mind nor Herculean heart and force are guiding the human figures in this Rome. No trash or litter sullies Rome's gorgeous streets, only scattered decapitated trunks the heads of which are now strung up in an orderly line with scarcely an anachronistic lock, French mustache, or Renaissance beard out of place. The massacre has not dirtied the murderous soldiers or made them sacrifice their gracefulness and poise; nor does any one of them have a wrinkle in his gold braid, his pretty embroidered hose, or his shimmering body shirt of gold, pink, burgundy, sea green, or robin's-egg blue. In the foreground an immaculately dressed soldier has his hand deep within the breast cavity of a grayish cadaver, yanking out the victim's heart in a variation of a traditional iconographic symbol for civil war. In the heavens a cluster of red horses races across the sky, whipped by (Mars's?) red horsemen (fig. 3a). At the upper center of the canvas, just below the serene Pantheon, Temple of All Gods, the Triumvirs sit in state in the Flavian amphitheater, variously called Vespasian's or the Colosseum. They await the centurion Lerna, who brings Antony the grisly head and carbonadoed hands of the newly executed Cicero. Everywhere are the inescapable contrasts between Roman order and disorder, between Roman dedication to the arts—architectural, literary, political, military—and Roman entanglement with barbarity and inhuman powers. Rationality encloses, nurtures, and perpetuates the demonic, savage, and feral in Roman life. And perhaps the reverse is also true. To Caron, the extraordinary proscription and the Colosseum's customary homicidal sports are mere variants of a single urge: the predictable attraction of civilized Rome toward disorderly violence.

The painting pays as much attention to Caron's own time as to Antiquity. Not a single severed head is clean shaven as in the popular Antique fashion, but most have been to a French barber. And the choice of Roman buildings includes a Medieval belfrey, Michelangelo's staircase for the Capidoglio (middleground, right), and an adaptation of a famous new French staircase (middleground, center) created in 'homage to the antiquizing [*antiquisante*] French architecture' of de l'Orme (Scailléirez 2; Ehrmann 180). It is an obvious departure from history and realism to seat the Triumvirs in a structure depicted half built, or half destroyed. In 43 B.C. the Colosseum was a century away from being constructed, and a millennium and a half away from being deconstructed to provide material for the palatial and ecclesiastical programs of Renaissance Rome. Like the classical ruins dotting Renaissance painters' Nativities, the truncated Colosseum reminds viewers not just of the vagaries of Ovid's all-devouring *Tempus edax* but also of the passing of the pagan epoch.

Caron is no Michelangelo, and his *Massacres* used to be unfairly dismissed as a mere record of court ballets (Murray 143). This view is an interesting error that points to this painting's meta-artistic anachronisms. Furthermore, the delicate costuming of his soldiers indeed hints at the proximity of court ritual to brutal street murder. The theatricality, like the other anachronisms and anachorisms in the picture, intensifies the artist's intentionally outrageous combination of attitudes toward Roman achievement and the achievements promised to France as it walks in the factious Romans' footsteps.

The painting is in a secular subgenre of massacres, the most famous examples of which depict Herod's Slaughter of the Innocents in Bethlehem. Works in Caron's subgenre are usually political and appear in inventories of, or are otherwise mentioned by, prominent members of both faiths in France. Sometimes the subjects are imagined, as with Caron's; and at other times the paintings are documentary reportage, as with Dubois d'Amiens's *Massacre of Saint Bartholomew* (1572, Musée Cantonal, Lausanne). Though Caron's piece predates that horrible subject, he does predict it, even down to the mixture of pageant and gore: for this day of slaughter occurred when the Protestant and Catholic aristocracy had gathered in Paris to celebrate a supposedly ecumenical royal marriage. Although Caron's allegiances were Catholic and royalist, his painting is not narrowly partisan. Instead it seems to preach to all sides the need to break out of the tragically absurd cycle of vengeful barbarity.

The Taxonomy of Anachronism

Anachronism, however it may be regarded by art historians, has not until recently been embraced by critics of Tudor-Stuart drama. Hitherto it has been treated either as an unintended joke or, as in Dr. Johnson's remarks on Shakespeare's Romans, as an irrelevancy. Even within the past half-dozen years, we still find a scholar taking Shakespeare to task for letting his Romans use, with an anachronistically interior sense, *noble* and *honorable*

(Miles 274–78): and thereby failing "to understand why his Roman subjects identified public performance and personal worth as persistently and as completely as they did" (282). More helpful perspectives on anachronism have been provided by Sigurd Burckhardt, Thomas Greene, Philip J. Ayres, Richard Hillman, Matthew Wikander, and Phyllis Rackin. Ayres, for instance, shows Jonson appealing to James's dynastic views by pretending to find prestigious precedent for them in the Julio-Claudian succession. Given the like of Tiberius and Nero, Jonson's play must here have done as much to problematize the English kingship succession as to endorse and defend it among people with even an elementary historical education.

Spectators come to historical drama, especially an English national one, in relative innocence, wondering what happened Back Then but soon finding themselves implicated in a metahistorical search. Elizabethans approached history plays with an attitude of emulative "nostalgia" (Rackin 122; cf. K. Burke, Pigman), an ingenuous and illogical urge to discover and reclaim their personal essence through recovering their nation's roots. But as Rackin explains, the playwright's use of metadrama problematizes both the quest and history itself. Meanwhile, the audience is encouraged to associate with the characters and to project itself into their situations. The upshot is contamination: spectators take political sides and incur guilt alongside the rebels and bad governors depicted onstage. Instead of providing an audience with the expected escape from a confused Early Modern Now into an attractively and logically analyzed Then, the play makes the Then a Now that urgently must be dealt with.

Dramas about Ancient pagan Rome evoke less Elizabethan audience identification and fewer moral scruples than English histories do, but Roman plays certainly deliver exhilaration, pathos, and tragedy. Here is the story of a civilization exhilarating because it carved for itself a life after death, a story pitiable not only because the culture died, but also because, when it lived, it seemed doomed to a repetitious, circular course.

For both Antiquity and the Early Modern era, Rome represented a short-term eternity—blasphemous or boring to some, challenging or reassuring to others. A dyspeptic author of the Geneva glosses at Revelation 17:14 duly notes that "no man can but marvaile" that Rome could "stand and hold out, in many mutations" from the time of Romulus to those of the popes. More enthusiastic is the voice of Horace, who in a poem imitated repeatedly throughout Renaissance Europe, tells his muse to take pride (*superbiam*) in his accomplishments. For though a poor boy from a rural locality, he has transferred Greek poetry into Latin, crafting for himself a little bit of immortality that will withstand time and weather. It will last for as long as the Roman pontiff and the vestal virgin ceremonially climb the steps of the Capitol, longer, in fact, than monuments of bronze last, or royal pyramids:

> Exegi monumentum aere perennius
> regalique situ pyramidum altius.
> *(Odes* 3.30)

As we shall see in succeeding chapters, poetry helped to give Rome *room* in the Early Modern English mind:

> Not marble nor the gilded monuments
> Of princes shall outlive this pow'rful rhyme,
> . . . .
> your praise shall still find *room,*
> Even in the eyes of all posterity
> That wear this world out to the ending doom.
> (Shakespeare, Sonnet 55)

Shakespeare finds new uses for the old words and thoughts, but still the sense of filiation persists, and with it the excitement of seeing that Horace has somehow triumphed over time and his own body, artistically *inscribing* himself and his message on the pages of history.

As for the tragic side of the Roman experience, G. W. Trompi's study of historical occurrence is instructive. He maintains that until at least the Reformation, Christian views of history are almost as circular as the views of pagans. Certainly, the history in most Renaissance Roman plays does not embody the linear view that some scholars maintain is the norm in Judaism and Christianity. Instead, these dramas project a society with an unchanging system of antithetical tensions: between civilization and barbarity, between tyranny and violent individualistic assertions of freedom, between factiousness and amity. And these dichotomies, in turn, make for Fortune's predictable cycle of actions and reactions, all contributing to a secular Tragedy of Man.

We shall see in the next chapter the extreme care that authors of Tudor-Stuart Roman plays take to refer frequently to the city-nation, to nationality, and to the place that identifies them. In literature as in life, place defines time and is in turn defined by it. For time is measured by the extent and motion of matter through space (cf. Čapek 389). The philosophic linkage in these concepts encouraged twentieth-century physics to invent the term *chronotope*, which Mikhail Bakhtin (84) borrowed for literary criticism a half century ago to signify time-place, the stopping of time in a given historical setting.

All literature employs multiple chronotopes simultaneously, though with an ever-varying configuration of emphases. Multiple chronotopes inhere in several familiar literary categories: quite obviously in allusion, typology, and intertextuality, but also in sequence, foreshadowing, dramatic irony, and all iterative motifs that ask us to move mentally from one time and place to somewhere, and some time, else. By the fact of physical presentation on stage, dramatic literature readily sensitizes its audiences to this chronotopic multiplicity in numerous ways. When characters take pauses, or dialogue and action are suspended in moments of scene change, spectators have time for personal reflection, including a sense of the chasm between their own world and that depicted on stage. During absorbing moments in the play, spectators can be involuntarily brought back to the mundane world by distractions—the cough or chatter of another spectator, or a loud noise from beyond the theater. The most interesting moments to analyze, however, are those when the dramatist prompts a spectator to travel from the play's chief historical chronotope to some present-day or eternal one. As with much classical Greek and Latin literature, Elizabethan and Stuart historical dramas are designed for spectators acquainted with the broad sweep of the stories. Such works provided the original audiences not only with advice and narrative information but also with the aesthetic pleasure of ironical endings—a sense that Clytemnestra will not escape unscathed and that destiny and Achaean survival finally preclude a Neoptolemus or Odysseus from being disastrously candid with a Philoctetes.

The Renaissance, a time of growing historical sophistication, invented the term *anachronism* (Rackin 91 nn. 12, 13), but certainly recognized that intentional anachronism had been a tradition for thousands of years. Vergil's Trojan hero of Homeric times, Anchises, prophesies the future of his progeny and addresses his son, Aeneas, as *Romane*. To any historically aware person, a moment's reflection would have revealed that this name was formed from that of Aeneas's descendant (Vergil, *Aeneid* 6.851)—a case of naming a person after his own great-great-grandson, as it were. At the very fountainhead of Western drama, Aeschylus makes his Archaic royalty familiar with such later Athenian inventions as rule by assembly (*Suppliants* 365–75) and the blood-guilt jury (*Eumenides* 59–67). In *Thyestes* (459–67), Seneca's titular hero is ostentatiously closer to the time of Caligula and Nero than that of the Trojan Wars. Thyestes shows an imperial Roman's familiarity with marine and littoral engineering, mechanical steam baths, the international gourmet trade, and kings whose altars displace those of Jove himself—a blasphemy of which no Greek potentate would be guilty, though several Roman ones were. Seneca's archaic Greeks are as well acquainted as Nero's Romans are with the Danube, the Spanish Tagus, the Red Sea, the grain fields of North Africa, the Armenians, the Chinese/ Seres, and even Rome's greatest enemy, the Parthians, who would not form a nation until many hundreds of years later (Frye). To insert an anachronism in a Renaissance Roman play must have seemed to write in an Antique manner.

The chronotopes of Early Modern drama reflect a Medieval as well as an Ancient heritage. Erich Auerbach (161–62) and Lawrence J. Ross (209) remind us of the "omnitemporalness" and Medieval feel of place and setting in such works. In England these plays long portrayed Romans like Augustus, Pilate, Tiberius, or Roman torturers in an anachoristic or anachronistic fashion, suggestive both of stage paynims and contemporary English bullies. The line separating a Roman tyrant from a Jewish Herod or Mohammed's favorite devil is often exceedingly fine. Romans, like other stage torturers, exist to satirize authority figures of the audience's own world, for they know far too much about names and places in that world (William 37, 51).

Sometimes such plays give half-serious witness to historic Rome's power, but the testimony may be designed to embody or convey something more flamboyant than historical fact. The Chester "Octavyan," for instance, governs the Roman Empire through something like voodoo dolls. Interest in local Roman color continues in a later Octavian play from France (*Mistère* 6.180–82). Here two senators bear the unintentionally amusing names of Cathiline and Cassius and amicably discuss with Octavien the murderous revolt of Brute and the heroism of the suicidal Cathon and Porcia. A late Medieval English pageant shows a better-informed interest in Roman politics and in Rome's complex paratactic connections with Christian chronotopes. The occasion is a Nine Worthies show in 1455, welcoming to Coventry Henry VI's queen, Margaret.

> I Julius Caesar soverayn of knyghthode
> and emperour of mortall men most hegh & myghty
> Welcum you prynces most benygne & gode
> Of quenes that byn crowned so high non knowe I
> the same blessyd blossom that spronge of your body
> Shall succede me in worship I wyll it be so
> all the landis olyve shall obey hym un to.
> (Worthies Pageant, *Coventry Leet Book* for 1455)

Terms like "blessyd blossom" and "benygne . . . quenes . . . so high" are usually reserved for a flower-decked Madonna and Child. Yet like Mary, Margaret is implicitly associated not only with flowers (particularly the marguerite) but also with Jerusalem. Because Margaret's father styled himself the king of Jerusalem, the Worthy Caesar's enthusiasm for Roman imperialism spills over into an implicit celebration of the Christian goals of the royal house of Jerusalem, of Joachimite apocalyptics (Reeves), and of various English patriots. Margaret's "blossom," the ill-fated Edward, has come into the world in the very year that the Second Rome, Constantinople, fell. The audience would sense that the play-Caesar wishes for the infant Plantagenet a future that denies the immediate past and reinstates versions of more ancient ones. Edward is being cast as the new conquering King Godfrey de Bouillon, who as the Crusader ruler of Jerusalem became the Ninth Worthy. On behalf of the "landis" that have just fallen to the Turk, Caesar is also predicting that Edward will become the successful leader of an ultimate crusade to regain the East; thereby Edward may implicitly become a "blessyd" *imitatio Christi,* the Tenth Champion of the secular tradition, or the Universal Emperor in Joachim's version of the Last Days.

Analogues to this portion of the Coventry Welcome can be found in many Tudor-Stuart Roman plays, but preeminently in Shakespeare's

Antony. Time in this golden tragedy shimmers iridescently, like shot silk: "the present is . . . distanced and appraised, and the past made uncomfortably alive by this duality of time, which characterizes the Shakespearean treatment of history" (Bethell 52). Ironic parallels, archetypes, parodies, and prefigurations abound. Renaissance English worlds, with their billiards and boy actors, come to overlay the ancient pagan world. A collage, or photomontage, develops of the coprotagonists and such of their counterparts as Isis and Osiris/Seth, Hercules and Omphale, Mars and Venus, Aeneas and Dido, and Adam and Eve. Drawing on biblical phraseology, the dramatist asks us to weigh Antony as a potential creator of a "new heaven" and a "new earth" (Seaton) and as a "lord of lords" of "infinite virtue" (IV.viii.17), betrayed by a suicidal "master-leaver" (IV.ix.22), who will not wait upon his leader for two hours, though requested to do so at a last supper (IV.ii.31–44).

Shakespeare's Cleopatra, like the grandfather of her frequently mentioned friend Herod, is sometimes an archetypal tyrant in attacking "innocents" (II.v.77). In dying, Cleopatra is at once Lilith, or some other evil snake handler (Adelman, *Common Liar*), and Mother Eve. Yet she is also Mary, the New Eve, with the "lord of lords" at her breast. And finally, she is two women in Revelation: the holy one treading upon Genesis's snake; and the Whore, riding the Roman Beast in Babylon, carousing lasciviously with the kings of the earth. As Fichter observes, the phrase an "eastern star" "nursing the serpent like a baby" constitutes a juxtaposition "both visually and morally incongruous," for "Cleopatra's death is an inversion of the moment it prefigures" (109). The scene is a tour de force of time and tense. Her presented Egyptian action, which took place in a past that is pluperfect to Christians, both prefigures and disfigures the Incarnation: that Judean event that has not yet come about, and that has since become something like an eternally present redemptive action.

Behind the chronotopes of *Antony* lies not just Medieval but also earlier Renaissance precedence, as in Garnier's *Cornélie*. There the pagan Cicero cautions against imperialism, using words that advertise origins in the *De officiis* yet also, with overt anachronism, in the Bible:

> Heaven delights not in us, when we doe
> That to another, which our selves dysdaine:

> *Judge others, as thou would'st be judg'd* againe,
> And *do but as thou wouldst be done unto.*
> For, sooth to say, (in reason) we deserve
> To have the selfe-same *measure* that we serve.
> (*Cornelia*, trans. Kyd, I.126–31)

In the surviving works of the historical Cicero, his language is nowhere near so close to that of the Golden Rule. Nor, of course, does Cicero echo the Gospels' advice about measure for measure and judging not that we be not judged (Matthew 7:1, Luke 6:37). True Ciceronian morality can often be comparatively prudential and selfish: for example, the observation that "no one should do any hurt to another, unless by way of reasonable and just retribution for some injury received from him" (*Offices* 1.7). Though Cicero says that "reason makes all men by nature to love one another" (1.4), this love seems often to consist for him in agreeable conversation and mutual exchange of benefits, rather than in selfless service. Kyd's and Garnier's editors and critics are apparently silent about the function of the Christian element in these lines; yet surely both scripts ask humanist readers to plunge the historical Cicero into the baptismal font and consider him as a prophet of Christianity, and as an anti-imperialistic counselor to the many would-be Caesars of sixteenth-century Europe. This sort of synchronicity and leap in time contains anachronism, it is true, but of a very different kind from the anachronistic *slip* that most literary critics have long tried to teach us patronizingly to forgive in such texts.

No work can entirely avoid anachronism, for there will always be some isolating detail inappropriate to the work's dominant chronotope. If original spectators can be assumed to notice an anachronism, it must be an intentional one; if not, it is to some degree involuntary or pro forma. Convenient instances of the latter category are provided in the so-called Peacham drawing (fig. 4), which seems to reflect features of the appearances of actors at some early production of *Titus Andronicus*. The beard, hair, and clothing styles are not particularly Antique from a modern viewpoint, and there is an incompleteness in the attempt to suggest Roman military costume. A leather skirt, a breastplate, a sash, greaves, a victor's crown—these say Antique Rome audibly enough and are distributed variously to the Roman general and such of his battlefield opponents as the Moor and two kneeling Gothic princes. The fact that the princes live in a partially Romanized fringe of the empire helps explain their half-Ancient costumes. In turn, the gender of their mother and the low status of the two guards probably explain why no like attempt is needed to "other" those three characters: their anachronistic appearance in Renaissance garb is likely to have been a pro forma feature of Roman plays, something spectators might possibly understand if explained to them, but not something that bothered them at all.

Intentional anachronism can be conveniently divided into several categories. The first two are inevitable and, for most commonsensical purposes, inconsequential. One is due to changes in language and dialect—for instance, Romans speaking English, or Medieval Englishmen speaking Early Modern blank verse. A second anachronism is equally unlikely to cause protracted negative comments: the anachronism whereby the author reorders, rearranges, or otherwise refashions relatively unknown historic events and speeches to achieve a satisfying aesthetic and thematic structure.

A more significant category of anachronism is discussed by the Renaissance theorist Giraldi Cinthio (and briefly commented upon by Allen H. Gilbert, 270, and Thomas Greene, 305 n. 68). Cinthio suggests that if our age's aesthetic standards are more refined than those of the age that we are describing, we must silently substitute our own details. In his treatise on romance, Giraldi Cinthio defends anachronism when employed to "harmonize" the manners of the original in keeping with a modern understanding (ch. 57). An approved precedent and example that he gives is Vergil's choosing to use Roman funeral customs of the Augustan Age in preference to those of the Homeric Age, when Vergil's characters presumably lived. A parallel example occurs some twenty chapters earlier, when Cinthio recommends Romanizing Homer's depiction of the Princess Nausicaa to enhance her "majesty," because "majesty with face royal and full of reverence . . . appeared together with the excellence of the Roman empire; majesty which (though the greatness of the empire is past) has endured in a high degree even to our day" (266). In Homer the princess encounters Odysseus at the brookside while she is doing the family laundry. But in a more decorous rendition, she should be depicted in accordance with the notion of true "majesty," which we have since been able to learn from Rome.

Certain anachronistic details seem required for artistic verisimilitude. The theater of Regency England modeled the embassy scene in *Coriolanus* after the famous painting of the event made by Claude Lorrain a century and a half earlier than the productions. Orgel compares to this the habit of Hollywood directors who safeguard their work's seriousness of tone by avoiding use of outdated hairstyles, which otherwise could titillate and distance an audience ("Counterfeit").

Of those anachronisms that are meant to be recognized as intentional, the chief ones are the literary, theological, and political. We have touched already upon a few Herodian and other Judaeo-Christian allusions. Some plays echo one another, so that audiences witness multiple presents: the day on which the spectators are going to the theater, the years the play pretends to be about, and the fictive moment in the play that this play is imitating. For instance, Jonson's tragedies have a reverberating half-life in *Nero, Roman Actor, Agrippina,* and *Messallina* (Briggs; Butler 139) so that a photomontage of two chronotopes emerges for frequent theatergoers. The like examples of literary imitation are myriad. First there are the plays that make audiences remember other classical stories, and thus other time frames, as does *Titus* with its Lucrece, Virginia, Senecan Thyestes, and Ovidian Philomel stories. Another species of literary imitation occurs in Fletcher's *Bonduca,* where English spectators are expected to appreciate how Fletcher has turned traditional details of *Romanitas* and *Britannitas* on their heads. When audiences hear the noble British warrior Caratach criticize Queen Bonduca and her sexually compromised daughters for their war policy and suicides, which have left "the Land . . . a wilderness of wretches" (V.i.15), many auditors would remember from Tacitus's *Agricola* another noble British warrior who made a similar (and more memorable) charge against the invading Romans: they conquer the land and its women, and "when all is waste as a wilderness, that they call peace" (30–31, trans. Savile, R5r). In a parallel flashy Fletcherian turnabout that alludes to Stoic Roman suicides in earlier plays, Bonduca and one of her daughters erroneously claim that their deaths outdo those of Roman ladies and that the best Romans must learn to be filled with British souls (IV.iv.115–53). (The manipulation of chronotopes also involves here an implicit nondramatic contrast: between the patriarchalism of Jacobean England and the limited feminism of Elizabethan and, far earlier, Celtic times.)

A good Renaissance imitation yokes the energy of its literary subtexts, while still doing justice both to the pastness of the past and the past's limited presence today—openly acknowledging the tensions created by modern alienation from past modes, customs, and themes. Thomas Greene recounts that when Goethe contemplated the gap between the Archaic epic past and the Hellenic tragedies created from it, he came to believe that "*alle Poesie*," all creative literature, "lives and breathes only in anachronisms." This last term, Greene says, involves not just the "commerce between texts" but also the (Cinthian) urge to render the past "vivid or bearable" according to modern decorums (Greene 305 n. 68).

A well-placed anachronism lets a drama bear on pressing contemporary issues. If we knew for certain the dates of *Coriolanus*, which seems to allude to English corn riots, or of Webster's *Appius*, which seems critical of England's custom of undersupplying its soldiery on the Continent, we might know more precisely the ways in which topicality functioned. But in Webster's case we can be sure that there must have been a decided impact if a production was mounted a little after 1625–27, when two-thirds of some twelve thousand ill-equipped, ill-fed English troops died while simply trying to get to the Rhineland (ed. Lucas l.125). The play's Roman army is similarly neglected—but not from any authority in the historical sources. The troops anachronistically compare their plight with that of some starving "Dutch" soldiers, a likely cover for criticism of the Stuart military debacle. In *Cymbeline*, Leah Marcus argues, a different topicality obtains: there is an "unease" of halfhearted temporal allusions; the play "subtly highlight[s] its own deconstruction," allowing itself to be read either as an attack on James's absolutism or, mutatis mutandis, an endorsement of it, moving an audience to some more mystical affirmation of the king's political positions (159–60).

Phyllis Rackin makes the further important suggestion that anachronism is "double-edged" and able to perform two functions simultaneously: alienation and identification. Anachronism deliberately dislocates action, "dissolv[ing] the distance between past events and present audience" (*Stages of History* 94), with the audience almost simultaneously being made to experience some sort of Brechtian "alienation device." For instance, some detail too obviously Ancient, or too blatantly Early Modern, breaks into the world of art and destroys our sense of the wholeness of our dramatic experience, and therefore of the easy continuity of past and present. Metatheatrical and metahistorical anachronisms cooperate to make an audience aware simultaneously of the age in which it lives and of what it wants to believe about the age in which the characters live. Besides, audiences can be confronted with additional temporal questions that have interested humanity ever since the pre-Socratics: the fact that the present is identified not just by the past but also by the future—which itself is defined and predicted by the past, a past read retroactively with preconceptions and expectations that, though inherited from the past, must be revalidated in the present.

The metatheatrical play of stage prediction—whether curse, blessing, or prophecy (Farrell)—is another device that problematizes the audience's self-consciousness about time in a history play. Because stage predictions in history plays usually come after the fact from the audience's point of view, they have a special aesthetic, thematic, and metaphysical force. The historical Antony at the Capitol in 43 B.C.—had he really cursed the conspirators as Shakespeare's Antony does when he prophesies a civil war—would not have had the same effect on a historical Roman eavesdropper as the allegedly predictive words of Shakespeare's Antony have on an Elizabethan spectator. Questions of language and fiction aside, we recognize that the Ancient eavesdropper would have had less reason to credit the truth of these predictions than the Renaissance spectator has for believing those of the fictive stage counterpart.

An Early Modern Roman play like *Caesar* exists in multiple chronotopes and tenses: especially the simple past of recent real-life Europe, and the "progressive future" of the series of theatrical and political representations of assassinations from the year 1599 until practically the crack of doom. Audiences found and find these carefully manipulated bits of foreshadowing an exciting experience: an experience at once legal and spiritually hygienic, but affording imaginative participation in all those oracular, prophetic, and necromantic activities that were forbidden by church and state, as destabilizing to the underlying continuities of a peaceful society and an integral soul.

In commenting on the endings to Shakespeare's Roman plays, G. K. Hunter argues that *Titus*, *Caesar*, and *Antony* have a "folding back or self-sealing structure" ("Roman" 108). The dramatist's intention in *Antony,* in this view, is to make the play look not forward but backward at the tragic deaths of the principals, and thus to commemorate "the closing of the book of the Civil Wars." Allegedly, Octavius's prophecy of a "'universal peace' is never energized in the play as part of its dynamic; it is a blank wall erected against the end of the action, with little more content than 'lived happily ever after'" (109). Critical opinions like these are still common, obscuring both a real sense of sequel and the long series of Renaissance reincarnations for Cleopatra as boy actor, gipsy strumpet, milkmaid, lass unparalleled, or Elizabeth-like "president" of a nation.

Sequel is frequently foreshadowed through Sophoclean irony and sudden suspension of illusion along with metatheatrical comment. In the aftermath of Caesar's death, Shakespeare's conspirators chillingly exclaim:

> *Brutus.* Let's all cry, "Peace, freedom, and liberty!"
> *Cassius.* Stoop then, and wash. *How many ages hence*
>   Shall this our lofty scene be acted over,
>   In states unborn, and accents yet unknown!
> *Brutus.* How many times shall Caesar bleed *in sport,*
>   That now on Pompey's basis lies along,
>   No worthier than the dust!
> *Cassius.*   So oft as that shall be,
>   So often shall the knot of us be call'd
>   The men that gave their country liberty.
>   (*Caesar* F2 III.i.110–18)

As Shakespeare and his audience felt it would do, the popularity of Cassius's "tragic scene" has continued, both "in sport" and offstage. The original London spectators knew that their theater was in a state that, from an Ancient Roman perspective, was unborn and that would nurture accents yet unknown. Further, the Londoners, living in an age of colonization and shifting boundaries, knew that there would be additional states and accents to employ Caesarian skits (as Polonius did)—and assassinations—in a long future time to come. Indeed, three centuries after the London staging, a son of Junius Brutus Booth played Cassius in New York and then visited a theater in Washington. There, he shot a pistol, jumped to the stage, waved an utterly extraneous knife, and is said to have exclaimed like an Ancient Roman republican: "Sic semper tyrannis."

One Roman play after another has its explicit or implicit sequel and doubtless was not originally designed to be understood without it. In *Wounds* the peaceful demise of Scilla, amidst otherworldly song, highlights his prediction that no succeeding Roman dictator will ever voluntarily relinquish his power (V.v.249ff.)—a likely prognostication of the tragic career of Julius Caesar, Cinna's son-in-law and Marius's nephew by marriage. Shakespeare's *Caesar* foreshadows the impending split between Antony and Octavius and thus faintly the whole train of events leading to Actium and the establishment of the Augustan principate along with its many inglorious successors. In Daniel's *Cleopatra* the tutor to Julius and Cleopatra's child prophesies the boy's assassination and the fact that Augustus will have no successors among his blood descendants since the progeny of Cleopatra's conquered lover Antony will rule (IV, 1018–51). The audience at *Sejanus His Fall* might generally be aware that Macro and Tiberius, too, were overthrown. But even spectators who did not share this knowledge could easily grasp that bad days were ahead for Rome, if only from the open hint that Macro's tyranny would be worse than that of the fallen titular hero. Similarly, in the ironic conclusion to *Catiline,* Cato and Cicero think they have saved the Republic, but we—and the play's silent bystander, ascendant Caesar—exist in other chronotopes and come closer to the truth. For Jonson, Shakespeare, and several of their fellows exploited and manipulated the obvious "tension between the humanist and providential ways of looking at the past" (Wikander 3): between what history, logic, chance, or God dictated would be and what man's sentiments would have had it be.

Sometimes hints of sequel are tantalizingly vague, encouraging audiences to fill out whatever the characters are ignorant of. At the end of *Titus Andronicus,* there is temporary peace and therefore an equilibrium. But it is an ironic one, because to reestablish Roman tranquility, the putatively great savior Lucius has had to use Goths. This people, the audience knows, will never finally relinquish its traditional enmity to Rome so long as the empire stands (Broude, Kliger). In the same way, in *Antony and Cleopatra* Shakespeare undercuts the wonderful coprotagonist when he has her term Octavius a "paltry" "ass / Unpolicied," doomed to an unhappy life of divine "after wrath" on earth (V.ii.2, 307–8, 287). The dramatist wants her misjudgment here to be obvious, for Caesar has been an effective Machiavel and his principate will be relatively successful, both politically and personally. Shakespeare uses Cleopatra's error to distance her as Phyllis Rackin notices that we are distanced from Henry V, when he wrongly forecasts that his infant son, the disastrous Henry VI, will reconquer Jerusalem. Octavius may be every bit as cold and unglamorous as King Hal (in most productions) is bluff and attractive. Yet Octavius has the better mantic inspirations. He sees the olive branch of pagano-Christian "universal peace" (*Antony* IV.vi.4) and is a better judge of some future political and spiritual realities than Antony and Cleopatra have been, with their oddly untraditional Elysium, where Dido loves Aeneas and Antony can proposition Iras.

No audience enters the theater completely ignorant of cultural history, and no one ever leaves without a sense of what goes on after the last act. No sensible spectators at *Coriolanus* worry whether Aufidius's perfidy will allow the Volscian empire to replace the Roman one. All will fall to Time's sickle. So too, at the ending of *Valentinian,* audiences know of the sequel: the coming centuries of barbarian invasion and Byzantine intrigue. Thus few in the audience are likely to share the characters' relief at the death of Rome's latest monsters. The denouement of *Messallina,* written a mere seven years before the closing of the theaters, is similarly suffused with historical irony: the unfortunate and overuxorious Claudius assures the audience that he has learned his lesson: after being cuckolded hundreds of times and all but cheated of his crown, he swears that he will never marry again. Many in the audience would guffaw, remembering that Claudius quickly allowed himself to be seduced by his niece Agrippina, who with her delightful son (and eventual lover) Nero, disposed of Claudius's elder son and Claudius himself. From an audience's perspective, this and other history plays occasion their own sequels and are never really brought to thorough closure.

Misprised Chronotopes

MacCallum (65ff.) and Schelling (2: 17) complain about Lodge's violation of decency: using clownish Renaissance figures like the Ancient Gaul Pedro and the Roman plebeians Curtall and (offstage) Dority to popularize "antique themes with vulgar frippery from the present" (MacCallum 68). Houppert cites Lodge for anachronism in *Wounds,* when an upper-class Roman alludes in the past tense to Crassus's defeat of "Spectacus," or Spartacus (II.i.91), an event supposedly not to occur for a dozen years into the future. The same editor, uncertain about a reference to a "second Brutus" (IV.iii.76), thinks it alludes proleptically to Marcus Junius Brutus, not Lucius Junius Brutus, and therefore represents the same "Elizabethan disregard for historical accuracy." Through probable oversight, this editor silently ignores a still more startling anachronism when Young Marius is said to die "with more constancy than Cato died" (V.v.57)—a demise thirty years in the future. Which, if any, of these ahistorical details are in fact intentional and noteworthy contributions to the text?

The Spectacus/Spartacus anachronism is of course too inconsequential to count at all, because it would never have been noticed in the theater. Just as the compressing of two separate events in a history play is not a real anachronism but an aesthetic device, so too is the Spartacus reference. In a century or so of civil war, the Spartacus slave revolt, like the revolt of the Latin allies, was regarded by Ancient historians as a minor diversion, and most Renaissance audiences would be a little vague about this bit of chronology.

The reference to Cato is, however, likelier to have been an intentional anachronism that the audience was meant to notice and relish. Roman history would be known to counterparts of the lower-class characters in *Love's Labor's Lost* and *Measure for Measure.* These stage figures automatically understand that Caesar and Pompey were rivals. If spectators were hard pressed, they would recall that Romans committed suicide and even that Cato did so. When *Wounds* refers to Scilla's favorite lieutenant as Pompey, audiences would correctly sense that this was the famous Pompey, soon after whose death Cato slew himself. The dramatist is connecting two violent ages: that of Marius and Sulla and that of Caesar, Pompey, Cato, and his son-in-law, Brutus. A like process occurs in Shakespeare's *Troilus,* where Homeric figures specify familiarity with Aristotle, and in *Lear,* where the fool anticipates by several centuries the life of Merlin (II.ii.95–96). Lodge's rationale, and maybe in part Shakespeare's too, is to suggest strong cultural continuity in the old civilization.

When Young Marius urges a follower to become a "second Brutus"—

> Woe to that Scilla . . .
> That gapes with murder for a monarchy.
> Go, second Brutus with a Roman mind,
> And kill that tyrant . . .
>
> (V.iii.74–77)

—whether or not the follower is himself of the Brutus family, we are confronted with a virtuosic combination of chronotopes. One "Brutus" is the Marcus who prevented the "tyrant" Caesar from "gap[ing] . . . for a monarchy" when, as perpetual dictator, Caesar started dressing like the Ancient Roman kings. Another is the first Brutus, the regicide Lucius Junius, who, some five hundred years earlier, did indeed abolish a monarchy. Yet again, another Brutus may be the treacherous Decius/Decimus, close follower of and betrayer of Caesar. Enticing anachronism operates in tandem with straightforward allusion. To talk of Lodge's Brutuses, we need a new paradigm of tenses. Young Marius's present is an Elizabethan's simple past, and Lucius Junius Brutus's actions are in the pluperfect. But what of Marcus Junius Brutus's actions to come? Are they in a *future*-past, and is the unfulfilled action to which the third "Brutus" is urged an optative contrary-to-fact in a past-future?

Even today it is easy to forget temporal complications in literature and the rest of life. In analyzing Huguenot polemics, Mario Praz finds a consistent conflation of ancient pagan Rome with modern papal Italy (*Flaming Heart* 91–92). A similar anachronism occurs in English (Protestant) plays, where the Ancient Judaeo-Christian allusions are striking enough to make audiences confront the differences between pagan and Christian lifestyles, and between Latin Catholic ways and those of the predominantly Protestant English. In *Wounds,* written about the time of the Armada, the comically Catholic "Frenchman" Pedro swears by "Jesu" and "Maria" some eighty years before the Incarnation. Overall, the impression must have been of a patched Roman antic with an overlay of Early Modern Roman Catholicism. Other anachronistically Christian references can also be found in Lodge's submerged image of Herod's "soldiers," who are murdering "the innocents" (V.i.89). Similarly, a Rowley character refers to Britain's being "tributary to that conquering *See*" of Rome (*Welshman* I.i.36). Chapman's *Caesar and Pompey* mentions Julius's holding the "chair of universal bishop," a clear allusion to the pope's simultaneous holding of the title pontifex maximus (a post that Julius also held) and the chief episcopal *cathedra* (chair) of the Catholic (that is, universal) church (III.i.48–50). In Shakespeare there are similar attention-getting "Romish" references: to "holy water" tears (*Cymbeline* V.v.269) and "penny tribute" (II.iv.20; cf. the hated Peter's Pence, abolished by Henry VIII); to the "relics" of (Saint) Julius (*Caesar* II.ii.89); and to the "popish" pagan Lucius Andronicus, who haunts a Roman countryside in which a local "monastery" has become "ruinous"—a fate we would expect in sixteenth-century England but not in fourth- or fifth-century Rome (*Titus* IV.i.76, 21). To ascribe these and like anachronisms to simple ignorance is silly, as silly as the putative offense of ignorance that used to be so casually laid at the writers' doors.

In Kyd's translation of Garnier's "les blons Germains" as "the flaxen-haird high Dutch," MacCallum saw only "a very innocent slip" (56). Another editor, of Heywood's *Rape of Lucrece,* complains of the dramatist's "absurd" piling up of English anachronism "until it is the occasional Roman allusion which seems misplaced" (Lucas, *Webster* 1: 36). Nowhere does the editor wonder about the play's relation to recent history, particularly the Gunpowder Plot, which was unraveled a year or so before Heywood wrote his play. Echoing the modern event, Heywood's play speaks of establishing a new line of succession by killing the king as he is assembled "in Parlament / With all the Senate and Estates of Rome" (130–31), "*all the Peeres* and Senators" (124). Though the details of the two plots are different, Heywood's phrases must have reminded some Englishmen of their struggles for parliamentary rights and of the restiveness of the French estates as they sat in their various regional *parlements*.

Typically, anachronism makes a Then into a Now (as above) or one Then into another Then (as with the Brutus reference in *Wounds* and the Aristotle reference in *Troilus*). Most editors of *Caesar* miss the second sort of anachronism in the ambiguous phrase "triumph[ing] over Pompey's blood" (I.i.51; see Ronan, "Pompey's Blood"): they wrongly think that the only blood is of Pompey's sons because that is what the *historical* Caesar's triumph was over. But only the most erudite playgoer in the audience would remember this. Though Shakespeare does not want to alienate such an auditor, he lets everyone else's mind dwell on the fate of Pompey the Great and the bloodiness of his civil wars—which are also a part of

"Pompey's blood." This phrase, like the play's later references to Pompey's theater and Pompey's bloody statue, is part of a series of reminders that dead Pompey is mighty yet, a symbol of the national factiousness turning swords into the rivals' entrails. Mere historicity is beside the point. This is poetry, which according to Aristotle should be more philosophic and serious than history.

Critical progress (Velz, "Ancient World") has been made since the time of Paul Stapfer, who a hundred years ago satirized *Coriolanus,* saying that its "hero wipes his bleeding brow with a 'mailed hand,' ladies fling their gloves, scarves, and handkerchiefs upon him as he passes, [and] mention is made of theaters, and of drums; and Alexander, Cato, Galen, and Censorinus, are prematurely named, as also graves in the 'holy churchyard'" (109). The functions that these details served are numerous, like the repeated tolling of a Roman-era clock at 3 A.M.—in *Caesar* and a decade later in *Cymbeline*—even if we cannot now agree which functions are the most certain, important, and serious.

In a Jonson play where war insignia are consigned to a "chapel" (*Catiline* III.iii.78), the editors hurry to defend their author when he has the Catilinarians drink the blood of a slaughtered slave in a strengthening "*sacrament*" (I.423–24). Almost all the textual notes forestall any Roman Catholic connotations and tell us that *sacramentum* is the Latin for "military oath"; by implication we are forewarned that Jonson would not want us to find here an inversion of the Last Supper. Equally fallacious is the editorial view implicit in the notes on *Sejanus* I.36, where a minor character observes the protagonist as a watch does a clock. At this juncture readers are told that Roman lords used to set a watchman by the water-clock to observe the time (Herford, Simpson, and Simpson). But surely an Elizabethan audience would also think of two modern chronometers, and Jonson was far too accurate a scholar, and far too intelligent a craftsman with words, to forget it. So too were the other playwrights, whose anachronisms once were, and perhaps still are, wont to set the High Tables on a roar.

By its very nature a history play will reflect language, beliefs, and customs not just of the age during which it is fictively set but also of the age when the dramatist and his audience are living. Every period has its rules of what constitutes indecorous or ignorant anachronism. Historiographical maturation allowed the sixteenth century to understand anachronism in ways that we do today. Increasingly, the artists had the conscious option to abide by, or wildly deny, the now-familiar decorums regarding historicity.

Elizabethan Roman plays conjure up a generalized Rome, replete with old dangers, and old victories, in personal, military, and political life. This habit helps convey the Romans' conquest of time and their casting their shadow even into the modern period. Ancient authors especially themselves enforce the dramatists' powerful sense of Roman circularity and historical return (Trompi). Lucan, for instance, sees the struggle of Pompey and Caesar as part of an eternal rivalry, a polarized oscillation, programmed by that of Romulus and Remus and doomed to be repeated again and again under the Caesars of his own age and later: 'We will *always* have Liberty, and there will always be a [threatening/regularizing] Caesar' ("semper habemus / Libertas et Caesar erit"; 7.695–96). Statements also about characters' being the "last Roman of them all" are widely dispersed among Ancient authors and their Renaissance followers. Bacon applies the epithet to the sixth-century emperor Justinian (*Advancement of Learning*, sig. CC4r). Shakespeare, following Plutarch (Bullough 5: 124), confers the title on two Republican Romans: Titinius and Cassius (*Caesar* V.iii.99). Jonson not only gives it to Cassius (following Plutarch also) but also extends it by implication to the post-Republican Germanicus (*Sejanus* III.392, I.86–159). Fletcher follows Procopius (Hadas, *History* 238), who may also be imitating Plutarch, and gives it to the fourth-century Aecius (*Valentinian* IV.iv.294).

Greene (193), Quinoñes, and others have stressed the Renaissance belief that unique individual achievements coexist uneasily with possible returns of the past. Anachronisms and similar devices emphasize that Roman history is "a repetitive phenomenon" (Kranz, "Clocks"). Any stereotyping of the customs of a thousand years of Western history (550 B.C.–A.D. 450) must blur distinctions and, paradoxically, depend on anachronism to achieve logical continuity. So it is not surprising to find one Roman play after another using the same motifs, ideas, verbal images, episodes, scenes, and physical gear (costumes, flags, eagle standards, triumphal regalia, tombs, city backcloths). Works keep repeating the names of the same gods, places, customs, and political offices and keep reenacting such stock "Roman" situations as the suicide, the triumph, and the sudden fight in a political forum. Moreover, the dialogue becomes a litany of names repeatedly assigned to characters or invoked by them in their speeches: Brutus, Scipio, Cinna, Portia, Octavia, Cornelia, Lepidus, Antony, Cato, Caesar, Piso, and Silius—all names that tell a story of Roman history's recycling itself. In *Wounds* alone, the dramatis personae include not only a Brutus but also a Mark Anthony, Scipio, Octavius, Cinna, Pompey, Lepidus, Metellus, Cethegus, Fulvia, and Cornelia, each of whom is carried over into, or has one or more counterparts in, the *Julius Caesar* of Shakespeare and several other authors' Roman plays.

The continuity that names provide in plays has historical counterparts in the funeral and naming customs of the Romans themselves. In actual upper-class Roman families, daughters bore as first names the father's family name. The sons inherited any honorific granted in the father's line. And at any funeral there was a procession of ancestral death masks and political regalia—as if all the generations were coeval. Occasionally, a Roman play will convey a similar sense of the magical/superstitious idol and ancestor worship prevailing in Ancient Rome. One may be reminded here of such details as the displaying of the Cornelius family images on triumphal arches in *Fulgens and Lucres* (Bevington 46–48); the worshipping of Marius's eagle in *Catiline;* or the superhuman power accorded statues in *Sejanus* and *Caesar*. By necromancy or not, the resurrection and metempsychosis of some dead Roman is expected, sought, or dreaded: play after play attends another Tarquin, Lucrece, Brutus, Marius, Sulla, Cicero, Cato, or Nero redivivus.

In dozens of dramas what some characters call the old-style Roman virtue never dies out but is always confronting factionalism, the "new" opportunism, and constitutional innovation. The histories and legends keep being repeated—those of a seductive African or Eastern queen (Dido, Sophonisba, Cleopatra, and in the Restoration, Berenice), the raped woman (Lucrece, Virginia, the Lavinias of Shakespeare and Fletcher), the misappreciated soldier (Aecius, Virginius, Lucius Andronicus, Antony, Coriolanus), the revolutionary reaffirming virtue and liberty (Lucius and Marcus Junius Brutus, Piso, Silius), the scores of suicides seeking to save face and liberty. And somehow the undular, spiraling flow of historical Roman continuity is made compatible with a sense of the life of England as at once its double and its antinomy.

Shakespeare's *Titus,* which is set near the end of Roman history in the West, is an especially full model for national continuity. This tragedy applies to the raped and apparently barren princess Lavinia, the name of Aeneas's wife: a fertile consort and cofounder of that Trojano-Latin line that harkens back to the predawn of Roman history. Further, this latter-day Lavinia is also given a plight explicitly like that of Virginia (V.iii.36), who had been threatened with rape a half-dozen centuries earlier than Titus's daughter had. Further, *Titus* summarizes Roman political history: there is a recrudescence of powerful political institutions that historically fell into desuetude (an independent tribunate, election by plebs; cf. T. J. B. Spencer), and the crucial invasion of Rome by the Goths recalls/foreshadows how that nation captured Rome in both the early and the final days of the city.

Ever since Antiquity Roman history had been very tightly unified around central parallels that linked contrasting events. Lucan's Pompey and Plutarch's Caesar, as Ian Donaldson notes (107), are each said to have wrapped their faces at the moment of assassination, and Caesar to have covered his privy parts—all actions that are probably unhistorical and are written in literary imitation of the death of Lucrece, a woman whose conventional need for shame and sexual concealment would presumably have been greater. The effect, in the case of Caesar, is to juxtapose in montage two events involving two different Brutuses. The straightforward and ironic parallels create a "doubleness of vision" through a "process . . . circular and incremental" (Donaldson 107). *Not* to have used this anachronistic recall in a Roman tale like *Caesar* would have been un-Roman and, in essence, anachronistic.

Whenever historiography was imbued with *Romanitas,* the dramatists tended to resort to the typological and to suggest that each moment in Rome contained part of her rise and fall and was as likely to have brought forth some moral freak, some paragon of constancy, some stalwart, or some confused wayfarer like Arruntius or Marcus Brutus. We have already noted the complicated references to the Bruti in *Wounds.* In the early Empire of *Sejanus,* Jonson's Silius, Cordus, and most Germanicans try keeping alive the Stoic spark that glowed in Republican Cassius and Brutus (I.93, 104). In *Valentinian,* as Rome fades into Byzantium, one of Fletcher's Romans voices a metatheatrical/metahistorical lament, recalling the Romans of Lodge, Shakespeare, and Jonson: "O *Brutus,* / We want thy honesty *againe*" (V.iv.18–19). In one of Shakespeare's and Lodge's possible sources, the Kyd-Garnier *Cornelia,* the chorus expects Pompey's widow to become a "Lucrece once againe" and then prays for "another Brutus" to save Rome from the Tarquin-like "tyrannical proud insolence" of Caesar, the heir of "cruell Tarquins tyrannie" (II.394–III. i.32). In *Coriolanus* Shakespeare decides to retain the name Brutus as the name of one of the two tribunes he chooses to identify out of a much larger group. Though this name is authorized by Plutarch, Shakespeare was free to have ignored or changed it; but undoubtedly he enjoyed making this tribunitial revolution recall the earlier constitutional changes under Lucius Junius Brutus. And of course Lucius Junius Brutus is crucial also to *Caesar,* where Marcus feels that a revenant Lucius is ghostwriting (as Marjorie Garber might put it) a part for him.

Early or late, major or minor, the English plays ambivalently tested historiographical orthodoxy, Ancient and Early Modern: glorifying Rome's early Republican virtues, regretting her subsequent Republican decadence, and tolerating or praising the imperial Principate as a necessity. In this view the constituents of Roman character were fixed, though their proportions might vary over time. Supposedly there would always be some Roman in every era of Roman history ready to fight for his faction, for empire, for personal honor or power or slight—to die, if need be, at his own hand "like a Roman." Or perhaps "true Romans," as one of William Rowley's characters says, ever swim "in a st[r]eame of blood" (*Shoemaker* II.ii.52–53), and may have done so since the time of Romulus (Alexander, *Caesar* I.137)—a proposition that the average Roman play forces spectators to contemplate, affirmatively or not, over and over again.

CHAPTER TWO

Rhomé: Power, Place, Politics

Rome was th' whole world, and al the world was Rome.

SPENSER
Ruines of Rome

The Chester *Processus prophetorum,* as we briefly noticed in the last chapter, followed the *Legenda aurea* in tracing Rome's power to "nigro mancye." Supposedly, in the Temple of Peace every province was represented by an idol, and if a revolt arose, Rome's idol automatically moved into action and brought the rebel idol—and thus the province involved—into decorous submission. The Chester author has a dim sense of the firmness and extent of Roman political power, even if that power must yield to the supernatural power of Christ, the true "prince of *postie*" (*Chester Cycle* 180). Here, as in later Roman plays, the heart of the matter is *postie,* the Englished form of the Latin *potestas,* 'power.'

The Medieval *Gesta Romanorum* presents all kinds of powerful Romans, though none are described with any more serious regard for historicity or political reality. The opening tale is quite typical. There we hear that the king-emperor Pompey has a daughter who dallies with "a certain duke . . . who regarded her with impure and improper feelings" (73). These stories, like the half-serious celebration of Antiquity in the Worthies Pageant of *Love's Labor's Lost,* remind us of the wide and quirky range of Medieval and Renaissance response to Rome's power—a range that could accommodate even the palindrome of *Roma/Amor.*

Power and Place

Beyond its having a direct relevance to Early Modern politics, Rome's experience loomed like a colossal ruined Tower of Babel, but a monument of history rather than myth, ambivalently testifying to both the futility and the romance of ambitious exertions of human power. Physically and psychologically, Early Modern Europe was strewn with remnants of Roman power and affluence—walls, fortifications, buildings, mosaic floors, coins, statues. In England, Rome's walls stretched across Cumbria, encircled York and countless other towns, and were the rumored basis of the Tower of London (*Richard III* III.i.69–71). In addition, there were such nonmaterial relics as oratorical traditions, literary monuments, the international language of Latin, and memories of Rome's reputation for helping, and hindering, the work of God's holy people. And Rome's philosophy, law, and military "disciplines" (*Henry V* III.ii, vi) set the standards of prestige and excellence. It is easy to share the thrill of Shakespeare and scores of other Renaissance poets when they reflect upon, and toy with, Horace's and Ovid's vaunts: that their verse will be known wherever the *Romana potentia* extends over the dominated earth (*domitis . . . terris; Metamorphoses* 15.877) and will be more lasting than monuments of bronze (*Odes* 3.30.1)—a challenge, and a boast that has been made good, serving as no small part of great writers' motivation in the West even now.

Everywhere one looked, one found fragments and survivals of Roman *potestas,* which the Renaissance was quick to recognize. The Middle Ages, with its Holy Roman Empire, use of Latin, and habit of traveling for international trade and on crusades and pilgrimages, might well have been expected to grasp the immensity of Rome's imperial achievement; but it did not. Nor did it see the pathos in the incomplete success of Rome to make good its boasts that its political, religious, and artistic achievements would be immortal. Instead, that double task of awareness fell to the age of increased exploration, discovery, mercantile trade, conquest, setting out of plantations, and colonization. To a European mind relatively unaware of the full temporal and spatial dimensions of the Egyptian pyramids or the Great Wall of China (not to mention the 140-million-year reign of the dinosaurs), Rome was a potent symbol of "aspiration and creative control over nature" and even over time itself (Paster 18). A Montaigne might admit that ordinary Greeks were objectively more distinguished than many famous Romans, but he had to acknowledge "that great and farre-spreading lustre of the Romane names, which still are tingling in our eares, and never out of our mindes" ("Défense de Sénèque et de Plutarque," *Essays*

2.32, trans. Florio). And in *Essays* 3.9 he says that Rome's very ruins are "marques et image d'empire *ut palam sit uno in loco gaudentis opus esse natura* [Pliny, *Natural History* 3.5]": 'the stamp and image of empire, as if in this one place alone Nature took delight in her handiwork.'

Until even the present day, only two empires—the late-departed British and Soviet ones—have covered more of the earth's inhabited surface than Rome did; and only the British ruled as high a proportion of the world's population. But neither of these recent empires existed at its height for more than a small fraction of the time that Rome's greatness prevailed. The Icaran/Herculean/Faustian aspirations of Renaissance Europe were quite properly stimulated by a new sense of Roman scale and possibility. Romanized Tamburlaine's conquistadorial boasting springs from a deeper understanding of Senecan imperial geographic rant. Suetonius's Nero or Caligula would not be at all surprised at the Shakespearean Antony, who treats "realms and islands" like small change dropping from his pocket (*Antony* V.ii.91–92); or who gives "a kingdom for a mirth" (I.iv.18); and in antic play freely abuses his power over half the earth: "With half the bulk o' th' world *play'd* as I pleas'd, / Making and marring fortunes" (III.xi.64–65). The size, wealth, and power of the empire, joined to its longevity, allowed it and its citizens to make their mark on the world in every conceivable human endeavor. The Roman Empire gave its citizenry a site, stage, status—or what Samuel Daniel calls "state"—for realizing themselves: "the distribution of giftes are universall. . . . We must not thinke but that there were Scipioes, Caesars, Catoes, and Pompeies borne elsewhere then at Rome; the rest of the world had them in some degree of nature, though not *of state*" (*Defense of Rhime*, qtd. in Rackin, *Stages of History* 144). And by realizing themselves so fully and recording in ink and stone their accomplishments so well, Romans preserved for all humankind our shared potential, in realms worthy and not.

Guillaume Du Vair, for instance, luxuriates in what he regards as man's promise of divine power through Roman Stoicism: "God is sovereign power. What does man wish for besides authority and command? Everyone aspires naturally to command; and those who know how to do it well are . . . a species of demigod. . . . God contemplates himself and admires himself; man considers himself, marvels at his own excellence, . . . [and can, through] imitation of divine actions, virtually deify himself in this life" (*De la constance,* trans. and qtd. in Braden 85–86).

Renaissance imperialists like Bacon paid particularly close attention to the Roman foreign policy of going quickly to war to aid allies or to safeguard "Borderers, Merchants, or Politique Ministers"; such a policy promised to enlarge an empire while waylaying the "heat of a Feaver" of civil strife at home (Bacon, *Essays,* "Greatness of Kingdoms"). Philip Edwards (*Threshold of a Nation* 83) recounts the new enthusiasm that the schoolmaster Camden shows for the Roman conquest: a development bringing the "society of civil life" and "brightness of that most glorious empire" to Britons, whose minds might otherwise have languished in "savage barbarism." As colonizers in Ireland and the New World, Early Modern Englishmen repeatedly perceived analogies between their own military and civilian power and that of the ancient Romans. The colonial official Sir John Davies sees Tudor Ireland as another Britain, fortunate to be conquered by an imperial power at "the height of civility" (qtd. in Edwards, *Threshold of a Nation* 85). Another more famous Anglo-Irish colonizer speaks of erasing the Irish language because "It hath been ever the use of the conqueror to despise the language of the conquered, and to force him by all means to learn his. So did the Romans always use" (Spenser, *A View of the Present State of Ireland*; qtd. in Edwards, *Threshold of a Nation* 86). Edwards also cites the marginalia in Strachey's report regarding Virginia, where Purchas queries: "Were not we ourselves made and not born civil in our progenitors' days? And were not Caesar's Britons as brutish as Virginians? The Roman swords were best teachers of civility to this and other countries near us" (83). Thomas Hariot's 1590 *Report* contains engravings of "the inhabitants of the Great Britain" designed to remind viewers that Britons "have been in times past as savage as those of Virginia" (*Tempest,* ed. Orgel, 34, figs. 9, 10). Less enthusiastically, the Jesuit de Acosta urged his readers not to "scorne . . . as fooles, or abhorre . . . as divelish" the New World Indians because "the same things, yea, worse, have beene seene amongst the Greeks and Romans, who have commanded the whole world" (2: 296). Such views pressed the question whether imperialism was a mark of man's glory or merely the stuff of empty "fooles" and "divelish" men. Further, as Braden writes (23–24), the suicidally self-repressive aspect of Stoicism made it seem "but the inner form of imperialism"; a war against time and emotional insurgency in order to stabilize one's "boundaries," to use Seneca's own term *finibus* from *Dialogues* 7.9.3.

In the Early Modern mind, history illustrated the ineffable Roman "character"—achieved self-confidence, restraint, pride, hauteur—character that has been excitingly, even glamorously, described again and again. Yet Tudor-Stuart drama also helps define, as Conrad's *Heart of Darkness* was later to do also, the way empires work and how their advance men risk losing their civilization and becoming demonic, subhuman, or subanimal. To Early Modern Europe, "Rome" gave a local habitation and a name to the tyrannically brutal as well as the humane; and it provided a paradoxical model of the potential hollowness in vast power. Pompey, the legitimate but empty hero of the old Republic, is equated by Lucan with some sacred oak, now rotted but standing by its own weight until a firm blast of wind upsets it (*Pharsalia* 1.70–239). In a similar vein, Montaigne's "De la vanité" (*Essays* 3.9) apocalyptically pictures a Rome where "all is totring, all is out of frame" but lingers on for supernatural reasons because 'men are the balls and playthings of the gods' (Plautus, *Captivi* Prologue)—and for natural reasons, because all structures survive by their own entropy.

> If the extention of rule, and far-spreading domination, be the perfect health of a state, . . . that of Rome was never so sound, as when it was most sicke and distempered . . . not a Monarchie founded in her limits, but so many nations, so different, so distinct, so evill affected, so confusedly commanded, and so unjustly conquered. . . . The contexture of so vast a frame holds by more than one naile. It holds by its antiquity: as olde buildings, which age has robbed of foundation, without loame or morter, and neverthelesse live and subsist by their own waight. (trans. Florio)

In the original the final tag "pondere tuta suo est" (1.239; 'fixed by its own weight') reveals the debt to Lucan's lines, which du Bellay (and his English translator) also noticed. Du Bellay has Lucan in mind when he pictures Rome as a feeble old "oke," "rotten and unsound," "halfe disbowel'd," and at the mercy of the next storm (Spenser, "Ruines of Rome" 28).

Yet if the Romans were merely "hollow men" (to use the Shakespearean phrase that Conrad and Eliot echoed), the Renaissance should have experienced few difficulties in emulating, and surpassing, the "Antike Roman" accomplishments. But the old Romans remained formidable rivals and helpers, offering means to assess human power and passionately to explore humanistic studies, Stoicism, suicide, paganism, gender privilege, imperialism, political absolutism, constitutionalism, civil law, and conquests in every area of life.

For a long time Rome stood preeminent with Jerusalem/Judaea as one of the two major barometers of life's opportunities, value, and dangers. The story of Rome, Augustine's *City of God* maintains, is the story of Cain-like Man, who thinks life is defined by power. Impressed with his own oligarchic or monarchical and patriarchal power, the other stage Romans share the belief of Massinger's Domitian: that the gods are oblivious to the fate of the powerless masses, for "mankind lives / In few, as potent Monarchs, and their Peeres" (*Roman Actor* III.ii.34–35). Romans were thought to act as alleged tyrants like Sophocles' Creon or Shakespeare's Caesar and Coriolanus: as if their city contained but one MAN (*Antigone* 736–39; *Caesar* I.ii.157), who could "be every man himself" (*Coriolanus* III.i.264).

Just as authors of morality plays deemed the name king fit for man in all his power and vulnerability, so too to many other writers, "Roman" came to symbolize the most, if not the best, that man could be. "Roman" meant "man" to the superlative degree: stereotypically masculine man the ruler, the killer, the Stoic, the builder, the wielder of words—someone self-secure enough to protect (when so inclined) weak and vulnerable females, children, subject peoples, or artists.

As for Roman women, they are sometimes patronizingly termed "masculine," but oftener freakish, whorish, or ripe for being violated and victimized. Stage Rome's obvious inability to treat women as people thus points to an instability, a hollowness, in two cultures: the Ancient and the Early Modern.

If style can reveal a dramatist's degree of interest in Roman culture in general, and in politics in particular, it will be significant that the word *Rome* and its cognates appear seldom or never in Medwall's *Fulgens*, the Nuce translation of Seneca's *Octavia*, and R.B.'s *Apius*, but an astounding 224 times in Lodge's *Wounds of Civil War*, a work originating several decades later, about 1585–87. This stylistic feature is far more striking in *Wounds* and other English Roman plays of the late 1580s and the 1590s than in Garnier's French or even in later English Roman plays (see table 1, p. 175). When Thomas Kyd published his translation of Garnier's *Cornélie* in 1594, he used twice as many loconominative references to Rome as the French author did; though they appear with considerable frequency in the French, there is nothing like the remarkable number used in Lodge. Whereas Garnier repeats *Romme* and *romuliste* some 31 times, Kyd uses *Rome* and cognates 63 times.

Loconominative terms, a reflection of setting, appear an amazing 123 times in Shakespeare's *Titus Andronicus*, and in his *Caesar* and *Coriolanus*, a still gigantic 68 and 106 times respectively. This count is higher than that in all but two other Shakespeare plays: *Troilus* (84) and *Henry V* (93). These last have a high count because they are about warfare with a foreign enemy—an explanation that does not apply at all to *Caesar* or explain the extreme largeness of the count in *Titus* or *Coriolanus*. Another striking use of this stylistic device appears in *Caesar's Revenge*, written by an anonymous scholar alert to fashion and renowned for gross acts of plagiarism against early Spenser and Shakespeare (Ronan, "*Revenge*" 172, 180–81). Predictably, *Rome* and its cognates appear in this voguish work very often, 117 times.

What is operating here is the desire to import dignity through reference to the supposed best of Antique civilizations. But added to this is an attraction to the many quibbles traditionally associated with Rome. *Antony* III.ii.57 and the episode of the muffled conspirators in *Caesar* II.i suggest that Shakespeare may have indulged in private wordplay with the terms *Rome* and *rheum*. Too, the characteristic conquering spirit of Rome may disclose certain associations with *roam*ing. But for educated English speakers, the chief quibbles would involve those between *room* and *Rome*, between the Latin *urbs* ("city") and *orbis* ("world"), and between the Greek *rhomé* ("strength") and *Romé* ("Rome").

In the upper border of his much-reprinted 1570 map of the Roman empire, Ortelius writes that Rome's imperial destiny to rule is contained in her very name: "Roman Tuam Nomen Terris Fatale Regendis" (cited in Gillies 204 n.45; cf. p. 60). Onomanticists had long seen Rome's fate in her name: "Some thincke that the [proto-Greek] Pelasgians, after they had overcome the greatest parte of the world, . . . dyd staye them selves in that place [Rome] . . . : and for their great strenth and power in armes [*hoplois rhomein*], they gave the name of Rome unto the cittie, as signifying power in the Greeke tongue" (Plutarch, "Romulus," *Lives* 1: 68). In his treatise on names and their alleged ability to forecast a person's future, William Camden (Jonson's mentor from Westminster School) includes the following entries under the Christian names Romane and Valens:

> *Romane,* Lat. Strong, from the Greeke; answerable to Valens. . . .
> *Valens,* Lat. Puissant.

Puissant, derived from the French word for power and capability, is itself associated with Roman valor in more than one play. With his own British "*puissant* might" (*Welshman* I.i.29–37), one heroic Caradoc is said to "outdare" the "*puissant* hoste" (IV.85, III.v.1–2) and "huge . . . Romane strength" of the "valiant Romanes" of "powerfull Rome" (IV.7, 2, 11).[1]

In all languages, Rome connotes power and expanse over time and space. Rome seemed a world, *the* world. The street guide ("plan") to Rome, writes du Bellay, is the "carte du monde" (*Antiquitez* 26.14). As his translator Edmund Spenser puts it, "Romane greatnes" embraces "All that the Ocean graspes" and thus forms "the map of the wide world" (*Ruines* 26, 351–63). Underlying this rhetoric is the tale of Alexander, weeping because there were no more worlds to conquer. Lucan's Caesar and his veterans accuse each other of a similar obsession. His men decide his motivation for civil war is imploding ambition: 'What can satisfy a man for whom Rome itself is too small?' ("Quid satis est, si Roma parvum est?" 5.274). And Caesar responds that their own greed exceeds the world's boundaries ("his non sufficit orbis," 5.356).

Various manifestations of this trope appear in several classical authors and their Early Modern imitators. Ovid is the most obvious (*Metamorphoses* 15.872). Muller (21) cites also Rutilius; and Gillies (203 n.45), Juvenal, Seneca the Elder, and Tertullian. It doubtless inspires the geographic rhetoric of *Tamburlaine, Antony,* and *Henry V*. The poet Donne, himself a sexual conqueror, wished to "possess one world" and make "one little *room* an everywhere" ("The Good Morrow" 11–14). The dramatist Jonson also adds the English quibble to the Latin one when he translates Lucan for *Catiline*: "unto whome / *Rome* is too little, what can be enough?" (III.ii.46–47; cf. ed. Herford, Simpson, and Simpson, *Catiline* II.281 n.). Fletcher and Massinger use similar locutions. Apology is made that the "narrow Stage" at *The Prophetess* "wants *Room*" to present so great a figure as Dioclesian (V.i,

p. 362; cf. V.iii, p. 389). And the British queen in *Bonduca* seeks to prevent Rome's making "the world but one Rome and one Caesar" (I.i.6). Shakespeare's attraction to these puns is evident in Sonnet 55, *John* III.i.180, and repeatedly in *Caesar:*

> When could they say, till now, that talk'd of *Rome,*
> That her wide walks encompass'd but one man?
> Now is it *Rome* indeed and *room* enough,
> When there is in it but one only man.
>
> (I.ii.154–57)

When Shakespeare's comic cobbler claims to meddle with *all* (*awl/ withal*), insofar as he represents a Roman voter, he would indeed have had control over *all* the Eurocentric world (*Caesar* I.i.23).

Elizabethans would have no trouble understanding the ambivalent verdict of a modern writer: that Rome's story is "*at the heart of Western civilization* [and] above all a *story of cruelty*, consumption, greed, and moral degradation. Founded in *fratricide*, the city survives from century to century, sacked, looted, conquered, occupied. But . . . [with a] history of *human and artistic endeavour without parallel*" (Hibbert, qtd. in FitzHerbert 769). Descartes, writing in 1637, explains that he had crucial doubts, a couple of decades earlier, regarding Roman views on suicide, parental authority, and political self-assertion, as these matters are recorded in "the Ancient heathen" authors. As a young man he concluded that their ethical and political writings were "most proud and stately Palaces" ("palais fort superbes, & fort magnifiques"), but built upon mere mud and sand; and that what the Ancients call "vertues" is actually "une insensibilité, ou un orgueil, ou un desespoir, ou un paricide" (*Discours de la methode* 13)—nothing but "a stupidness, or an act of pride, or of despair, or a parricide" (*A Discourse of a Method*). Here Descartes implicitly touches on several essential Early Modern stereotypes of Rome: namely, (1) the supposedly kingly dignity conferred upon those powerful and wealthy enough to dwell in "proud and stately Palaces"; (2) the Stoic aloofness that may be a cover for mere *insensibilité* and stupidness; and (3) the pride that could lead variously to imperialistic cruelty, parricidal violence in the family and *patria,* and readiness for defiant yet despairing suicide.

Descartes's simultaneous admiration and disapproval of the cultural "palaces" that Rome has left us are also paradigmatically built into countless other typically Renaissance comments. And some comments are obviously even more disapproving. To readers of Revelation 12:5–9, no characterization of the Ancient city could seem more negative than the identification there of Rome with the seven-headed "red dragon" Satan, the spirit of cosmic Evil (cf. Geneva glosses).

A convenient résumé of other negative ideas on Rome can be gathered, as T. J. B. Spencer points out, from title pages of Elizabethan Roman histories. Factiousness is the theme on the title page of William Fulbecke's *Historicall Collection of the Continuall Factions, Tumults, and Massacres of the Romans and Italians,* a work of 1601, advertised as "revealing the mischiefes of discord and civill discention . . . and ambition . . . [and] complotting in darke conventicles against superiors" (qtd. in T. J. B. Spencer 29–30). When we open the 1578 translation of Appian (*Auncient Historie*) we further read that Romans are thievish in foreign policy (title page; cf. Barroll 334), while at home they fall prey to tyrants (cf. Machin's *Every Woman* C4v) and conspiracies. This Appian volume is allegedly an "exquisite Chronicle of the Romanes Warres, both Civile and Foren. In the which is declared"

> Their greedy desire to conquere others.
> Their mortal malice to destroy themselves.
> Their seeking of matters to make warre abroad.
> Their picking of quarels to fall out at home.
> All the degrees of Sedition, and all the effects of Ambition.
> (Qtd. in T. J. B. Spencer 30)

Nevertheless, Christianity teaches that God's Providence has authorized all government, including Rome's. In Jasper Fisher's *Fuimus Troes,* the Romans who invade Britain are no saints, yet are described in orthodox Stuart terms as Heaven's "viceroys on earth" (V.vi.534)—so strong could be the belief in the providential role of Augustus's Pax Romana in ensuring the peaceful birth and preaching of Jesus. An Early Modern spokesman, echoing Saint Paul, says that the "governaunce" of any "empyre" is the "gyfte of and ordinance" of God (Carion 87; Romans 13:11). And at the very start of Genesis, prelapsarian man is defined as a natural ruler: endowed by his Creator with plantations and livestock preserves, and given Godlike "dominion" or *over*ness. But for Rome to follow the advice of Vergil's Anchises, to crush an arrogant enemy—even if he supposedly started a war unjustly—needs something like an answering arrogance. So too does the effort to expand a Roman or an English empire. For Jesus resisted the temptation to rule the kingdoms of this world, at a time when most of the known Western ones were under Roman control; and whatever assaults he launched upon Caesar, or upon the things that are Caesar's, were indirect.

Inconsistency and ambivalence about those who wield power is strong in the Judaeo-Christian tradition. The Bible castigates monarchy itself, as in 1 Samuel 8, or implies that its abuses are all but inevitable, as in the Magnificat: "He hathe put downe the mightie from their seats, and exalted them of lowe degree" (Luke 1:52). And it is "the devil" who, in showing Christ "the kingdomes of the worlde," is not contradicted when he boasts of his ability to deliver them into whomever's hands he wishes: "And the devil said unto him, All this power wil I give thee, and the glorie of those kingdomes: for it is delivered to me: & to whomesoever I wil, I give it" (Luke 4:5–6). The Bible, then, helped increase Renaissance apprehension concerning power and the archetypal secular repository of power, Rome.

The extent to which Rome governed consistently and well from place to place and age to age has always been subject to considerable debate. The Greek historian Appian remarks on the justice and rational borders of Rome, noting that no other empire was ever so large and long-lived, and so little burdened with unprofitable territories and peoples (*Roman History*, Preface, 7–8). And to judge from an encomium like Aelius Aristides' in the second century (a famous text, available since 1519 in a Latin Aldine translation), Rome aimed at efficiency, professionalism, and an openness of opportunity to all: "If one considers the vast extent of your empire he must be amazed that so small a fraction of it rules the world, but when he beholds the city and its spaciousness it is not astonishing that all the habitable world is ruled by such a capital.... Whatever any people produce can be found here, at all time, and in abundance" (*The Roman Oration*, trans. and qtd. in Hadas, *History* 142–43). Rome governs by law, enforced by a self-controlled and self-respecting administration: "You alone of the imperial powers of history rule over men who are free.... Careers are open to talent.... Rich and poor find contentment and profit.... Your soldiers and officers you train to prevail not only over the enemy but over themselves. . . . You have . . . filled the wastes with posting stations, introduced orderly and refined modes of life" (143–45).

Yet ever since Antiquity the image of Roman power has tended to be mixed, combining glamor with horror. In one of the few classical Latin works to describe Britain at length, Tacitus praises one great Roman administrator yet also echoes Diogenes' commonplace about the brigandage of imperialism and (anticipating Augustine) says that Romans are "robbers of the world" and "search also the sea" with equally "ardent affection" for "glorie" and "wealth": "To take away by maine force, to kill and to spoil, falsely they terme Empire and government; when all is waste as a wildernesse, that they call peace" (*Agricola* 30).

Shakespeare hailed Essex as a Caesar in Ireland (*Henry V*). When England's new imperial Caesar, James I, made his triumphal entry into London (fig. 5; Jones, "Stuart *Cymbeline*" 92–93), he too was surrounded by *Romanitas,* finding applied to himself the lines that Vergil wrote in explanation of Augustus's and Rome's destiny, *Aeneid* 6.851–53: 'Whereas other nations may be renowned for scientific and artistic accomplishment, a true Roman's fate is to govern well [*regere;* cf. *rex*], sparing the tractable and crushing the arrogant.'

Despite Rome's recurrent, even endemic, instability, she has served, and has continued to serve, as a storehouse of dignified political furnishings. Governments and politicians of every stripe have had or sought Roman associations to dignify their status, as Medieval and Early Modern republics enlisted Roman precedent in running, for instance, Italian city-states or even (as in Cola di Rienzo's case) Rome itself. Henry VIII, disengaging England from papal suzereinty, proclaimed his realm an *imperium* (as had Anglo-Saxon kings), and his successors wore the crown imperial. For centuries all Europe has envisioned a *translatio imperii,* as is evident merely from titles—tsar (of the Third Rome), kaiser, despot of the Romans, consul, emperor, count, duke—and objects such as laurel crowns and military sashes (figs. 2, 4, 5) and decorative *grotteschi* (figs. 1, 2).

A classical setting itself carried prestige, and in plays like several we have just considered could have aesthetically reinforced the political message. For as Hobbes argues in a somewhat analogous case regarding Roundhead command of the classics, the study of such books put good language and Republican ideals simultaneously before left-wing parliamentarians, leading them also to praise "popular government . . . by that glorious name of liberty," and swaying their modern fellows with the glorious Ancient eloquence (*Behemoth,* qtd. in P. Burke 96).

Nevertheless, the fact is that history validates Rome's immortality more through its arts than through its political borders and structures, thus compromising its heroic autarky and giving both horror and pathos to that greatness. Ancient writer after Ancient writer boasts that Rome's buildings, cults, institutions, borders, and arts are immortal. But as du Bellay, Spenser, and numerous other Renaissance authors realize, Rome's life was becoming less and less likely to be coeval with Time. Pride, at once fulfilled and frustrated, lurks in Vergil's boast of Rome's vast, endless "imperium sine fine" (*Aeneid* 1.279). Ovid too is at once absurd and presciently Faustian when (like the Horace of *Odes* 3.30) he records vatic prophecies of Rome's immortality and hence of his own—"omnia saecula fama":

> All the world shall never
> Be able for too quench
>   my name. For looke howe farre so ever
> The Romane Empyre by the ryght of conquest shal extend,
> So farre shall all folk reade this woork. And tyme without all end.
>   (*Metamorphoses,* trans. Golding, 15.877–79)

Thinkers of the Middle Ages, and its Antique predecessors in Christian, Hebrew (Hadas, "Allusion"), and pagan culture, had some sense of Rome's power. In 1 Maccabees 8, Republican Rome is a model of justice and efficient political management, but in Daniel and Revelation it is a bloody monster, irresponsible and somewhat inefficient (Simmons 59). Its citizens were given to "civil warres and continual discordes among them selves" (Geneva gloss at 2:41), exactly what one would expect of a nation the clay feet of which were a "sign of disunion." Thus the Romans "destroyed themselves after arriving at the highest pitch of fortune" (John Calvin, qtd. in Simmons 59).

A nation's potency can turn hollow, as Lucan hints. When Augustan Vergil and other Romans rededicated the nation to supposedly equitable imperialism, they did so despite the unbelievable rapacity of their governors and the conspicuous consumption of the nobles, particularly in late Republican and early Imperial times. As numerous accounts of the first century before and after the Nativity attest, this was the age when oxen were traded for a box of Caspian caviar (Plutarch, "Marcus Cato")—a time when the immensely wealthy gourmet Apicius slew himself as soon as he found that he had literally *eaten* through his millions in six months, and when, as Suetonius fascinatingly documents, emperors were known to indulge the cruelest, most humiliating, and most obscene whims. No one sees more clearly than Jonson this decadent world, and conveys a sense that Rome wastes and dirties all nature. The

> women wear
> The spoils of nations in an ear,
> Changed for the treasure of a shell.
> (*Catiline* I.555–57)

"To please / Their wanton taste" and effeminate lusts, Romans ever seek the "new and rare . . . , not the best," scouring "quarries deep"; they "hunt all grounds . . . draw all seas, / Fowl [i.e., also *foul*] every brook and bush" (*Catiline* I.553, 570–73).

The quibbling commentators of Early Modern England accorded to each noble Roman the stereotypical *strength* and *room* to be a *man:* a hard, armor-plated male whose freedom of decision and mastery was as great as humanly possible. And the dramatists indicate that in striving for royal and godlike self-realization, the Roman sometimes succeeded but risked tumbling back into the allegedly effeminate, the demonic, the befouled, the bestial, the trivial, the hollow, the merely antic.

Political Topicality

One might well ask whether the repetition of the loconominative markers of Roman nationhood, reinforced by the habit of equating Rome with power, made Roman plays into unusually political instruments. Surely, the nominatives establish an exotic setting, recall for the audience "the city's stake in the action" of a play (Paster 92), and provide honorifics that evoke, for humanist audiences, expectations of old-fashioned noble behavior (Haywood, Paster 70, Barton, "Livy" 128 n. 20; Ronan, "Onomastics" 49–59)—and create ironies when such expectations are frustrated (Lloyd). But do the iterations of *Roman* ever really perform any *incisively* political function? Do these repetitions of *Rome* and *Roman* boldly (or even disingenuously) encourage truly *pointed* English applications of a play's politics? Or do the iterations merely emphasize Rome's cultural difference and otherness?

If Massinger's character's remark about Caesars and senators in the non-Roman *King and the Subject* was derogatory enough to make Charles I censor it as "insolent," audiences at Roman plays must have sensed continual analogies to English politics. For in Stuart times particularly, the monarchs were called emperors (cf. fig. 5); less flatteringly, the Speaker of the House of Commons was likened to a Roman tribune, and the king's favorite was customarily termed a "Sejanus" (Patterson 56–57).

Even where we can look at governmental records, or glance over the shoulder of a dramatist as he or she adapts sources, it is hard to distinguish truly topical political intent from a mere desire to seem interesting. In *Catiline* Jonson may have intensified the parallels between the ancient insurrection and the Gunpowder Plot (DeLuna 329–34, 360). But in view of the unattractive pomposity of Jonson's Cicero, would such parallels really marshal much additional English support for James? In *Poetaster* (*Jonson*, ed. Schelling, xvii) Jonson had temporary legal problems over his satire on lawyers, and in *Sejanus* over, presumably, his own Catholicism and alleged equating of James with Tiberius. But no more serious repercussions came of the charges against Jonson; nor did Massinger's work suffer much more severely from his tangles with the censor over *Believe As You List.* Perhaps because everyone knew that drama is symbolic action, nothing was done about the playwright's explosive line in *Roman Actor,* where we hear that under the "great name" of "Caesar . . . / All Kings are comprehended" (I.iii.53–54). The censor could have been resigned to the idea that, inevitably, "what great ones do, the less will prattle of" (*Twelfth Night* I.iii.33). As the antitheatricalists warned, dramas do create the antihierarchical illusion of making greatness familiar, letting us see extraordinary power wed to quite ordinary emotions: "The like passions sway ["Princes"], the same reason, that makes a Vicar goe to law for a tithe-pig, and undoe his neighbours, makes them spoil a whole Province, and batter downe goodly Cities with the Cannon" (*Duchess of Malfi* II.i.104–9). These lessons could enflame some spectators, while being construed by others as overgeneral or imprecisely applicable. Plays were written to interest theatergoers, not just writers and actors. Sin itself is more attractive than sermons, and the excitement of vicarious rebellion is as much a safe thrill as that of vicarious sensuality, heresy, blasphemy, or other self-aggrandizing fantasy. And it may be safer for governments not to repress the fantasy life of potential rebels. So long as thoughts are uncontrollable, a wise government will not discourage their cauterized and antiseptic use. Patterson justly notes how underestimated the "functional ambiguity" has been regarding political ideology in many Tudor-Stuart dramas (60). Clearly, many plays encourage a variety of ambivalent positions (Leinwand 488). Timid intentional quietism alternates with "subversion or legitimation" (Patterson 60) and vigorous political containment, and all make way for monetary and aesthetic opportunism.

Like history writing proper, a drama of history advances partisanship less than it encourages relativism and tragic ambivalence. As Bacon says, history comes to no final conclusion about the "doubtfull" case of Lucius Junius Brutus's executing his sons, for any decision must be based on social good—the "good respecting Society" "*comparatively*"—and must reflect such contingent considerations as "the weighing of duties, betwene person and person, Case and Case, particular & publike" (*Advancement of Learning* Vv4v–Xx1r). No English Roman drama propagandizes so unmistakably and unrelievedly as Eisenstein's brilliant *Potemkin* does. There was no political party sponsoring the hustling artists of the time, and the political interests that spectators brought to the theater were widely diverse. Audiences contained future regicides like John Bradshaw and the fellow traveler John Milton (Butler 167). But they also included the politically passive, the positive supporters of the monarchy, and the trivially curious. Thus almost any popular drama would have in it something of seeming political relevance, or irrelevance, for everyone, according to taste.

Occasionally Roman plays do turn overtly political and attack imperialism by revealing its complaining victims. Or plays briefly discuss constitutional questions, as in the Caesar plays (e.g., Alexander's [III.i.1288–89] and *Coriolanus* [III.i]), or display an equivalent of class warfare as in, again, *Coriolanus* (Zeevold) and *Appius*. Yet the liveliest political disagreements in Roman plays tend to be over strategy and personality, not ideological difference. Usually constitutional issues are left vague, typically reduced to slights and grudges, or a misty conflict between tyranny/monarchy and "liberty." The plays are skewed toward upper-class vantages, with few serious revelations of lower-class dilemmas. Not many hungry stage plebs simmer with outrage at their own prudent servility and self-humiliation. The causes of Rome's internal problems are presented as many. One is upper-class factiousness; another, the hydralike mob (Tupper)—the "rot[ting]" and "slippery people" (*Antony* I.ii.185–87, iv.41–47), who "wander" mist-ridden (*Catiline* IV, Chorus 21, 53), ever "covet[ing] change" (*Messallina* 1791) and (as *Caesar, Sejanus,* and *Coriolanus* vividly demonstrate) occasioning murderous destruction. Like male mob members, women are a further portion of society that male power brokers and politicians try at their peril to ignore. These pressure points, along with the nation's military and imperial traditions, formed Rome into a place of "wrangling stryfe" (*Octavia* III.48, trans. Nuce) and "garboils" (Marlowe's Lucan 1.68; *Antony* I.iii.61; and, as T. J. B. Spencer notes [30], *Aeneid* 1.1, trans. Stanyhurst).

Since Antiquity connections have been discussed between various kinds of conquest, with Plato maintaining that sexual self-restraint is a key to fitness to rule (*Phaedrus*), while the opposite theme is tentatively proposed by Shakespeare in *Antony* (arguably, II.ii.228–29). Historically, the great users and abusers of power included sexual conquerors like Antony and Caesar and outright rapists like Tarquin, the kidnappers of the Sabine women, and, by intention, Appius. In fact, as the plays demonstrate, several of Rome's crises were instigated by sexual attack on some eminent woman, an act occasioning a sympathetic rupture in the body politic. In a quarter of the Roman plays, rape is discussed and/or attempted, and dramas like *Titus* and *Lucrece* (or the narrative "Lucrece") were obviously crafted to suggest the vulnerability of the entire fabric of society to the predatory male.[2]

Political subjects in Roman plays also include the failure of the government to reward properly its soldiers, the factious selfishness of oligarchs, the alarming plight of the unstable poor, the Machiavellian diplomatic and intelligence machinery by which a government keeps itself in power, demagoguery and the effective generating of patriotism, the problematic role of priestcraft and the supernatural in determining the course of a nation's history, and the methods by which tyranny—or freedom—can be eliminated.

Specifically, dramatists are strongly attracted to political crises. The works depict a city in political flux at home and abroad, undergoing a transition from monarchy to aristocratic republic (*Lucrece, Coriolanus*); from aristocratic to mixed republic (*Coriolanus*); from decemvirate back to republic (*Appius*); from republic to dictatorship or triumvirate (*Wounds, Caesar, Caesar's Revenge, Caesar and Pompey, Cornelia, Catiline, Cicero*); from triumvirate to empire (*Antonius, Antony, Poetaster,* Daniel's and May's *Cleopatra*) and early principate (*Sejanus*); from a pagan polity toward a Christian one (*Titus, Shoemaker, Virgin Martyr, Two Noble Ladies,* and, implicitly, *Cornelia, Caesar, Antony, Cymbeline, Fuimus Troes*); from homeland threatened by external enemies to one temporarily powerful (*Titus, Sophonisba, Hannibal, Faithful Friends*); and from a land threatened by palace rebellion to one representing a new stasis (*Titus, Sejanus, Faithful Friends, Valentinian, Prophetess, Roman Actor, Agrippina, Messallina*).

Ancient Rome's relations to other lands are treated as Early Modern imperialism is in *The Tempest:* namely, with a fullness that permits spectators to reflect upon victims' cries for freedom. In Garnier's Antony play, Egyptians fear some axe-bearing "Romaine madly bent" (*Antonius* 813–16). Typically, Renaissance stage Roman invaders are unrepentant about violations of the *lex gentium*, and conquest becomes, at best, a glamorous form of robbery. The anecdote of Alexander and the pirate (land versus sea theft) lurks between the lines again and again: for instance, in *Antony* II.vi.86–94 (Barroll 334), *Caesar's Revenge* 762–63, or, earlier, Kyd's translation of Garnier, where Romans ask what "right" they ever had to invade Asia (*Cornelia* I.132):

> Are we not thieves and robbers of those Realmes
> Whose mournfull cryes and shreekes to heaven ascend,
> Importuning both vengeance and defence
> Against the Citty, rich of violence?
>
> (143–46)

The *Antonius* is pitched in the same outraged Augustinian register. There the chorus complains that fruitful Egyptian "corn" has been "pill'd from hence with thevish hands" (780–81). In yet another Romano-Egyptian play, *The False One*, we hear how an expanding nation is necessarily drawn to parricidal bloodlust. Conquerors kill whoever is, or soon will be, a neighbor or kinfolk. Perimeter defenses are defined, "Cemented," and "manur'd" by a sticky but nutritive helping of blood and blood meal. "The globe" and glebe "of Empire must be so manur'd" and "her walls water'd with a Crimson show'r / Drain'd from a Brothers heart" (V.ii, pp. 359–60). The precise degrees of topicality that a passage like this would have for a cluster of normative Stuart spectators are hard to gauge at our present remove, but it is likely that this conversation must have been arresting to many in the audience.

The unmistakable continuity in the various stage Romes may have encouraged anachronisms that brought ancient Roman experiences directly into the Tudor-Stuart ken. English spectators at May's *Cleopatra* would catch the author's proto-republicanism in Lucilius's sneer at Octavius for his "most royall Caesar-like dissimulation" (V.i.63). So too an audience at *Nero* in about 1624 would hear that *all* courts and stately homes are lascivious:

> Chastitie, foole! a word not knowne in Courts:
> . . . .
> [It] never comes to great mens Pallaces,
> Where ease, and riches stirring thoughts beget.
> (*Nero* I.i.44–49)

A reader or spectator's sense of the distance between Jacobean England and Neronic Rome would antically dissolve in cynical laughter, an effect consonant with that of another device in this same play: the transference to pagan Rome of glaringly non-Roman, Moslem ideas of sensuality in the afterlife (IV.vii). The pagan Rome of *Nero* is thus simultaneously itself, another non-Christian chronotope (an Islamic Mediterranean one), and a model of Stuart England—all, apparently, with the transparent purpose of satirizing English court decadence, but not in any obviously trenchant fashion.

The handling of the arrest of Carbo, a legitimate consul sitting on his throne, must have been especially absorbing to audiences in Lodge's *Wounds of Civil War* (c. 1587), a few years before the politically sensitive *Richard II*, with its abdication scene. On constitutional and religious grounds, Carbo refuses to submit to the humiliation required by fellow noblemen Scilla and his assistant, Pompey, who have just illegally grabbed power from him and the constitutional state. "What no obeisance, *sirrah, to your lord?*" the jocular thug Scilla asks.

> *Carbo.* He that thrice hath borne
> *The name of Consul scorns to stoop* to him
> Whose heart doth hammer naught but mutinies.
> *Pompey.* And doth your lordship . . . disdain to *stoop?*
> *Carbo.* Ay, to mine equal, Pompey, as thou art.
> *Scilla.* Thine equal, villain? No, he is my friend,
> Thou but a poor anatomy of bones.
>
> . . . .
>
> *Carbo.* Scilla, *I honor gods, not foolish men.*
> [*They throw him down.*
> (V.i.39–SD52/53)

The biblical Jesus too refused to "fall downe" (before Satan; Luke 4:7), and with varying degrees of sincerity, so too Shakespeare's Julius Caesar and Jonson's Tiberius forbid citizens to indulge in genual obeisance (the latter episode fascinatingly analyzed in Goldberg 178–85).

Early-seventeenth-century England would also have been intrigued by the proto-Quaker retort of Prince Caradoc/Caratach/Caratacus in *Valiant Welshman,* when the hero was asked to stoop to the Emperor Claudius Caesar, alleged master of the Southern as well as Northern Hemisphere.

> I was not borne to *kneele, but to the Gods,*
> Nor basely bow unto a lumpe of clay,
> In adoration of a clod of earth.
> Were Cesar Lord of all the spacious world,
> Euen from the Articke to the Antarticke poles,
> And but a man: in spite of death and him,
> Ide keepe my legs upright, *honour should stand*
> Fixt as the Center, at no Kings commaund.
> (V.v.13–20)

The message is political: the equality of all gentlemen. Yet its secular theme also has a faintly sectarian ring. Caradoc's reference to "adoration" of a "lumpe of clay" may refer both to Protestant iconoclasm and the clay feet of Rome's idol in the Book of Daniel, while Caradoc's reference to the

Southern Hemisphere and to bowing to a "*Kings* commaund" might bring home the scene's relevance to Jacobean church and imperial world-state.

Such passages as Lodge's and R.A.'s touch the issue of any Christian's bowing and kneeling. Triumphalist bending and bowing of the subjects were enforced at court by Elizabeth and the Stuarts alike, in imitation of customs rooted in pagan Roman Antiquity—and the liturgy of Roman Catholicism. Communicants knelt in both Tudor and Stuart times. The controversial "Black Rubric" was in force in Edward VI's reign, warning that kneeling did not constitute idolatrous adoration of the sacramental bread and wine. But this admonition was tactfully removed under Elizabeth and her successors (Booty), tacitly permitting the faithful to believe what they wished regarding the reality within communion ritual.

Caradoc is a kind of Reformation Patrick Henry when he further goes on to announce:

> Tis inough for Sicophants and slaves,
> To crouch to Tyrants, that feare their graves.
> I was not borne when flattery begd land,
> And eate whole Lordships up with making legs.
> Let it suffice: were Cesar thrice as great,
> Ide *neyther bow to Rome, him nor his seate*.
> (V.v.26–31)

The word *seate* is probably meant to evoke antipapal reaction in an audience, while Caradoc's hints about courtiers who must "mak[e] legs" to the king in order to receive royal grants of land constitute obvious social, economic, and political satire of the type that a Jonson or Swift provides. R.A.'s audiences would have a cause to reflect that the good Roman "king" Claudius allowed a spirited Briton to maintain self-dignity through actions disallowed politically and ecclesiastically by Elizabeth and James—and never tolerated by their royal successors until scores of years later.

Like *Gorboduc* a half century earlier, *Welshman* is an illuminating specimen of a drama that repeatedly hides not just libertarian but also chauvinistic political messages under the disingenuous guise of anachronism, a trait heralded even in the play's title. In compliment to Henry Prince of Wales, the activist patron of theater company and a prince who sought a measure of independence from his monarch/father, the playwright exhibits an example of princely courage and self-sufficiency, while he also diplomatically compliments the Celtic background of the Stuarts and Tudors, and the supposed openness to peace upon which James prided himself.

Complexly ambivalent anachronisms suggest topical political reference to Rome's relations with Britain. For one thing, there is the paradoxical fact that British excellence has had to be tested on the battlefield and recorded in the histories by entirely *Roman* agencies. Second, from the play's start we know that the line between imperial and papal Rome will be hard to draw, for the Emperor Claudius is said to have made the "Bryttish Ile / ... tributary to that conquering *See*" of Rome (I.i.35–36). Such phrases obviously bring us anachronistically to the worlds of King John's submission to the pope and of Henry VIII's Act of Supremacy. A third source of cultural complexity and ambivalence is that the play's most subversive political remarks are given to characters whose villainy is in the Italian manner of a Machiavelli or a Romanized stage tyrant like one of Seneca's and Marlowe's. Out of a wish to exploit the audience's interest safely, censurable ideas are put into the mouth of a usurper, who titillates hearers of numerous political persuasions with the following delicious attack on monarchical pretension:

>   salutes
> Of *villany,* and ambition, best *befits*
> *The royall thoughts of Kings:* Read Machiavell:
> Princes that would aspire, must mocke at hell.
>   (I.iii.93–96)

In the same vein is the advice of the wicked Earl of Gloster to his king: "Maintain the quarrell with your awfull power, / Be it *right or wrong*," for "onely *Kings wils are Lawes* for other men" (III.i.10–14).

Welshman's audiences were treated also to less cynical political advice, even if it is equally capable of antimonarchical construction: for instance, the proposition that a king is royalized by his care for his subjects—"Kings in this are known, / That for their subjects lives neglect their owne" (IV.ii.55–56). More complex is the way that the play's Antique Chorus, a Welsh "Bardh," speaks to modern interests when describing the date of the dramatic action:

58 "Antike Roman"

> Before faire Wales her happy Union had,
> Blest Union, that such happinesse did bring.
> (I.i.56–57)

The words "Blest Union" surely recall not merely the incorporation of the principality of Wales into England in 1522 but also James's pursuit of a complete union between Scotland and England (with Wales) to make a Great Britain.

Obviously, some of the political doctrines in *Welshman* are ingratiating to a patriotic audience. The narrative traces how the heroic "Welsh" prince Caradoc (Caratacus) nobly spares the Emperor Claudius on the battlefield and is later captured, transported to Rome, and welcomed as a hero by the emperor. This historico-romantic drama is tied to *Cymbeline* (which it sometimes copies) and such other Brito-Roman romances as *Bonduca*. Cymbeline's son Guiderius appears, and the play has themes of British courage and chivalry, the dangers of British civil wars, and resistance to the paying of tribute. And like *Bonduca*, *Welshman* includes a "Caesar," a Bonduca/Voada, and of course a Caradoc. There are battle cries against Roman pride and baseness, while in a similarly unsubtle fashion, the British heroism of Caradoc is starkly contrasted not only with the perfidy of a Roman rapist and a lone treasonous British noble but, less predictably, also with the comic bluffness of the Welsh Earl of Anglesey (a title held by a Catholic in Stuart times) and the idiocy of his "foolish" son. The earl speaks stage Welsh; and his son, in heat over the Fayry Queene, crawls about the stage naked. Together, father and son do little to suggest Welsh dignity and therefore are employed to pander to the chauvinism of an English audience The bard and Caradoc, by contrast, speak perfect English. Thus the play both celebrates and mocks the acts of political, religious, and ethnic union. The audience pays its money and takes its own choice of how to respond to the new inclusion of Celtic—Welsh and Scottish—strains into English life.

If an indifferently written potboiler like *Welshman* could include interestingly ambivalent or otherwise complex political messages—libertarian, constitutionalist, chauvinistic, Machiavellian—is it surprising that the works of cleverer or more profound authors could also seem cogent? Is the supposed theme of political quietism in Jonson's Roman plays "deploy[ed]" so "as to give it the attraction of Resistance idealism" (Hill 125)? Or is the theme mainly deconstructive? A variant of this quandary is seen in Fletcher's *Valentinian,* where a character expresses a view of royal privilege so hyperbolic that, for most auditors, it must have been repulsive and self-undermining: "*Majestie* is made to be obeyed / And *not inquired into*" (I.iii.27–28). The politically volatile Machiavellian dialogue in the Fletcherian *False One* has already been cited. There, dangerous satire on a whole range of topics is prudently put in the mouth of villains, as they discuss their assassination of Pompey. We are cogently reminded that victors write the history books and that kings came into being through their own ambition, not divine will or a social compact.

> *Photinus.*   *if we prosper*
> *'Twill be stil'd lawfull,* and we shall give laws
> To those that now command us: stop not at
> Or loyalty, or duty: *bold ambition,*
> To dare and power to do, gave *the first difference*
> Between the King and subject.
>   (V.ii, p. 359)

The whole play is opportunistic and shallow, but the occasional brilliant shard makes it worth attention today and performed the same function almost four hundred years ago.

Believe As You List presents especially interesting issues of politically pointed anachronism. Until Massinger had trouble with the censor, this Roman play had a late-sixteenth-century setting and concerned Don Sebastian, pretender to the throne of Portugal, and a man harassed by Spain, even during a long residence in Elizabethan England. In its original form of 1630, *Believe As You List* was disallowed by the royal Master of the Revels, Sir Henry Herbert, who cited in support of his ruling the sensitive fact of "ther being a peace sworen twixte the kings of England and Spayne" (in *Plays* 2:293). What was Massinger's original purpose in choosing this pathetic tale of a holy yet ineffectual pretender, supported abroad by his countries' merchants and yet betrayed by his supposed friends' cowardly or selfish collusion with his enemies? Probably the intent was first to criticize Elizabeth's manipulation of Don Sebastian and then to show her successors' (especially Charles I's) lack of support of and protection for both his English merchants living abroad and the wandering royal relative, the erstwhile king of Bohemia (Edwards, *Threshold* 182–84; cf. Gross).

Massinger's new title is surely designed to intimate the ambiguous nature of the play's fictive time. The prologue states that in concocting "this strange historie," the "author" of this play is said to have misapplied geographies and histories; but "beleeve you as you list,"

> yf you find what'[s] Roman here,
> Grecian, or Asiaticqe, drawe to nere
> a late, & sad example,
>
> . . . .
> . . . be it new, or olde,
> the tale is worth the hearinge.
> (Prologue 3–22)

The modern Oxford editor exaggerates when he speaks of Massinger's process of revision as "going over with a paint brush to make [the work] look like ancient history," but with "the original play . . . show[ing] up under the paint work" ("Pretenders" 20 n. 2)—a judgment that implies that Massinger's revision is sloppily transparent. Instead, as with Middleton's multiply chronotopic *Game at Chess,* Massinger's *pentimento* ably enforced anti-Spanish and anti-Habsburg sentiments. Massinger's patriotism, as well as his showmanship, encouraged him to endow Sebastian not only with an anachronistic Habsburg or "German lippe" (I.ii.184) but also with a set of Christ-like experiences, while turning the Spaniards into Satans, Pilates, spouters of Machiavelli, coarse manipulators of Sebastian's priests and merchants, and stereotypical Renaissance Latin villains. The author smoothly transfers to Rome the connotations of the Black Legend, whereby Spaniards were believed by Elizabethans to be unusually cruel, greedy, and uncivilized imperialists (Maltby)—and therefore supposedly the English's Other.

In response to this censorship, Massinger reset, or pretended to reset, the work in Hellenistic times, with a historical Antiochus the Great's being unhistorically exiled from his native land by his Roman enemies. This event imitated the fates both of the modern Portuguese Don Sebastian, resident in England and mistreated by Spain, and of Carthaginian Hannibal, Ancient victim of Roman oppression. Spectators with a smattering of history would know, or be soon able to discover, that the play's Quintus Flaminius, the chief Roman persecutor of the fictitious Antiochus, had indeed cruelly plagued the historical hero Hannibal. The play's Antiochus, then, is meant to be perceived in almost simultaneous multiple fashion: now as dignified Hellenistic monarch; now as the defeated Carthaginian general; now as badgered sixteenth-century Portuguese prince; and now again as Christ. This last is because the play's hero is part embodiment, part parody of Jesus; he is distinguished by such experiences as speaking on a mountaintop, ritualistically rejecting a trio of demonic temptations, and being derided with a signboard listing his supposed crimes above his head as he rides bound upon an ass in a mock Palm Sunday–like procession through "Calipolis." The name Calipolis means "beautiful city" and had recently been applied to London itself by Jonson in his masque *Love's Triumph Through Callipolis,* presented at court two days before Massinger was refused a license for the first version of his play (Harbage 126; *Massinger,* ed. Edwards and Gibson, 3: 293) and four months before the revision was accepted.

The charge that Cruickshank made several years ago against *Believe* seems unjustified: this tragedy is not a "fiasco" (140), the "ineffectiveness" of which is likely due to the revision of the setting (180). As Ure says, the work exhibits a "sense of different cultures in conflict" ("Marston's *Sophonisba*" 82). As a matter of fact, this effect becomes only the richer when an occasional revision is incomplete. Paradoxically, this makes the work even more like Caron's Roman painting: an Early Modern vision, the object of which is to distance an audience and reorient its time sense in a fashion proleptically Brechtian. As with the irrational details in the manneristic Gothic revival of the sixteenth century, the multiplicity of chronotopes in such dramas as *Believe* was relished for each of their own sakes. The original audience in 1631, if it had had clairvoyance, would have especially enjoyed what Edwards calls the play's "strangely prophetic" quality. By switching the story from a consideration of a repressive (Spanish) monarchy to a repressive (Roman) republic, the author helped foreshadow the problems of the English commonwealth and of later republics, associating "the ethos of modern expediency and progress . . . with republicanism" ("Pretenders" 35). Doubtless, one reason for multivalent chronotopes in Roman plays is their unique capacity to accommodate and empower so many Early Modern political, literary, and other cultural agendas. A "Roman" setting can excitingly allow a re- and pre-presentation of heteroglossic voices for countless groups: past, present, and future.

PART TWO

PLAYING STOICS AND TYRANT-KINGS

The matter of tragedies is . . . all kind of heroyick evils.

JOHN GREENE
Refutation of the Apology for Actors

CHAPTER THREE

Nobilitas and *Majestas*: Munificence, Clemency, and Sensitivity to Slight

Plumed troops and the big wars / . . . make ambition virtue!

SHAKESPEARE
Othello

As we have seen in chapter 2, Rome's long-lived fame and persistent, huge, and rich empire encouraged the newly centralized states and emerging empires of Early Modern Europe to model themselves on Rome. As this and the next two chapters seek to demonstrate, stage Romans could seem empowered far beyond the ordinary in at least seven areas. The first four are military and governmental achievements, humanistic patronage of the arts, an ostensibly king- or godlike clemency, and the powers of self-control and self-denying *constantia* (ch. 4). To this list we must quickly add a majestic pride that could shade off into unflattering traits like factiousness and a sensitivity to insult (to be discussed in this chapter), a fondness for rituals of superiority (particularly the triumph and humiliating "insultment" (discussed in ch. 5), and downright savage cruelty (ch. 6).

An initial sense of the dynamic according to which these diverse traits fit together can be gathered from two documents: William Thomas's description, and William Rogers's engraving, of Rome. For Thomas in 1577, for instance, the ruins of Rome produce the essence of ambivalence, looking simultaneously majestic, tyrannical, sadly tragic, and religiously inspirational.

> [When I] beheld . . . the *wonderful majesty* of buildings . . . , imagining, withal, what *majesty* the city might be of, when all these things flourished I remembered again the occasions whereof these *glorious* things have grown, what numbers of wars the Romans have maintained *with infinite blood shedding,* destructions of whole countries, ravishments of chaste women, sack, spoil, tributes, oppression of commonwealths, and a thousand other tyrannies without the which the Romans could never have achieved the perfection of so many wonders as mine eye did there behold. Then perceived I how just the judgment of God is, that hath made those antiquities as a *foul* spoil of the *Roman pride,* and for a witness to the world's end of their *tyranny*. (*History of Italy*, qtd. in Einstein 136–37)

Man's proud and majestic achievements—often purchased through cruelty, greed, and foul lusts—are both glorious and despicable; and their ruined remnants alike connote the depths of human pathos and the heights of divine power.

Another fascinating reminder of Rome's intertwined traits is provided in figure 6 by the great native engraver William Rogers, at work about 1590. Rogers draws an orderly Rome among beautiful hills, but surmounted by looming monsters: a demonic crowned locust (the Romish clergy), a leaping ram (the pope), two multiheaded beasts (one of them named "Satan"), and a triple-tiared whore carrying (as in Dürer's *Apocalypse*) a ciborium or covered chalice. Once again the message is that Rome's vaunted civility is counterbalanced with demonism, bestiality, blasphemous strivings, sensual excess, and bloodlust. The noble Roman ever risks being enslaved by an obsessive effeminizing appetite—whether it be a sexual appetite like that which allegedly possessed Shakespeare's Antony, or some bloodlust and *libido dominandi,* or even a self-mutilating Stoicism.

In many cultures the king is coterminous with his country, and the kinship of the rulers with the gods is a matter of faith. That such beliefs did not obtain in Rome was historically a source of inconvenience or embarrassment to Julius and Augustus Caesar, who during their lifetimes were worshipped as divinities throughout Asia but not Italy. But in the Early Modern view Rome and Romans were like Shakespeare's Julius Caesar: noble, putatively royal, and perhaps even divine as well. The city was dreaded for "marveilous *puisaunt roialnes*" (Rainolde L4v) and "majesty" (William Thomas, qtd. in Einstein 136). Thanks to an empire that was the first of its kind, Rome invented the conception of "majesty with face royal and full of reverence" (Cinthio, *On the Composition of Romances,* qtd. in Gilbert 266).

Jean Tixier (Textor, *Epithetorum* s.v. "Roma") records that Statius terms Rome a city 'crowned with kings' ("regum diademate") and that Mantuan calls it a people fertile in kings ("gens regum . . . ferax"). Mantuan also talks of Rome's consuls as being *crowned* with a thousand senators ("*corona / mille senatorum,*" 21), and the political theorist Charles Merbury alleges in 1581 that "a Senator of Rome was thought any kinges compagnion" (A1v). In the *Tragedy of Cicero,* Rome is described as a "royal city of senators" (II, Dv), and as Lodge puts it, a Roman senator is "a sovereign of this town" (*Wounds* II.i.133). The tendency to royalize a whole class of Romans is at least as strong in England as on the Continent. Garnier speaks of the "visage *franc*"—the free, open confidence on the face—of Pompey's father-in-law as he prepares for suicide, and Kyd renders the phrase "*princely* visage" (*Cornelia* V.312). What belongs to a free man in the French (*franc*) becomes a prince's in the English. In sum, England's Rome is a state full of prestigious senators and other nobles, almost all of whom feel the equal of anyone else in the world, kings and emperors notwithstanding. And that this makes for plays that are conflict-filled, and emotionally and intellectually stimulating, goes without saying.

Sovereignty in the Arts

In one English Roman play after another, the capital city itself is characterized as "royal Rome" (*Titus* I.i.11), "Queen / Of all the world" (*Catiline* I.109–10), "the worlds Queene" (*Cornelia* III.ii.1), "the supreme head of majestie" (*Two Noble Ladies* 1682), a land of "globes and scepters" (*Believe* III.iii.131). Early Modern writers strike a note of enthusiasm that is missing from, say, Chaucer's Roman references (e.g., in *Legend of Good Women*), for the Renaissance grasps the hugeness of Rome's empire and the majestic marvel of the human constructions that adorned her physically, emotionally, and intellectually. First of all, as naive Fluellen reminds us, there is Rome's crowning preeminence in the "Roman [military] disciplines" (*Henry V* III.ii.73) of "the royal occupation" and "peril" of war (*Antony* IV.iv.17, viii.35). Rome's neighbor in *Coriolanus* views his republic's army as "most royal" (IV.iii.43). Martial bravery also royalizes the son of a provincial Roman official, for when a daughter of the Emperor Dioclesian contemplates marriage to such an underling, she asserts that "a prov'd soldier / Is fellow to a King" (*Virgin Martyr* I.i.345–46). And careful "Tullie" on the homefront (fig. 7) is equal "Captai[n]" with royal martial "Caesar" (Whitney 47).

Early Modern times felt empowered by classical learning, not just in government and warfare but also in architecture, law, philosophy, history, and the verbal arts (cf. Velz, "*Orator*"). The Deity himself assured the survival of classical oratory to empower mankind with effective speech. In a view that Bacon shares (*Advancement of Learning*), Ascham argues that "the providence of God hath left unto us . . . onelie in the Greke and Latin tong, the trew preceptes and perfite examples of eloquence" (*Scholemaster* 1: 22). Tudor-Stuart Roman plays contain numerous scenes of debate and references to, or appearances of, men of letters—all letting us know that Rome is a place where words count as much as actions. Poets and other writers appear in *Caesar, Catiline, Valentinian, Nero, Caesar and Pompey, Agrippina*. In *Sejanus* a Roman historian defends the writing of history, and in *Roman Actor* a player speaks at length on behalf of the whole histrionic tradition.

Although Jonson's *Poetaster* admits that Rome had also some poor writers, it suggests that good words are a "liquid *marble*." Poetry, says Jonson's fictive counterpart to the great builder Augustus, surpasses the "cold forms" of monuments and "hollow statues" (V.i., 2370, 2374), and

> can so *mould Rome and her monuments*
> *Within the liquid marble* of her lines
> That they shall stand fresh and miraculous
> Even when they mix with innovating dust.
> In her sweet streams shall our brave Roman spirits
> Chase and swim after death, with their choice deeds
> Shining on their white shoulders; and therein
> Shall Tiber and our famous rivers fall
> With such attraction that th'ambitious line
> Of the round world shall to her centre shrink
> To hear their music. And for these high parts
> Caesar shall reverence the Pierian arts.
>
> (V.i.2380–91)

Jonson's Augustus is making it clear that *majestas* can be conferred by poetry—English as well as Roman.

But it must be admitted that plays' evocation of imagined or real *visual* testimony to Rome's regality counted at least as much as references to her literary preeminence. Let us put aside for a moment the question of the regality of purple and gold in Roman costume. There remains the mention and use of kingly processions, rituals, representations of royal heraldic beasts.[1] Beyond this, there is additional suggestion of Roman physical munificence in architecture, statuary, coins, medals, cameos—specimens, fragments, and imitations of which were scattered all over Europe. When Giovio seeks to praise a modern "castle and bridge," he refers to them as "worke worthy of the noble minde of a Romaine" (G4v). When a great building celebrates a great man, it becomes "a piece of State"—a political statement—serving "the advancement of the Monarchie" by infusing "Magnificent and Majesticall desires, in every common person" (Wotton 107). As Vitruvius says of Augustus's building program, "The state was not only made greater through you by its provinces but *the majesty of empire* also was expressed through the eminent *dignity of its public buildings*" (*De architectura* 1, Preface, 2, qtd. in Paster 8–19; cf. Heuer). Architecture was the incarnation of noble/royal/divine Roman excellence. The true Renaissance "prince" will manifest his or her majestic soul in building programs as monumental as those of the "auncient Romaines," "which be a great witnesse of the prowesse of those *divine* courages" (Castiglione 4, 288–89).

Since at least the mid-sixteenth century private and public theatrical performances alluded to the Roman statues and structures, either verbally or through painted curtains and onstage buildings. In 1566, in order to simulate the classical ambiance of the play that would soon be presented there, an Oxford hall was decorated in a style that we might call Old Roman Palatial: "Nothing, now, more costly or magnificent could be imagined than [the drama's] staging and arrangement. . . . The hall was panelled with gilt, and the roof inside was arched and frescoed; in its size and *loftiness* you would say that it [was] copied after the *grandeur of an old Roman palace,* and in its *magnificence* that it *imitated* some model of *antiquity*" (Bereblock, *Diary,* trans. Schelling, *Drama* 1: 108). In the Revels Accounts for a court performance of a lost "Pompey" in 1581, there is a "new" "great city" and "a senate howse" (Schelling, *Drama* 2: 27), while in Henslowe's list of Admiral's properties in 1590, there is mention of a "sittie of Rome," probably a backcloth adequate for Doctor Faustus's aerial tour of Rome.

This scene (*Faustus* viii) omits mention of Saint Peter's, the dome of which was finished in 1590, but specifically refers to "pyramids"—like Cestius's or obelisks (OED)—and to the premedieval "castle" Angelo, Hadrian's Tomb. A backdrop for the Marlowe play would thus be suitable for many dramas with Ancient Roman settings. In another Admiral's play in which such a backdrop might well serve, Rome is a place of "matchless sovereignty," looking like the bejeweled "palace of the morning sun," with the noble Tiber "lead[ing] out" in elegant procession "the stately buildings of the world" (*Wounds* I.i.221, 289–90; IV.i.227). Three decades later in a King's Men play, another Faustian aerial tour takes place, probably before another backcloth, on which would be displayed the "lofty Towers" and

> These spacious streets, where *every private house*
> Appears *a Palace* to receive a King:
> The site, the wealth, the beauty of the place,
> Will soon inform thee 'tis imperious Rome.
> (*Prophetess* II.iii.341)

Shakespeare could be certain of awakening an audience's sense of Rome's architectural majesty—and the princely status of its great lords—when he placed onstage the Andronici's tomb "sumptuously reedified" (*Titus* I.ii.351). Or when he has Antony prefer Cleopatra to the "clay" brick "*arch*" of empire—a triumphal Roman arch, not a Gothic one (*Antony* I.i.33–35). Or, again, when Romans speak of both Antony (III.x.18) and the dead Julius as a "noble *ruin*" (*Caesar* III.i.256).

Shakespeare's *Caesar* repeatedly, of course, summons up Rome's palatial private dwellings, elaborate public fountains, buildings and theaters with statuary. Representation of statues are called for also in *Sejanus* (V.171–94) and *Roman Actor* (V.i.SD180–81). Among the numerous other Roman plays that refer to Rome's architectural and sculptural preeminence is the anonymous tragedy *Nero*, where we hear an inventory of the monuments that fell victim to the Emperor's incendiary action. The architectural "majestie" of Rome is again explicitly indicated in *Agrippina* I.i.330, by the Republican-leaning Thomas May; this work also mentions Nero's "gorgious Palace" (Prologue 30), numerous other "marble Palaces," "Triumphall Arches, Pillars, Obeliskes," "Julius Temple, Claudius Aquaeducts, / Agrippa's Baths," "Pompey's Theater," and similar "monuments / Built with the riches of the spoiled world" (I.i.333–39). As the final phrase suggests, Rome's artistic sovereignty was not assumed to be an unmixed blessing but could also be taken as symbolic of all the proud imperial vices that plagued its thousand-year career, as William Thomas noted.

King's Fellows

Art in the broadest sense was not the only conventional basis for the stage Romans' claim to mastery. First, they were chiefly male, aristocratic, and possessed of great military and civic authority. Ever since Antiquity, non-Romans tended to equate Roman senators with lordship, an anachronism, for, as Plutarch reports ("Life of Romulus"), the local term *patres conscripti*, 'selected fathers,' is not aristocratic in denotation. Understandably, strong terms of control such as *lord* and *peer* are applied to Romans in several plays: *Virtuous Octavia* III.ii.17; *Caesar's Revenge* 967; *Sejanus* I.60; *Lucrece* 124; *Believe As You List* I.i.79, ii.122; and repeatedly in Lodge's *Wounds*.

Roman achievements in political and numerous other areas encouraged an Early Modern sense of Roman *notabilitas*, 'worthiness of being known,' which some etymologists think is the basis of *nobilitas*, or the usefully ambiguous word *nobility*. To be noble signifies (1) mere possession of aristocratic forebears (whose excellences one is presumably striving to equal, or at least not disgrace) and/or (2) an achievement on one's own of a personal level of excellence that can be recognized by the society at large. Insofar as Roman *nobilitas* historically involved *notabilitas*, it obviously involved power, if only through Fame, which is the longtime control over persons' minds.

In a speech with interesting dramatic parallels, the Marius of the historian Sallust argues that his "scarres and wounds" indicate courage and compensate for lack of a pedigree:

> I confesse I am not able to alleadge (as witnesses of my desert) eyther a long drawne pedigree, tryumphall Chariots, or the Consulships of my progenitors; But if need were, of Speares, Ensignes, Barbes for Horses, and other like rewardes and ornaments of Chivalry; to which, if ye also adde, a body mangled with scarres and wounds, I could produce aboundance; This is my Nobility, not lineallie descending by course of inheritance, but with industry, sweat, and the expence of much blould, atchived. . . . To assaile the Enemy, . . . to lie

hard, and finally with equall patience to endure Heate, Colde, Hunger, thirst and travayle; here I am expert. (*Jugurth* 212)

Similarly mangled bodies are said to be eloquent not only in the Roman tragedies of Shakespeare but also in a work like the Fletcher-Massinger *False One:*

> Rather lose all your limbs, than the least honesty,
> You are never lame indeed, till loss of credit
> Benumb ye through: Scarrs, and those maims of honour
> Are memorable crutches, that shall bear
> When you are dead, your noble names to Eternity.
> (IV.iii, p. 353)

But as in Shakespeare, the dramatic context exerts a partial alienation effect on the doctrines being preached, for the speaker is a temporarily repentant villain, who history says will go on to do more evil. As with cynical Enobarbus at the Last Supper of Shakespeare's Antony, the sentiments tug at the heartstrings, and the hearers are touched despite themselves by his manipulative cliches. The impact of the scene on the mind and heart of the audience offstage must, of course, also be quite vertiginous and complex.

In an era when Early Modern monarchs were seeking to build up a loyal cadre of talent from new sources, "achieved" nobility, not "lineallie descending," was especially attractive and useful. And things Roman came to be of a special interest because of the Ancient city's emphasis on personal excellence and its relatively flexible social gradations, whereby citizenship, as well as senatorial and imperial rank, were extended to people of all social, racial, and geographic origins. As the Renaissance author Poggio Bracchiolini stresses, Roman *nobilitas* denotes a more interior and moral quality than the corresponding Greek category of *eu-geneia* ('good birth'; Braden 67). The honorific *noble* in the vernacular languages came to refer not so much to Medieval chivalry, or to equivalents of the Ancient *cursus honorum,* as to the revived traditions of the New Learning, especially neo-Stoicism. "Stoicism enters Renaissance literature as part of the metaphorics of nobility," satisfying "an appetite for classical dignitas" (Braden 77). For "Neo-Stoicism resuscitated a distinctly Roman ethos; to be a Stoic meant, in effect, to be a Roman" (Anson 13). Accordingly, to call a person or stage character "Stoical," "Roman," or "noble" soon amounted to the same thing. And as the next chapter will show, the strong rhetorical attraction of Stoicism toward the rhetoric of sovereignty over one's emotions made this philosophy especially hospitable to the new definitions of nobility, where this day's deeds and reputations command at least as much respect as yesterday's.

Tudor-Stuart dramatists' awareness of a connection between nobility and Rome originates at least as early as 1497, the date of *Fulgens and Lucres,* where the scholarly and pious martial hero outbids a member of the old aristocracy for the heroine's hand. Almost a century after *Fulgens,* when evidence of a sustained series of Roman plays emerges, we find in Lodge's *Wounds* a frequent use of *noble* and *nobility* (e.g., I.i.245; III.ii.47, 62; III.iv.68, V.v.79). The mindlessly imitative author of *Caesar's Revenge* (c. 1594) makes such a fuss over his many iterations of the word *noble* that he almost always spells it with a capital N. Chapman's Brutus is said to know what "fitted noblesse and Roman" (*Caesar and Pompey* IV.iv.36), as if the two categories were equivalents. Jonson's disreputable Sejanus courts the reputation of being "the noblest Roman" which ironically means using his agents "nobly," even if by that he intends nothing loftier than manipulating others through bribes (*Sejanus* I.268, IV.94). Shakespeare's Antony brags that he and his lady stand up "*peer*less," and their un-Roman behavior signifies the true "*nobleness* of life" (I.i.1–40).

In all his Roman plays Shakespeare enlists the code words of Roman moral nobility to question their meanings. "There's not a *nobler* man in Rome than Antony" (*Caesar* III.ii.116–17), the mob says when Antony's opportunistic manipulations are most transparent to the theatrical audience. But how much worse is Antony's claim to nobility than Caesar's, Brutus's, or Portia's, for each character's supposedly "noble" and "honorable" side is problematized. And *Coriolanus,* in which the word *noble* and its cognates occur almost twice as often as they do in *Caesar* (77 vs. 43), is another paradise for tracing irony and structural iteration.

Drawing on the Platonic notion that a control over one's passions was regarded as the mark of a ruler, Stoicism implies that its ideal Wise Man is beyond mere nobility and styles him king over himself. This general idea was also transmitted through numerous other channels. A popular maxim ascribed to Cato in the Middle Ages and Renaissance emphasizes that 'if you rule with/through/for your mind, you are a king; if you rule with/through/for your body, you are a slave' ("Tu si animo regeris, rex es; si corpore, servus," "Dicta Catonis" 624). According to Renaissance rhetorical practice (Ronan, "Multiplex"), all men can be described as kings and gods. In the Judaeo-Christian tradition, the kingship of all descendants of Adam is a traditional topos, allowing for the easy substitution of "Rex Mundi" for "Everyman" in English morality plays. The nature of a Christian king is bifold, as Bacon says when he advises kings to remember a paradoxical pair of ideas: that they are men and that they are gods: "All precepts concerning Kings are in effect comprehended in . . . *Memento quod es homo,* and *Memento quod es Deus*" ("Of Empire" [1607], in *Essays* [1607]). The kingship of God had been an Old Testament theme memorialized in Roman art since late Antiquity (Bianchi Bandinelli), and the obverse of this had long been also true, as Shakespeare's Company's patron explains: Scripture teaches that Kings are not only GOD's lieutenants upon earth, and sit upon GOD's throne, but even by GOD himself are called Gods" (James I, qtd. in Edwards, *Threshold* 40). The border between man and god is closer in the case of a king than of any other human. In view of the many excellences to which Romans rightly or wrongly laid claim, it is no wonder that the English Roman play is full of indications that Rome represented the *crowning* human achievement—and also the damningly blasphemous human ambitions to godhead.

Speaking in the same philosophical register, Montaigne articulates a protoegalitarian vision when he refers to every Christian as a "prince" of Rome, as if all believers were purple-clad cardinals ("De la vanité," *Essays* 3.9)—a doctrine close to that of the priesthood and kingship of all believers, or to the Ancient ideal of universal Roman suffrage.

From the start the dramas insist on the issue of not just the nobility but also the regality of Rome and Romans. In *Wounds of Civil War* the consul Octavius sits on the "throne" of Rome's "monarchy" (III.i.82; IV.78, 122). In V.iv an officer of the second rank is said to "enter in royalty" (SD1), that is, in purple and gold triumphal gear. When thus arrayed, the infamous leader of civil strife, Scilla, visualizes himself sitting in the quasi-divine "throne" of "matchless glory" and as being filled with "thoughts more greater than a crown, / And yet befitting well a Roman mind" (II.i.6–18). As in *Tamburlaine,* several of Lodge's principal characters are self-made leaders, but they and their entire families are handled like royalty. Hence, when captive princely born foreigners lower themselves and docilely drag

Scilla's victory chariot onto the stage (in what must really have been a familiar crowd-pleasing ploy), it is the noble Roman who can give *them* lessons in true princeliness:

> *Scilla.* For fear of death can *princes entertain*
> Such *bastard thoughts* that now from glorious arms
> Vouchsafe to draw *like oxen in a plow?*
> . . . .
> *Aristion.* I tell thee, Scilla, captives have no choice,
> And death is dreadful to a caitive man.
> *Scilla.* In such imperfect mettles as is yours;
> But *Romans* that are still *allur'd by fame*
> *Choose rather death than blemish* of their name.
> (III.iii.81–91)

Like a prince, a true Roman loves honor, fame, and "glorious arms," and would rather kill himself than suffer a diminution of his name. Scilla has taught these values to his wife and daughter, for they will soon comport themselves before Marius with a suicidal courage that he repeatedly identifies as a sign of a "Roman" and "princely majesty" (IV.i.385, 399).

In *Caesar's Revenge* not just the Caesarians (II.iv.1483–1500) but all their Republican enemies are *princes* and *lords* (I.iii.729, 291; i.96; II.i.729; II.v. 1526; IV.i.1882–83). Similarly, in Thomas Heywood's *Lucrece,* to banish "the Kings name" and to rule the Roman republic make one worthy, as the Republican Lucius Junius Brutus learns, of the oxymoronic title "royall Brutus" (2584). This satiric episode recalls Shakespeare's *Caesar,* where another antimonarchical Brutus is all but acclaimed a king when the mob yells—

> *2 Pleb.* Let him *be Caesar.*
> *3 Pleb*   Caesar's better parts
>   Shall be *crown'd* in Brutus.
> (III.ii.51)

Cassius snarls that although all noble Romans were "born free as Caesar" (I.ii.97), Caesar alone has gotten the royalizing "palm" and "start of the majestic" world (130–31), becoming Rome's *mon*arch, "one only man" and ruler (157, cf. 152, 155). To die without trying to grasp at world rule proves that one is no socialized Roman at all but, as Brutus puts it, a mere "villager" (I.ii.172). *Caesar* V.ii also presents a highly suggestive series of icons of royal *Romanitas:* Octavius, Titinius, Cassius (and possibly Brutus, and Antony) wear victory crowns, and certainly the message that Titinius "crown'd dead Cassius" (V.iii.95–96) underlines this ironic motif.

Jonson's Silius recalls that he and his fellows, before the end of the Republic,

> were born
> Free, *equal lords* of the triumphèd world
> And knew no masters but affections.
> (*Sejanus* I.59–61)

In *Antony* Sextus Pompeius reiterates Brutus's desire to "have one man but a man" (II.vi.19), indicating that Republican Roman sovereignty rests with the whole class, not three men alienating all power to themselves and pretending to be "the senators alone of this great world, / Chief factors for the gods" (9–10). Interestingly, Pompey defines senators as divine "factors" or makers/doers, almost as if they were meant to be *God*'s viceroys, a standard synonym for kings. Such doctrines are Montaignesque, and but a step away from the egalitarian notion of the Webster Virginia that every freeborn Roman citizen has a freedom equal to a king's:

> *Clodius.*   Thou art my slave,
>   And here I sease what's mine.
> *Virginia.*   Ignoble villaine,
>   I am as *free as the best King* or Consull
>   Since Romulus.
>   (*Appius* III.ii.109–13)

As late as 1635, not many years before England argued out similar beliefs on the battlefield of civil war, Silius and his companions in rebellion in Richards's *Messallina* are still preaching the royalty conferred on individual Romans by reason of their daring. These aristocrats tell the Emperor Claudius that they are "enobled, into / The eminent temper of true Monarches" (V.i.2332–33).

The costume of Garter Investiture for Frederick of Wirtemburg was described as having sleeves that were "wrought after the manner of a long pretext or senator's robe," "embroidered with needlework blue" (Rye lxxviii): nothing could be more majestic for this monarch than something on the Roman pattern. The normal Renaissance version of the "pretext" was probably purple and gold, though here blue is substituted in deference to the blue of the Garter.

In a poem on Cicero in *Tottel's Miscellany* (2.118), Nicholas Grimald refers to Cicero's wearing a "royall robe" (2.253), and Geoffrey Whitney's *Emblemes* alludes to the Romans as being traditionally "deck'd in Scarlet" (134). The fact that the Whore of Babylon is "red with blood" and "apparelled in scarlet" shows, says the Geneva gloss at Revelation 17, her urge not only to kill "licentiously" but also, like the "Romish clergie," to dress in "a robe imperiall and of triumph." And, as if in anticipation of the theories of Michel Foucault, George Sandys explains that the essence of magisterial power is to shed blood: for to be "cloathed in a robe of scarlet" is only proper to "Princes and Magistrates, expressing their power of inflicting death by that bloody colour" (65). Faith in the socially cohesive powers of a sovereign's gentler traits of clemency and munificence is apparently weak, and *regalia* are ultimately established by the royal right to deploy arms and the prerogative of the death sentence.

Actually, the amount of scarlet/purple (*purpura*) in genuinely historical Roman regalia seems less than the Renaissance thought. Roman military officers wore purple and gold (*Aeneid* 12.126). In civilian life senators and magistrates ordinarily wore white gowns striped and/or trimmed with purple (Johnston 177–85; L. Wilson). On the streets of Rome, one of the few times that a historic person would wear gold-encrusted purple was if he was being made an *imperator,* or perhaps under the Empire, if he was the emperor. The normal *imperator* was a successful general whose most recent campaign had occasioned thousands of enemy war dead (the actual number is disputed). He would have had his face painted in red like Jupiter Capitolinus, and would be dressed in the red and gold kingly regalia that customarily graced that chief cult statue of the Roman state. There can be little doubt of the role of royalizing/divinizing bloodrites here (and elsewhere, as ch. 6 indicates) in conveying a sense of the divine kingliness of a noble Roman. In stage Rome, any blood—not just the enemies' but one's own also, shed in battle or suicide (ch. 4)—could ennoble a person, raising him or her metaphorically to the purple.

The use of the *purpura* costume in English Roman plays is a documented custom of several decades' standing, continuing till the Restoration. In the Admiral's Company *Wounds* of the mid 1580s, the "imperial Senators of Rome" dress in "royal robes": namely, "scarlet gowns," the color of "purple blood" (I.i.113, 215, 222; V.ii.23; cf. V.i.7). And when a Roman general of the second rank is awarded a triumph and enters "*in royalty*" (V.iv.SD1), the audience is silently being reminded that royalty in ancient Rome extended to many nonroyal people and involved purple garments as well as golden regalia. The Children of the Queen's Chapel put on *Poetaster* in about 1601, and the closing lines of the play allude to "apes [being] apes," even though clothed in "scarlet" (3170). Since the play's Augustus was obviously clothed as royalty but should not be accused of being an ape, his subordinates— mere noble or prominent Romans—must have also been in scarlet regalia. In *Catiline*, a King's Men play and thus likely to tell us something about the costuming of Shakespeare's Romans, Jonson's senators are twice termed the "purple" (I.277, V.265), an inappropriate phrase if the actors were wearing the more historically correct white gowns with purple trim or stripe. In *The Virgin Martyr*, a Red Bull play of about 1620, a provincial official says that he wears "the scarlet robe of bold authority" (I.i.173). In *Faithful Friends*, recently ascribed (by the Malone editor) to the 1620s, a Roman senator is identified by "his Scarlet Gowne" (III.ii, 1680–81). If Beeston's Boys in the late 1630s exercised their rights to *Appius* (Harbage 120–21), the senators there would also have been dressed in gowns of "crimson," which the play defines as "bloud"-red "scarlet" (I.iv.74–77). In the university play *Fuimus Troes* of about 1625, there is a reference to characters' being clothed in the "scarlet of patrician blood" (III.ii.459), a probable quibble dependent on the play's Roman aristocrats' wearing purple vesture. Earlier, in *Catiline*, such apparel lends subtle point to the Allobrogian ambassadors' disgust that "the world's master" was "a mere clothed Senate" (II.15), while in *Julius Caesar* the *purpura* would reinforce the impression created by the assassins' purpled hands, giving further sarcastic force to Antony's reference to the senatorial conspirators as this world's "princes" (III.i.209) (fig. 7).

By their constitution Republican Romans had a shared distribution of powers, including the assignment of chief executive power to two consuls, not one. From the time of Romulus to at least that of Caesar, Roman history teaches that "Dire league of partners in a kingdom last not":

> Shall never faith be found in fellow kings.
> Dominion cannot suffer partnership.
> This needs no foreign proof, nor far-fet story:
> Rome's infant walls were steep'd in brother's blood;
> Nor then was land or sea, to breed such hate,
> A town with one poor church set them at odds.
> (*Lucan* 1.88–97, in "First Booke," trans. Marlowe)

Citing this same classic formulation of Roman factiousness, Augustine mercilessly parallels Romulus with the other "archetype" of emulous "envy," Cain. Romulus illustrates that "he that glories in dominion must needs see his glory diminished when he has a partner to share with him" (*City* 15.5). All in all, desire for power over space (dominion) and time (glory, fame) encouraged Romans to be argumentative and full of "garboils," as Marlowe's Lucan (1.68) and several other authors put it (T. J. B. Spencer). Not just a humane protection against tyranny but also a divisive factiousness is unfortunately built into republican Rome's contentious mixed polity. *Caesar* touches on the clash of Pompeian tribunes with those who would permit Caesar monarchical dignities, while *Coriolanus* explicitly alludes to the "double worship" at the core of Rome's popular-aristocratic constitution (III.i.142).

Where the nobility has power and aspiration approaching those of the "eminent temper of true Monarches" (*Messallina* V.i., 2332), pride and a sensitivity to slight will repeatedly lead to violence—a principle of which Elizabeth and Essex were both well aware. Rome is described in the opening of Appian's *Civil War* (*Roman History*) as full of *hybris acosmos:* the "uncomely contumely of every trifle, and foule contempt of law and right" that, since the time of the Gracchi, "did ever play a part" in Roman politics (*Auncient Historie* 1:2). Warlords acted "in power *like princes,* and as *Monarkes*" (*monarchikoi*), levying armies "in word against the contrary faction, but in deede against the countrey" itself. No wonder the whole last half of the great Roman philosopher Seneca's *De ira* ('Of Anger') is devoted to dangerous touchiness. Doubtlessly Bacon too had haughty and bloody Roman politicians in mind when he wrote that "they that are *glorious* must needs be *factious;* for all bravery stands upon comparison. They must needs be *violent* to make good their own *vaunts*" ("Of Vainglory," *Essays* [1612]).

No fewer than fifteen English plays on Rome make verbal reference to the stereotype of Roman "factiousness," and many plays demonstrate the proposition as early as the opening scene. By line 242 of the opening scene of Lodge's play, the meeting of the Senate deteriorates into a bloody brawl between Marians and Scillans; Heywood's *Lucrece* commences with Sextus Tarquin plotting to displace the incumbent king and boasting that "all the Peeres and Senators" "imbrace my *faction*" and "Love change of state, an new King to obey" (I, 124–27). Similar themes emerge from the brawling opening of *Titus* (I.i.214, 404, 451), *Coriolanus* (I.i.193; cf. V.ii.29), and *Caesar*. In the last mentioned, Romans are readily "factious for redress of [their] griefs" (I.iii.118; cf. II.i.77), and the action of I.i commences with the public confrontation of Pompeians and Caesarians. Perennial "*equality* of two domestic powers" necessarily "breed[s] scrupulous *faction*" (*Antony* I.iii.47–48; cf. Phillips). In *Tiberius* even imperial Rome is "rent" and "butchered" with "secret *factions,* compleate treacheries," "common set abroach by each degree" (1602–4). Warfare between social degrees and classes is evident repeatedly in Jonson's *Catiline,* where the titular protagonist attempts to project onto Cicero the rebel's own commitment to "contention" and "faction" (IV.iii.19–26). In *Sejanus* too the Romans bandy about insults concerning "factious" "traitor[s]" (III.350–52). The code word *faction* or its derivatives cooperate with the action, highlighting the contentiousness of Rome's political life in at least seven more plays: *Appius* V.i.4, *Welshman* V.iv.56, Alexander's *Caesar* III.70h, *Agrippina* III.i.274, *Roman Actor* I.iii.134, *False One* II.iii, p. 325, and *Messallina* 1846ff. Stage Rome is fractious, a "dangerous Rome / No Rome of safety" (*Caesar* III.i.288–89), a city that exports its aggressiveness imperialistically abroad, as such plays as *Wounds, Caesar, Antony,* and *Coriolanus* expertly show. Beyond constitutional and class questions, personal pride is an important source of political tension. In his *Moral Essays* Seneca writes that ordinary men of affairs, unlike the ideal Stoical Wise Man, are deeply bothered by slights that involve the loss of expected money, prestige, or power through the conscious machinations of enemies (*De constantia sapientis* 9.2–4). The ingratitude of patrons, the populace, or the whole state is surely such a loss-causing action and is the burden of many Tudor-Stuart

Roman plays, many more than of non-Roman plays. Though today we might think of *King Lear* as the archetypal study of ingratitude ("How sharper than a serpent's tooth it is / To have a thankless child," II.iv.288–89), this theme is not at the heart of most Tudor-Stuart tragedies with Christian settings, even if *Macbeth* is a striking exception. Instead, most studies of in*grat*itude—lack of *graci*ous acceptance—are to be found in tragedies with a pagan setting: in other words, beyond the customary sphere of *gratia*. *Timon*, more obviously pagan than *Lear*, is dedicated to the proposition that all Athens is ungrateful—that her senators extend no more true gratitude toward the great Alcibiades than the sycophants of Timon show to him. And if the age's Roman tragedies are examined, along with Roman tragicomedies like *Cymbeline*, it becomes manifest how tightly the theme of ingratitude is linked to the Ancient locale. Roman dramas constitute 30 percent of Shakespeare's oeuvre, and yet concordances suggest that these five plays and *Timon* contain fully 60 percent of the dramatist's four dozen uses of words like *ingrate*, *ungrateful*, and *ingratitude*. Shakespeare and his fellow dramatists seem to have viewed the Ancient world, particularly Rome, as stained with a cruel pride—self-interested, ungenerous, contentious, murderous. In fact, the Renaissance as a whole makes more of Roman ingratitude than Antiquity did. Probably because Machiavelli finds the Athenians more guilty of ingratitude to their chief citizens than the Romans were to theirs, he feels he must clear the Romans of this traditional charge and deal with this subject unusually early in the *Discourses*, bringing it up immediately after such more predictable topics as religion (1.11–15) and liberty (1.1–10, 16–27).

What Paster concludes of *Sejanus* holds for *Caesar* and many other Roman plays: that they are based on a "continuum" in which "celebration yield[s] endlessly to ingratitude" (62, 96; cf. Velz, "Undular"). Even Shakespeare's nonclassical plays exhibit signs of the tie between Rome and ingratitude, as when Faulconbridge calls rebels "ingrate revolts / You bloody Neroes" (*John* V.ii.151–52). Whether it be Rome toward its citizens or disaffected citizens toward Rome, each party jealously guards its power, casting the opponent as a being lethally unthankful. Rome's "civil broiles" and "factious ... tumultuous times" (*Agrippina* III.i.275–76) are usually caused by a need "to scourge th' *ingratitude* that *despiteful* Rome / Cast[s] on" the victims and their families (*Antony* II.vi.22–23). *Wounds* opens with Scilla's dismay at not being elected general in the Pontic campaign. He does not argue that the post should revert to him out of legality or military prudence, as we would expect a modern politican to allege, but instead, mainly on the basis of Rome's own honor and gratitude:

> Trustless Senators and ingrateful Romans,
> For all the honors I have done to Rome,
> For all the spoils I brought within her walls,
> Thereby for to enrich and raise her pride,
> Repay you me with this ingratitude?
> (I.i.160–64)

In Jonson's *Catiline* (1611), the spirit of this same Sulla and his arguments literally hover about, inspiring the titular hero and his crew with hurt feelings and a sense that their country has treated them shabbily. In an opening scene of plausible indebtedness to Lodge's, Jonson's Catiline complains that Mother Rome has unnaturally denied him the Pontic generalship: out of all her

> brood, mark[ing me] out for the *repulse*
> By her no-voice when I stood candidate
> To be commander in the Pontic war?
> (I.87–89)

And later in the same act Catiline initiates plans to burn Rome out of this same hatred for "th' ungrateful Senate and the people" (III.iii.159d). Similar notes are struck, usually verbally, in *Lucrece, Appius, Roman Actor, Titus, Coriolanus, Cymbeline, Hannibal,* and many other works.[2] And such remaining plays as *Valentinian, The Virgin Martyr, The Prophetess,* and *Believe As You List* are full of intimacies forestalled or betrayed, with family and political ties violated—all fueling the bitterness that ingratitude occasions.

Besides articulating Pompey's already cited view of Rome's ingratitude (II.vi.22), *Antony* displays Ventidius emphasizing his commander's potential for ingratitude (III.i.25–26). Too, Cleopatra expects that Roman Caesar will sympathize with her over the alleged perfidy and thanklessness of Seleucus. Additionally, *Antony* reveals Octavius's denial of "honorable" posts to those who have recently left Antony for him. Such men Caesar callously, even if prudently, places in the front lines, where the danger will be greatest (IV.vi.7–17). Especially fascinating is the way that *Antony* —like *Caesar* and *Lear* before it—appropriates a Christian chronotope in developing the theme of ingratitude, *Caesar*'s Julius drank at breakfast with those who would betray him, and so too Antony shares a momentary resemblance to Christ not only in his Last Supper-Gethsemane scene (IV.ii.30–44) but also in being abandoned by Enobarbus, an incipient penitent like Judas and suicidally inclined "master-leaver" (*Antony* IV.ix.22).

Mark Antony bragged that Rome's greatness lay not in what it took from the rest of the world but in what she gave to it (Plutarch, "Antony," *Lives,* cited in Montaigne, "De la grandeur romaine," *Essays* 2:24). Both Julius and Augustus Caesar sought, and gained, reputations for mercy. At their best, says Sallust, Romans have "governed by conferring benefits on their subjects, not by intimidation; and when wronged they would rather pardon than seek vengeance" (*Catiline* 9, trans. Handford). And the Augustan poet Vergil defines the Romans' task, as we have seen, to spare the humbled ("parcere subjectis," *Aeneid* 6.853), a goal Saint Augustine ambivalently viewed as the pompous "chief glory" of overproud Rome (*City* 1.5, trans. Healey).

Acting on behalf of a client's family, Cicero sought to rescind the banishment of one Quintus Ligarius, a minor enemy of Caesar (later allied to his assassins; cf. *Caesar* II.i). After the man's brothers had unsuccessfully hurled themselves at Caesar's feet, Quintus was formally charged with siding with a foreign enemy. Thereupon, in the famous oration *Pro Ligario,* Cicero directly addressed Caesar, who presided over the court, and said: 'Nothing pleases the people more than good will [*bonitas*]; no other of your many virtues is more admirable or gracious than your pity [*misericordia*]. Nothing that men do draws them *nearer the gods* ['is more *divine*'; *ad deos nulla re propius accedunt*] than the act of saving fellow men; no aspect of your good fortune is greater [*maius*] than your power to forgive—nor no aspect of your character more natural than your desire to preserve [*servare*] as many as you are able' (37–38). On another occasion Cicero wrote 'Nothing is so *kingly* [*regium*], so worthy of a free and liberally educated person [*liberale*], and so munificent [*munificum*]' as to help those in need.[3]

Seneca repeatedly expresses similar hierarchically phrased encomia on clemency. For instance, in the *Moral Essays* he says that to save a citizen, one rightly earns the (temporarily royalizing) civic oak crown, while to save a state full of one's citizens one should be regarded as godlike (*De clementia* 1.26.5). Godlike too is a prince who refuses to exact the full penalty from a wrongdoer ("Fragments," from *De clementia* I.448–49).[4]

To employ clemency is to act with what Duke Prospero would call "*nobler* reason" (*Tempest* V.i.26). With puns on the royal *super*iority of this virtue (cf. ch. 5), Bacon writes: "Certainly in taking Revenge, A Man is but even with his Enemy. But in *passing* it *over,* he is *Supe*riour: for it is a *Prince*'s part to Pardon" ("Of Revenge," *Essays*). When George Chapman sought the mercy and favor of James after the scandal of *Eastward Ho,* the dramatist appealed to the king's "Caesar-like bountie," saying that the ancient Roman "conquerd still to spare the conquered; and was glad of offences that he might forgive." In citing this passage, Jonathan Goldberg nicely observes the principle that Caesarian "power is displayed in self-defeat" (283 n.27), a proud and arbitrary conquest of one's own self.

In the early and influential *Wounds of Civil War,* Lodge makes clemency an obvious motif by elaborately dramatizing the forbearance that rival Roman princes could occasionally show. Scilla restrains his deadly anger against talky lower-class clowns, while Marius illustrates clemency by treating Scilla's captive wife and daughter, not as victims, but as "two welcome guests in whom the *majesty / Of my conceit and courage* must consist (IV.i.266–67). Then, like Alexander with the Persian royal family, he imperially frees his kingly captives.

In Brandon's *Virtuous Octavia* (V.iii, 2216) the eponymous heroine is Antony's widow, and she recounts her brother Octavius's "clemencia" in sparing those who left the elder of the surviving Triumvirs for the younger. Under the heading "Clemenza" in Ripa's emblematic dictionary, clemency is accompanied by the olive, an equation that may help explain Shakespeare's associating olives with Octavius in *Antony* IV.vi.6. For this prince was concerned not just with peace but also with forgiveness and clemency. However, in Fletcher's *Bonduca* (as in *Henry V* and *Measure for Measure*) a character—and the audience—are warned that mutiny is encouraged by "clemency" (I.ii.166–67). With equal authorial attention to casuistic complexity, a cynical Sabine in *Faithful Friends* expects insolent Rome to do no more than pretend to "clemencye" (II.iii, 1401; cf. 1386, 1403).

Webster's evil Appius wishes to be known for "princely grace and clemency" (*Appius* I.iv.43), however little he deserves it; and Jonson's Tiberius similarly seeks to steal a reputation for "mercy" (*Sejanus* III.345), as does his fellow in empire (I.268). With Tiberius and Sejanus, there is no truly noble and royal magnanimity, no gracious readiness to forgive an underling his actions. "Romes mercie" and "accustomde lenitie," and Marcus Scaurus's "clemencie," are also frantically and vainly invoked in *Believe As You List* (I.ii.112; II.ii.218, 227). Other references to clemency, often of a problematizing sort, are found in Shakespeare's *Antony* (V.ii.22–28), May's *Cleopatra* (V.ii.16–18), and numerous other conqueror plays. In *Virgin Martyr*, for instance, though Diocclesian is a persecutor of subroyal Christians, he ostentatiously shows mercy toward his fellow martial monarchs of other lands (I.i.241). Neither is the clemency of Shakespeare's "noblest Roman," Brutus, above suspicion: he spares Antony mainly because he thinks the reveler will be powerless if he is detached from the living Caesar; and though Brutus worries about prying hard-earned money from peasants, he has no regrets about using revenue that Cassius has wrung by similar extortion.

In language suggestive of *Titus* and *Merchant of Venice*, Alexander's Caesar claims that "the sweetest comfort which my conquests gave, / Was that I so might do to many good": "Of *clemency* I like the praise, more then / Of force"; "And *pity is the best thing in the Gods*" (*Julius Caesar* II.i.479–94). The last clause above may well remind us of how shocking the Andronicans' scandalous lack of clemency must have seemed when they spurned the Gothic royalty and incited the tragic action of *Titus*:

> Wilt thou *draw near the nature of the gods?*
> Draw near them in being merciful:
> Sweet mercy is *nobility*'s true badge.
> (I.i.117–19)

In this foreshadowing of the sentiments of Shakespeare's mistress of Belmont, we have three gradations of clemency: that of nobility, that of a god, and because the lecture is being delivered by a queen, that of royalty. In the Republican world of *Coriolanus*, Shakespeare's Cominius and Volumnia strike a similar note when they criticize the hero's unroyal, ungodlike recalcitrance:

86   "Antike Roman"

> I minded him how *royal* 'twas *to pardon*
> When it was less expected.
>
>   (V.i.18–19)

> Thou hast affected the fi[n]e strains of honor
> To *imitate the graces of the gods:*
> To tear with thunder the wide cheeks a' th' air.
>
>   (V.iii.153–55)

Whether Marcius' sparing of Rome is finally more than the thoughtless reaction of a mere mother's "boy" or of a subhuman (especially an eagle) with an uncharacteristically suicidal and defeatist disposition (V.vi.111–16), the above passages argue that clemency is in keeping with the honor of a nobleman, the disposition to pardon of a royal king, and the graciousness of a thundering god. The words of a lady "nothing undervalu'd / To Cato's" Portia (*Merchant* I.i.165–66) further reinforce these formulas when, in IV.i.188–96, she says that the attribute of mercy is a divine power, "above" the coercive scepter of the "mightiest" earthly "awe and majesty":

> mercy is above this *sceptred* sway.
> It is an attribute to God himself;
> And earthly power doth then show *likest God's*[gods'/gods]
> When mercy seasons justice.

And if we read the non-Roman play *The Maid of Honour,* we find Massinger weighing the twin Roman proclivities for triumphs and clemency: the "Lordly Roman" gravitated to cruel triumphs, when instead he should have sought to "draw neare the nature of the *gods,* / Best known for such, in being mercifull" (IV.iv.3–8).

Admittedly, Rome had a reputation for ingratitude, cruelty, sensitivity to insult, pride; and the city's building programs were often based on thievery and blasphemy. Yet it was also civilized and humane enough to be associated not just with munificence, artistic excellence, and *constantia* (ch. 4) but with *clementia* as well—the last being a central aspect of Aristotelian *megalopsychia* (*magnanimitas*) intersecting Ciceronian *humanitas* and Christian mercy, on the one hand, and Machiavellian monarchical policy, on the other.

Figure 1. "Loose Speech": Grotesque-framed Renaissance antic, Roman amphitheater, and the generation of vipers. Woodcut. De La Perrière's *La Morosophie* (1553). Courtesy of Bibliothèque Nationale, Paris.

Figure 2. Laureated Henri II in antic-decorated armor. Medal (1552). Courtesy of British Museum, London.

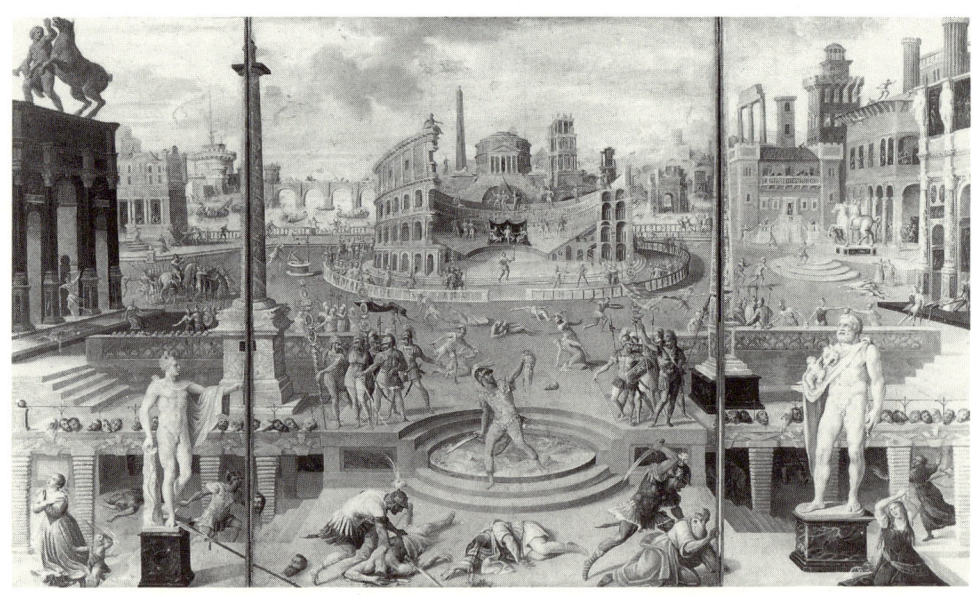

Figure 3. Caron, *Les Massacres du Triumvirat* (1556). Courtesy of Musée du Louvre, Paris.

Figure 3a. Detail of Caron's *Massacres:* Triumvirs, Pantheon, triangular buildings, ghostly riders in the sky, and Cicero's body parts.

Figure 4. Laureated imperator with sash. Peacham, *Titus Andronicus*. Drawing (c. 1595). Courtesy of the Marquess of Bath, Longleat, Wiltshire.

Figure 5. Laureated James I with sash, Emperor of the Whole Island of Britain ("Totius.Ins'.Bryt.Imp'."). Accession medal (1603). Courtesy of British Museum, London.

Figure 6. Majestic Rome surmounted by the papal Whore of Babylon and her monsters. Engraving by Rogers for Broughton's *Concent of Scripture* (c. 1590). Courtesy of Bodleian Library, Oxford.

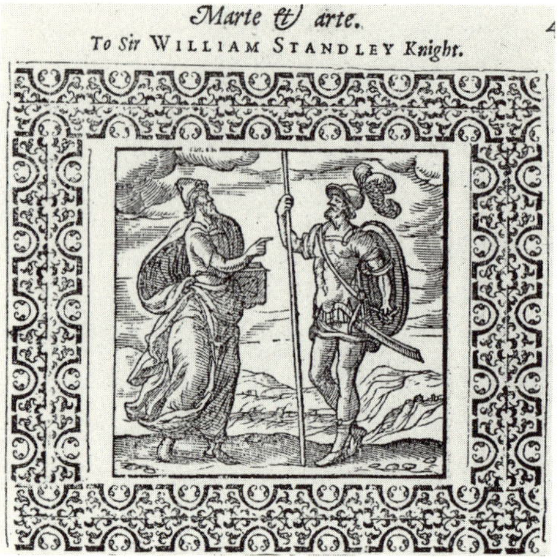

Marte & arte.

To Sir WILLIAM STANDLEY Knight.

Figure 7. Balancing *Ars* (Cicero) and *Mars* (Caesar). Woodcut. Whitney's *Choice of Emblemes* (1586). Courtesy of University Library, Glasgow University.

70 *Fortuna virtutem superans.*

To FR. W. *Esquier.*

Simile de Aiace seipsum interficiente (super cuius tumulum virtus plorans pro falso iudicio) apparet antè, folio tricesimo. Nam cùm Achillis arma per Agamemnonis iudicium, Vlyssi adiudicabantur, Aiax illius iniuriæ impatiens, & postea insanus, seipsum interficiebat, sic inquiens vt Ouid. habet 13. Metamorph.
Hectora qui solus, qui ferrum, ignémque, Iouémque,
Sustinuit toties, vnam non sustinet iram:
Inuictúmq. virũ vicit dolor, arripit ensem:
Et meus hic certè est, an & hunc sibi poscit Vlysses?
Hoc ait, vtẽdum est in me mihi, quiq. cruore
Sæpè Phrygum maduit, domini nunc cæde madebit,
Ne quisquam Aiacem possit superare, nisi Aiax,
Dixit, & in pectus, &c.

WHEN BRVTVS knewe, AVGVSTVS parte preuail'de,
And sawe his frendes, lie bleedinge on the grounde,
Suche deadlie griefe, his noble harte assail'de,
That with his sworde, hee did him selfe confounde:
But firste, his frendes perswaded him to flee,
Whoe aunswer'd thus, my flighte with handes shalbee.

And bending then to blade, his bared breste,
Hee did pronounce, theise wordes with courage great:
Oh Prowes vaine, I longe did loue thee beste,
But nowe, I see, thou doest on fortune waite.
Wherefore with paine, I nowe doe prooue it true,
That fortunes force, maie valiant hartes subdue.

Fides

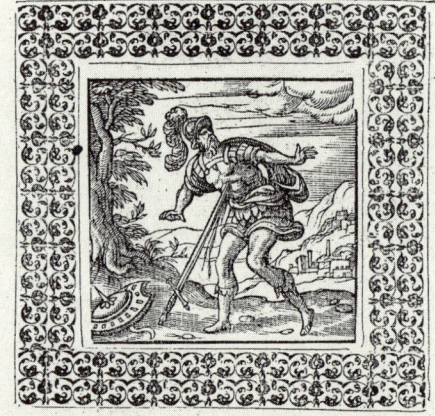

Figure 8. Ill-judged heroism of suicidal Brutus. Woodcut. Whitney's *Choice of Emblemes* (1586). Courtesy of University Library, Glasgow University.

Figure 9. The fire, hand, and patriotic constancy of Scaevola. Woodcut. Whitney's *Choice of Emblemes* (1586). Courtesy of University Library, Glasgow University.

Figure 10. Constancy with her column, Scaevola-like hand, and fire. Woodcut. Baudoin's translation of Ripa's *Iconologie*. Courtesy of Humanities Research Center, University of Texas at Austin.

Figure 11. Antique David and Goliath: pedal insultment and the triumph. Detail from Donatello's *Bronze David* (c. 1430). Courtesy of Museo Nazionale (Bargello), Florence.

CHAPTER FOUR

Suicide and the Dynamics of Stoical *Constantia*

> See how I regarded Caius Cassius,
> By your leave, gods!—this is a Roman's part.
>
> SHAKESPEARE
> *Julius Caesar*

In the last chapter we noted that all things Stoical enjoyed an Early Modern reputation for *Romanitas, regalia,* and *nobilitas* (Anson 13, Braden 66–77). Stoicism lays great stress on the power of the individual to rise above circumstance and escape the pressures of everyday life, which it admits are often daunting. It suggests that though we belong to society and the Powers of Life, we cannot long stay integral or happy unless we also feel we are partly our own persons. One thing that Roman plays problematize for Renaissance humanists is the Senecan notion of a heroic suicide not just as alternative to a heroic life but also as a fitting extension of it.

Not surprisingly, suicide is portrayed or discussed in 90 percent of the Roman plays (forty-one out of forty-five) from 1560 to 1635.[1] The four exceptions are rather atypical, being nonserious plays (*Every Woman in Her Humour; Shoemaker, a Gentleman; Two Noble Ladies;* and *Prophetess*) and therefore less representative of the Roman genre than the rest. No one can proceed very far into an understanding of the function of the Early Modern Roman play without facing the issue of suicide as it appeared in literature and life, Antique and contemporary.

Some suicides in Antiquity were juridical and mainly pro forma, like the death sentences of Socrates or Seneca. But heroic suicide proper was dictated variously by despair, self-affirmation, or personal loyalty (Dublin and Bunzel). Like such other legally and morally dubious activities as adultery, suicide was endowed with an ambivalent attractiveness. In the *Phaedo* Plato seems to discourage the act, but ambiguously enough to have helped inspire Cato on the evening of his death. In the *Aeneid* (6.434–39) Vergil condemns world-weary suicides to an unattractive corner of Hades, though, like his contemporary Livy and successor Lucan, he praises various political suicides.

Cato's and Lucrece's politically powerful deaths are the great test cases of moral casuistry in the Christian West. Augustine criticizes Cato Uticensis for being too proud to accept the clemency of Julius Caesar's (unconstitutional) regime, and also maintains that Livy's defense of Lucretia's death is illogical, warning his own contemporaries to eschew the example not just of Lucretia but even of canonized Christian souls who chose their own death rather than endure rape (Donaldson). Though Dante assigns a portion of Hell to suicides, he allows Cato the freedom of not living there but in fact of serving as governor of Christians' Purgatory. Similarly, though Montaigne unapologetically sought for himself a quiet literary retreat from French religious wars that he could neither stop nor win, he at first greatly admires Stoicism, echoing Seneca's praise of Cato's death as an act of "divine resolution" (Seneca, *De providentia* 2.9) and announcing that "this man was truly a patterne, whom nature chose to shew how farre human vertue may reach, and man's constancie attaine unto" (*Essays* 2.37, trans. Florio).

In 1586 Whitney wraps Brutus's death (fig. 8) in a mixture of heroism and patronizing pathos. The Roman's posture is drawn in a less than flattering manner, and the marginalia parallels this famous Roman with mad Ajax, laboring under faulty judgment ("pro falso iudicio . . . insanus"). According to Wymer's findings (16 n.52), English suicide rates had been on the rise since the middle of the sixteenth century, and the social stigma was being lifted from the act. Sir Philip Sidney did not escape Protestant canonization even though he fatefully chose to enter his final battle at Zutphen without his thigh armor. Jonson's mother bragged of being ready to take poison and to kill herself and her son if he was made to endure juridical mutilation (Drummond 283). And the imprisoned Sir Walter Ralegh probably thought he could win popular support for his release by attempting to take his own life. On the stage Roman suicide was guardedly but increasingly admired. An idea of the range of attitudes toward the act is provided in Shakespeare: from the selfless love to which Cleopatra and Romeo say they aspire, to the antic unmanliness of a "Roman fool," as Macbeth, Leonatus's jailer, and perhaps Hamlet conceive of the deed.

Bernard Paulin plausibly suggests that the Tudor-Stuart writers' interest in suicide reflects a Renaissance love of moral casuistry, of individualism, and of grand theatrical gestures (588–95). Literary suicide promised imaginative escape at a moment when the Renaissance nation-state strove to be as absolutist as the Medieval church. Under both these dispensations, a person's life was not at his conscious disposal. Those who willfully broke the laws regarding suicide could be deprived of Christian burial and of the civil right of bequeathing property, which was accordingly forfeited to the authorities. Thus the popularity of this stage subject reflects a safe vicarious indulgence in forbidden options that at least seemed to extend personal empowerment.

Suicide as Roman Art

The suicide motif in English Roman plays involves up to eight common features. Four of these have already been stated or implied in preceding pages: (1) an insistence on calling attention to suicide's *Romanitas* by the use of the word *Roman* and cognates, (2) a radical ambivalence about suicide, and yet a suspicion that it opened a highway to (3) inner and outer power and (4) hierarchically defined honorifics of praise and prestige ("manly," "noble," "royal," "divine"). Additional marks include (5) the structuring of the stage suicide as a highly public and histrionic/pedagogic presentation, complete with (6) litanies of Stoic Roman saints (Cato Uticensis, the Brutuses, Lucretia, Scaevola, Regulus, Seneca), (7) lists of specifically Stoical moral terms ("Wise Man," "Constancy," "Resolution," "Patience," "Fortitude," "Temperance," "Measure"), and (8) traditionally neo-Stoic images for the dynamics of the soul—especially the images of horse- and fire-management and of hard, cold, stony or metallic surfaces that are used for the containment and direction of fiery inner energies.

A brief review of the suicide motif in Shakespeare's *Antony and Cleopatra* will illustrate seven of the eight marks, the exception being the list of Stoic saints. In overall fidelity to history, *Antony* contains two possible and four certain suicides: the deaths of a suicidally inclined Roman (Enobarbus) and Egyptian (Iras) and the obvious suicides of the Roman conqueror himself and of three Greek-named individuals over whom Antony has had direct or indirect power—Eros, Charmion, and Cleopatra. Though only two of these deaths are suicides, the deaths of all four aliens take on Stoical *Romanitas*. Even if the queen is identified as the Oriental or "eastern star," the fact that she is stellified at all suggests a mythology at least as much Roman as Greek or Egyptian. Like a Stoic with his belief in the continuity between the fiery pneuma in the stars and in his own soul (Long 157), Cleopatra regards herself as "fire and air" and wants to ascend from her throne to the next highest level of prestige, that of divinity. If she "shackles accidents and bolts up change" through suicide, she will transform herself from queen to god. But like any other would-be Stoics so long as he or she remains in this world, Cleopatra must guard and direct her fiery soul-stuff by maintaining a divine immobility, a masculine toughness, and a hard exterior containment. Thus she speaks of escaping the pull of the "fleeting moon," symbol of her subjection to femaleness (with its mensual/menstrual and other biological rhythms) and to the mutable contingent world to which all humanity is bound. She tries to rigidify herself into a "marble" constancy and a masculinity/divinity in the "high Roman fashion" of Ancient Stoicism. Were she really able to do so, she would thereby resemble more the example of a Stoical Roman wife like Octavia: "holy, cold, and still," "more a statue, than a breather"; and there would no longer be truth in charges like those that Antony made to Cleopatra in his anger—that she could only barely "guess what temperance should be."[2]

For an English audience already torn between conflicting Christian and Stoical belief, the spectacle of Cleopatra must have become even more deliciously unsettling as she fluctuates between feminine indecision and the coldly Epicurean search for "easy ways to die." Spectator reaction would be further complicated by the scene with the Clown, where the supposedly high Roman Cleopatra turns into his antic. Her final idea of death *à la mode romaine* now includes an earthy woman's fantasy of making love to Roman dominator(s). Handling her snakes, she magnificently partakes of the Dionysian, the demonic, or at very least the irrational—categories quite far from Stoical stellar pneuma. Her death begs a complex response, even apart from any reflections on the problematic statesmanship and motherliness of her last earthly actions. And Rome is a necessary way station to her Oriental death, into which everything is finally subsumed.

The Metadramatic Pedagogy of Suicide

In a rhetoric textbook Seneca's father recounts what the oratory professor Latro would have said had he been asked to advise Cicero when Antony was threatening him: namely, "that it was dishonorable for any Roman, all the more for Cicero, to ask for life" (M. Seneca, *Suasoriae* 6.8). The formulation is rather low-keyed, and no other Ancient text that I know of states even that strongly the idea of the dignified *Romanitas* of suicide as it is embodied or discussed in play after play, Roman or otherwise, in Tudor-Stuart England. When Livy gives Lucretia a suicide speech, the closest he comes to calling her death a Roman act is her saying that she is trying to prevent later Roman wives from pleading rape to cover any sexual pollution. And in Plutarch the death of Antony is much less straightforwardly labeled Roman than it is in Shakespeare. A look at the odd opening of Tixier's famous Renaissance fact book, the *Officina,* can startle one with the centrality of the notion of Roman suicide in the Renaissance mind: the first—and quite long—entry is on deaths caused willingly or accidentally by the person dying, and great numbers of the suicides are Roman.

The true inspiration for associating suicide with *Romanitas* is the late-sixteenth-century preoccupation with neo-Stoicism, as Anson, Braden, and several other scholars have maintained. Throughout Elizabeth's reign the treatment of stage suicide, while remaining ambivalent, became increasingly dignified and Stoical. The differences in the two versions of Wilmot's *Tancred and Gismond* help make this clear. In the 1566–68 version, the heroine announces "I will not live and there to stay" (IV.iii.81), and the hero rushes offstage to rive his breast in "wrathfull ire" (V.iv.29–31). Into these moments of emotional excess, the 1591–92 revision inserts the now-modish Stoic term *resolve,* spelling out the neo-Stoic equation of kingliness, suicidal Stoicism, and the kinglike wisdom of the Senecan Wise Man, as defined in Seneca's *De constantia sapientis:*

> *Tancred.* A kingly deed the king resolves to doe.
> *Julio.* The *wise man* overrules his stars.
>   Undaunted should the minds of kings indure.
>   (V.iii, 1829–31)

Hints of divine immovability and of toiling in the "royal" profession of warfare (*Antony, Othello*) seem to inhere in the word *constantia,* a term that means 'standing with' and suggests the unchanging reliability and self-possession of a god or defensive soldier. Beginning at least by the 1580s, suicidal resolution or constancy was axiomatically regarded as simultaneously royal, Stoical, and Roman. A return to Lodge's *Wounds of Civil War* is instructive. In one of three invented episodes, Scilla castigates foreign princes for failing to do what Romans would do, slay themselves rather than endure humiliating capture (II.iii.81–92). The second episode occurs in IV.i.249–389, when the dictator Scilla's wife and daughter are taken prisoners and threatened with death: they repeatedly are said to demonstrate a "princely majesty" and suicidal bravery worthy of "Asian queens"—or "Roman ladies" or "dames of constancy," "Roman constancy." Similarly, in a later scene the historically private suicide of the defeated Young Marius is staged by Lodge in histrionic splendor before armies and hosts of civilians, while the chief actor announces that he will herewith "let thee see a constant Roman die" (V.ii.82).

"Romans, if any here be in this Senate" (*Sejanus* III.337) who would know from Silius or a dozen others how to "dye like Romans" (*False One* V.ii, p. 361), all they need to play this "Roman part" (*Caesar* V.ii.89) is "a Roman hand, / A sword and heart to dy" (May, *Cleopatra* V.i.3–4). Escaping from misfortune or disgrace in this fashion, one's death will supposedly be greeted with the exclamation "Thou art a Roman!" (*Valentinian* IV.iv.178). If not, characters might have to say there was "No Romane in him" (*Bonduca* IV.iii.48). Similar formulas appear in *Coriolanus* and other plays, Roman and non-Roman (*Hamlet, Macbeth, Volpone, Revenge of Bussy D'Ambois,* and so forth[3]). Everywhere, suicide is emphatically "a Roman's part" and for that reason worthy of having its dignity and morality carefully weighed (*Caesar* V.iii.89). With or without specifically suicidal implications, the Stoical code words *constancy, resolution,* and their cognates reecho throughout the many Roman plays: in the sixteenth century, *Titus, Caesar's*

Revenge, Cornelia, and Shakespeare's *Caesar;* and in the seventeenth century, *Sophonisba, Lucrece,* Alexander's *Caesar, Faithful Friends, Catiline, False One, Roman Actor, Jews' Tragedy, Virgin Martyr, Hannibal, Messallina,* and *Believe As You List.*[4]

Though often stage suicides or discussions of suicide are also dotted with problematizing deconstructive hints and details, the overall effect of transmission from history or literature into drama is an increase in the dignity and glamor of self-chosen death. Hence I have difficulty agreeing with Paulin and Wymer when they speak of a tendency for the stage treatment of suicide to be generally uncomplicated but to grow progressively less sympathetic in Jacobean than Elizabethan times.[5] It seems to me that there is a large element of ambivalence right from the start, and that it is usual for there to be a copiousness of complication. For instance, Lodge's suicidal Young Marius is first glamorized by being made younger than his historical counterpart, and his alleged "crueltie" (Appian, *Auncient Historie,* Marginalia 52) to fellow citizens is expunged; only then can he build a great scene, slaying himself in full view of immense and largely appreciative crowds, instead of, as in reality, after having "hid[den] himself in a Cave" (56). Garnier's *Cornélie* greatly amplifies the pathetico-heroic hints of Scipio's suicide in Appian's account (131). And in bringing Garnier's play into English, Kyd endows Scipio and his daughter with further dignity by using the Stoical code words *resolute, resolved,* and *constancy.* These Kyd employs oftener than Garnier does their French counterparts: "le front blesme" ('a face awestruck') becoming "resolute" II.321; and "main cruelle" ('a cruel hand') becoming "cruelly resolv'd" (V.321). Jonson's show-stopping onstage suicide of Silius, professing his moral authority before the full Senate, is also more theatrically Roman than Tacitus's tale of an accused extortioner whose suicide in an unspecified place is one in a series of accounts of several Romans who slew themselves, usually at home, rather than face Tiberius's agents in court (*Annals* 4.19).

In *Caesar's Revenge* and *Tiberius* we find sentimental/heroic suicides of widows whom history never records having killed themselves at all. Further, the historical deaths of Sophonisba, Antony, and Cleopatra are invariably romanticized in Nabbes, Marston, Shakespeare, May, and Brandon—even though probably implicitly problematized also. *Caesar's Revenge* neither dramatizes nor alludes to the lurid medical details of Cato's repeated act of self-disemboweling; for the real Cato "tare himself asunder with his hands (like a wilde beast) the sowing up" (Appian, *Auncient Historie* 130). Chapman's treatment of the same event is also more emphatically dignified than the historians'. With not just a Stoic or Socratic mantle but also a radically Protestant Mosaic one, this Cato kills himself, guided by the "light and fiery pillar" of his own "reason," than the which "th'eternal law of heaven and earth [is] no firmer" (*Caesar and Pompey* V.ii.42–44).

Oftener than not, a Roman's suicidal "part" is played out attractively in high style, with an educative "smatch of honor" (*Caesar* V.v.46) for the inspiration of various audiences: onstage, in the house, in the heavens, and in climes and future times, then or now unknown. Few suicide scenes have mean or ghastly touches. There is nothing in the Roman plays that compares, for instance, with the indecorous grandeur of Seneca's accounts of a newly enslaved Spartan lad and a German. The one brained himself rather than empty a bedpan (*Ad Lucilium* 77.44); the other, forced to train to fight wild animals, choked himself on his gladiatorial school's latrine brush (70.22).

The element of pose and display in Ancient Stoicism is strongly reflected in the Renaissance stage treatment of suicidal constancy, where there is only a fine line between heroism and heroics. Tacitus's father-in-law, Agricola, was not a suicide, but it is difficult to read of his life without contrasting what the historian says of him and what the mythos was of the Stoic stage-Roman suicide. While Agricola was on duty in Britain, news reached him that his only son had died in Rome: 'The father grieved, but in moderation and with dignity' (*Agricola* 29, R4v)—'and not as others do, full of ambition [*ambitiosi*] for self-aggrandizement.' For he was not like many other Romans, even strong and "good men," who "doate" on their "glorie," indulging in "ostentation of vertue," or celebrating themselves by any other "artificiall meanes" (R1r).

Tacitus would not have had the same compliment to pay to Shakespeare's Brutus. The theatrical personage, who admires the "formal constancy" of "Roman actors" (*Caesar* II.i.226–27), receives news of Portia's death in an obviously *staged* fashion, whether the dual announcement is authorially intended or not. When Messala tells him to "bear the truth" "like a Roman," Marcus (unlike Macduff in another culture) feels compelled to illustrate a great Roman's Stoic patience to bear and endure by not weeping (IV.iii.187–94). The lines suggest that he is teaching the great national meditative art that he practices:

> *Brutus.* With meditating that she must die once,
>   I have the patience to endure it now.
> *Messala.* Even so great men great losses should endure.
> *Cassius.* I have as much of this in *art* as you,
>   But yet my nature could not bear it so.
>   (IV.iii.190–94)

For Brutus one's life is an educative histrionic creation to be shared with others. He views his own death as something that must be performed decorously, because it forms the final improving chapter in the book of his life: "Brutus' *tongue* / Hath almost ended his life's *history*" (V.v.39–40).

The Romans in this tragedy may not equally share the "formal constancy" of Roman actors (II.i.226–27), but they are all, certainly, histrionically didactic. The conspirators kill themselves in the same way that they killed Caesar: with a clear awareness of spectators, of an audience—of the Roman Senate and People, of the world of spirits and gods, and of posterity, even those in "States unborn, and accents yet unknown."

> Brutus, come apace,
> And *see* how I regarded Caius Cassius.
> By your leave, gods!—this is a Roman's part.
>   (V.iii.87–89)

Titinius recognizes that his act is probably ungodly but excuses it on "a Roman's" cultural grounds. He and his creator cue this portrayal of patriotic and personal loyalty so that it will impress Brutus—and anyone who has bought a theater ticket.

An even more theatrical death occurs in Massinger's *The Roman Actor*, where the protagonist has to kill himself in a play onstage, and in the same author's *Believe As You List*, where a constant half-Roman bravely stage-manages his own execution:

> there's noe torment of a shape soe horrid
> can shake my *constancie*. where lyes the *scaene* now?

> thowgh the *hangings of the stage* were congeald gore
> the *Chorus* flintye executioners
> and the *spectators,* yf it coulde bee, more
> inhumane than flaminius, the *cue* gieven
> the *principall actor's readie.*
>
> (2607–13)

Such rhetoric is enforced by Roman Stoicism, which encouraged the tendency to regard life as theater. As Marcus Aurelius, Stoic and emperor, wrote in *Meditations* 10.27, actions in today's highest governmental circles are scenes or "dramata" that have occurred in the past, and will occur in the future, even though the cast of characters differs and changes (trans. Casaubon). We live both as spectator at God's cosmic entertainment and as "one of the players, and must plaie the parte, which the authour there of shall appoint" (Epictetus 22). God "hath no Need of a discontented Spectator. He wants such as may share the Festival; make part of the Chorus"; "if it is not worth your while, depart" (Arrian 4.1, 1.29). And the most important part in our life's script to *act* well is our *clausula,* or final rhetorical periodic phrase—our death: "It fareth with our life as with a *Stage-play;* it skilleth not how long, but how well it hath beene *acted.* It importeth nothing in what place thou maketh amend of life: die where thou wist, thinke onely to make a good *conclusion* [*clausula*]" (Seneca, *Ad Lucilium* 77.20, trans. Lodge). Our actions are on continual display. As Seneca says of Cato's death, "I do not know a spectacle [*spectaculum*] more worthy of God" than Cato's calm resort to suicide when all the state lay in ruins (*De providentia* 2.9).

The least expected feature of Tudor-Stuart Roman suicides is not their theatricality so much as their strongly didactic and pedagogical flavor, continually stressing that Stoicism is a learned "art." Of course, the social doctrines of Stoicism encouraged good example and mutual exhortation to virtue, but the number of times that stage Roman suicides refer to classrooms is truly remarkable and without parallel. In his suicide Lodge's Young Marius is an instructor as well as a performer. This teacher has a series of lessons: "Kill that tyrant" as the first Brutus did; "Go, second Brutus"; "See," friends and enemies, see and "follow" "a constant Roman" (*Wounds* V.iii.81–88).

> I press in place [*Stab(s himself)*].
> To let thee see a constant Roman die.—
> Praenestians, a wound, a fatal wound,
> The pain but small, the glory passing great.
> Praenestians, see a second stroke.
> > [*Stabs himself*] *again*.
> > (81–85)

His demonstration includes visual aids and pedagogical reinforcement through repetition; and Marius's Praenestian pupils respond antiphonally, "We follow thee, our chieftain, even in death. . . . *Moritur*" (90–92). If history is, as Cicero puts it, the schoolmaster of life (*magister vitae*), the lesson that is impressed on English spectators is *imaginative* participation in another culture's historic mores. The audience is taught emotional anthropology, though not actually urged to follow this leader into self-chosen death. (In fact, the audience will also soon hear Scilla explore the antic side of this death, calling its perpetrator a "brainsick" "silly boy" [V.v.71, 78].)

A pedagogic metaphor is clear too in Webster, where Appius plays schoolmaster to Clodius and future Roman evildoers:

> *Learn* of me Clodius;
> *I'l teach* thee what thou never *studiest* yet,
> Thats bravely *how to* dy.
> . . . .
> Those that succeed me
> That so offend, *thus punish*.
> (*Appius* V.ii.138–43)

And Heywood's Lucrece is partly a school "dame" with the entire world as her classroom:

> Let all the world, learne of a Roman dame,
> To prise her life lesse than her honor'd fame.
> (*Lucrece* 2488–89)

May's and Shakespeare's Antonies are stunned that a servant or an alien "woman / Should *teach*" them "how to die" (*Cleopatra* V.i.23–24):

> Thou *teachest* me, O valiant Eros, what
> I should, and thou couldst not. My queen and Eros
> Have by their *instruction* got upon me
> A nobleness in *record*.
>
> (*Antony* IV.xiv.96–99)

And Fletcher's Romanized British princess in *Bonduca* wants to teach by the "example" of a guiltless womanly suicide, unimperialistic and unblasphemous:

> would ye learn
> How to die bravely. Romanes, to fling off
> This case of flesh, lose all your cares for ever?
> Live as we have done, well, and fear the gods;
> Hunt Honour, and not Nations with your swords;
> Keep your mindes humble, your devotions high;
> So shall ye learn the noblest part, to die.
>
> (IV.iv.127–33)

Other Fletcher plays tell the same story. In *Valentinian* a Roman captain slays himself to teach a lesson to a friend: "Behold and find I was no traitor" but "die as I do!" (IV.iv.175–76). Thereupon a survivor laments that the world now lacks living instruction: "Of whom now shal we *learn* to live like men?" "O thou alone a Roman, thou art perishd" (290–95). Another of the play's characters is conscious not just of an earthly classroom but also of "blessed spirits" bearing witness to his death. Falling on his sword, he adds: "Oh, that posterity / Could learn . . . / There is no pain at all in dying well" (IV.iv.263–67). In the Fletcher-Massinger *False One*, when Roman troops close in on Cleopatra, she advises her timid sister to "*study* to dye nobly" (p. 369) and "*learn* in my death / . . . to imitate" me (p. 366). And in the anonymous *Faithful Friends*, which is sometimes associated with Fletcher and his school, the heroine's suicide is temporarily forestalled by a brave friend who promises first to "*teach* [her] how" (III.ii, 1662).

When Jonson's Silius commits suicide in *Sejanus*, he too casts himself as ethical teacher as well as a histrionic performer in a mocking political skit. He tells his fellow senators to learn from him how to be simultaneously senatorial, satiric, and suicidal in the Roman manner:

> Romans, if any here be in this Senate,
> Would *know to mock* Tiberius' tyranny,
> Look upon Silius, and so learn to die.
> (III.337–39)

But of all statements of Stoical pedagogy in English Roman plays, none is more unmistakable than that of this play's ironically ineffectual anti-Tiberians, who think that they should "study" Lepidus's "arts." These may look to them to be full of fortitude and patriotically Roman—

> *Arruntius*. What are thy *arts*—good patriot, *teach* them me—
> That have preserved thy hairs to this white dye,
> . . . .
> *Lepidus*.   *Arts,* Arruntius?
> None but the plain and passive *fortitude*
> To *suffer and be silent; never stretch*
> These arms against the torrent; *live at home,*
> With my own thoughts and innocence about me,
> *Not tempting* the wolf's jaws: these are my *arts*.
> *Arruntius*. I would begin to *study* 'em, if I thought
> They would secure me.
> (IV.290–300)

But since the theater audience never learns of anything that the prudential survivor Lepidus has done to mitigate the horror of the rule of Tiberius and his favorites, lessons in Lepidus's "arts" would hardly seem to be seriously recommended by the dramatist. Quite the reverse, a sort of negative pedagogy.

The Dynamics of Constancy

Without specialized knowledge of Early Modern symbology, who would have predicted David Lindsay's understanding of how the Book of Daniel represents Rome, the Fourth World Empire? Lindsay says that the iron and steel of the Roman idol's loins and limbs indicate Rome's "diligence" to gain power and "abuse all uther Natioun" ("Monarch" 3, 3756–60). To understand the pervasiveness of references to Roman constancy in various plays, it is useful not just to review the abstract statement of this motif but also to make forays into Renaissance iconology. In Shakespeare's Roman plays, such critics as Wilson Knight and Maurice Charney find "austere imagery of hard, cold material objects and the practical business of state" (Charney 16). To this list Wilson Knight would add horses; Anson, fiery sparks; and Braden, perhaps, volcanoes. When further amplified from the sciences of the time, these images form an important part of the language that several dramatists apply to archetypal Roman harshness, toughness, dedication to duty, and, of course, constancy.

Constantia is represented all over Renaissance Europe with an inextinguishable light and some hard and imperturbable object. The title page of Saxton's *Atlas* of 1579 (Hind pl. 39) and the Cecil tomb sculpted in London between 1609 and about 1612 (Whinney 236 n. 42) are two of many English examples in which Constancy is accompanied by her commonest attribute, the column. Columns, says the great Continental iconologist Valeriano Bolzani, indicate every sort of firmness, including virility (2: 404, trans. Chappuys). Further, he mentions that other signs of *firmitas* include stone and the builder's square (bk. 49). A modern student of Renaissance iconology, Guy de Tervarent, adds that Constancy is represented by a draftsman's compass (as in Donne's "Valediction Forbidding Mourning"), craggy rocks beaten by the sea (as in Whitney's Emblem 96), and the perpetually cool salamander immersed in flame. If we comb Henkel and Schöne's mammoth anthology of European Renaissance and Baroque emblem books, we find that constancy and allied virtues are symbolized also by the anvil (1409), a steady lamp (1364), and storm-resistant houses, towers, trees (113, 145–46, 1213–14). Mount Olympus is said to stand for "securitas" (60–61), while the volcano Mount Aetna, battered by the four winds, symbolizes the light that shines amid adversity (64).

Cesare Ripa's late-sixteenth-century *Iconologia* contains three separate descriptions of "Costanza." One is of a youth unfazed by a charging bull. Another is of a female firmly placed on a square pedestal. The base is a sign of her being stable and balanced. One of her arms is aloft, and the other is propped on her staff. In a third version, Costanza leans against a column. Since the iconologist says that the staff in the second representation symbolizes Constancy's need for outside support, the column in the third example must perform the same function. We should infer that the staff would be of wood and the column of stone, both materials that possess a toughness beyond that customary for our human flesh.

In the earliest editions of Ripa, the right hand grasps the staff or column, and the sword is borne in the left. This hand is thrust "voluntariamente" toward a flame, which usually emanates from a vase. In that the "sinestra mano" is traditionally the less pure, the flame must be burnishing and tempering the steel of constancy. The vase enclosing and feeding the fire implicitly hints at an alliance between constancy, containment/continence, and the management of emotion. For as Shakespeare's *Caesar* II.i.178–89 reminds us, the dynamics of *constant* Brutus involves his "stir[ring] up" otherwise mastered emotions so that, after their mutiny, he may "seem to chide" them and finally subdue them even more thoroughly than before.

Though Ripa does not say so, the juxtaposition of sword, hand, and fire automatically evoked the favorite Renaissance motif of Mucius Scaevola, who punished himself by bravely burning off his own *dextra*—the standard Latin word for sword hand (fig. 9). The subtext of the Scaevola story is further strengthened in three French Ripas (fig. 10), which reverse the hand placement in obvious allusion to the stoical Roman youth.

Livy and others relate how Scaevola (meaning "Lefty") went on an assassination mission to the camp of the Etruscan king Porsena, who was besieging Rome. Mucius's attempt failed; he was captured. Furious at his wayward hand, he announced, "Romanus sum." 'I am a Roman come to kill you but am equally prepared to die for it. For both to act and to endure are what Romans are strong at' ("et facere et pati fortia Romanum est" [Livy 2.12]). Thereupon he thrust his *dextra* into the king's sacrificial fire, alleging (fallaciously) that the Etruscans could expect a whole series of Roman youths from the same suicide squad. And then, the story goes, Porsena was so impressed that he not only freed Mucius but also congratulated Rome on its courageous citizens and lifted the siege. Hence, when Whitney selected the sword-fire-hand icon, he alluded to it as the symbol not just of "heart" (*anima, megalopsychia, magnanimitas*) but also of desire for "fame" and love of "patria" (fig. 9).

Constrained and controlled greatness is also signified by horses. The prestige of saddle and chariot horses of warfare, like the prestige of birds that kill their prey, has traditionally been very high, standing for the aristocratic reputation for loftiness that their owners have enjoyed—unlike such baser folk as the keepers of draft horses, oxen, or gamecocks. The riding and war horse, Wilson Knight properly maintains in his remarks on *Antony*, has long been a sign of aristocracy, of the officer and landowning classes (*Imperial Theme* 212–14) and of the mystique that inheres in them. As the *Hieroglyphica* puts it, the horse is a symbol of "*Emprise & maistrise*" (bk. 4, trans. Chappuys, vol. 1, G3v), 'control and imperial rule.' Caron's painting (fig. 3) depicts two of the most famous statuary groups displayed in Rome during the Middle Ages and Renaissance: the equestrian Marcus Aurelius and the horse-taming group usually known as Alexander and Bucephalus (Haskell and Penny 252–54, 136–41). It is not surprising that the aspiring Roman lords of Shakespeare and his fellows are frequently associated with horses and that the Ancients' allegedly noblest traits—*constantia* and energetically noble aspiration—are seen as horselike. Few symbols besides that of the horse are so capable of indicating active *constantia*.

A look at Plutarch's "Life of Antony" reminds us of some of the other ancient significations of horses. Antony, the biographer says, was a man of *unbridled* appetite. Images of bridles and of tempered steel frequently accompany pictures of horses, and the iconographers work all three into Renaissance programs of Temperance (Tervarent, s.v. "Tempérance," "Mésure"). Since the prehistoric invention of the legendary centaurs, and in written literature since at least Plato's *Phaedrus*, horses have symbolized uncontrolled libido. Horses stand for rule but also the need to be ruled—not just surging strength, martial nobility, soaring mettlesomeness but also various chaotic drives. When the spoiled and drunken son of Tarquin the Proud indulges in sexual fantasy in Shakespeare's poem, he develops a horselike

> Lust . . . in his pride, no exclamation
> Can curb . . . or rein his rash desire,
> Till like a jade, Self-Will himself doth tire.
> ("Rape of Lucrece" 705–7)

Dramatic sources of the English playwrights' habit of comparing spirited Romans to horses include French Roman plays (Grévin's and Muretus's, according to MacCallum 55; also Garnier/Kyd, *Cornelia* IV.155–60). In Lodge's *Wounds* (III.iii.82–83) Scilla claims that Romans are different from oxlike foreigners with their "imperfect mettles." Shakespeare's Andronici see themselves as steel-backed horses: they are "metal, . . . steel to the very back," with "backs" so used to bearing that they are now "wrung" (*Titus* IV.iii.48–49). The image recalls *patientia* or passive *constantia,* and yet glances at the men's mettlesome nature and their similarity to heroic equestrian statues and horse-taming Temperance. In *Julius Caesar* the resolute Roman is not a "hollow," "deceitful jade" (IV.ii.23, 27) but a creature whose high "spirits" and "insuppressive mettle" is spurred (II.i.123–35). Casca's odd, and implicitly unequine, behavior puzzles Brutus, who expects him to retain his "quick mettle" (I.ii.296). Like the country itself, the hero of *Coriolanus* keeps breaking "strong link" and "curbs" like a runaway horse (I.i.69–72). Despite a pathetically intermittent lack of discipline, he is a fine Roman animal, dedicated as Valeriano would have it, to conquest and empire—and fated, as many of the best horses historically were—for civic sacrifice to his patron and namesake, Mars (Simonds, Carcopino 228). He is the essence of lively constancy on the battlefield, but he cannot move from casque to cushion. Martius's constancy is as ambivalent, shifting, paradoxical, and indeterminate as so much else that vivifies a Roman play.

Less active than unstable equine *constantia* is the defensive side of Roman constancy as it borders on apathy and cruelty. This constancy is evocatively rendered in images of wood, trees (e.g., *Sejanus* V.241–62; cf. Seneca's *De providentia* 4.16), ice, stone, public buildings and statues, or other inflexible, inanimate objects. Though Seneca alleges that the heart of the Wise Man is not 'as tough as either stone or steel' ("lapidis . . . duritiam ferrive," *De constantia* 10.2), Early Modern Englishmen tend to regard the Roman heart as having hardened beyond *constantia* into cruelty. In discussing a Roman's heart, Robert Garnier uses the abstract word *endurci* ('toughened'; *Cornélie* V, 159), which his English translator renders with an image, making the organ into a specifically icy and "*stony hart,* that nere dyd Romaine good," but "would *melt with nothing* but theyr deerest blood" (*Cornelia* V.272–73).

Stone imagery is especially prevalent in the Roman drama of Bible-reading England perhaps because Scripture repeatedly speaks of sinners' stony hard-heartedness (e.g., Ezekiel 11:19). In pagan Latin literature, too, flint is a standard image for the cruel heart (Lewis and Short, s.v. "silex"). Massinger not only has his constant, sexually restrained half-Roman hero called a "man of snow" (*Believe* IV.ii.227) but also invents a Roman jailer who confesses to be as emotionally restrained as "flint" or "marble" (IV.ii. 3–4). Perhaps not in the last instance but often elsewhere, references to marble and other stone permit a playwright to hint obliquely at the Romans' praiseworthy Stoic patience, monumental majesty, rocklike courage, magnanimous concern with architecture and public display, as well as at their less admirable proclivity to cruelty and self-destructive passivity.

Erasmus, in *Praise of Folly,* dismisses the Stoic Wise Man as a figure of "flint or rock," a mere "stony semblance of a man" (trans. Wilson, qtd. in Anson 14). *Taming of the Shrew* echoes the old canard about Stoics' making man unspontaneous, like stocks and stones (I.i.31), and in *Caesar* and *Sejanus* we find a world where men and statues are confused. This malady becomes explicit in *Antony,* where pure-minded Octavia seems more a "*statue, than a breather*" (III.iii.212).

In Lodge's *Wounds* senators are called pillars, towers, and pyramids—a suggestion not just of Rome's majestic wealth and urbanity but also of the rulers' toughness and constancy. The suicidally constant ladies in *Wounds* are termed "two the fairest *stars* of Rome" (IV.i.269), beautified by "*snow-white wrists*" and "milk-white necks" (393–94)—tropes indicative of emotions firmly under control. Such ladies will supposedly have a miraculously chilling effect on Nature wherever they wander, turning rivers and "fierce" gulfs "smooth as *crystal ice*" (IV.i.397–99).

Images of metal operate similarly to those of stone, even occasioning subtle allusion to both the warlike prowess of the Romans and their enthusiasm for majestic bronze monuments. Iron is a (martial) substance traditionally *tempered,* and it symbolizes endurance in time of trial ("In miseriam humanae fortis"), as Pegma (178–79) puts it in 1555. Hints at Rome's combination of *constantia* and savagery can be seen in implicit references not just to *ferrum,* "iron," but also to its cognate *ferrumen,* "solder" or "cement" (Lewis and Short).

To evoke a constancy more active than what could be represented by ice, stone, and metal, not just horses but fire is often evoked, if only to mold and temper the metal/mettle. Images of sparks are added also, usually from lightning, stars, or, more humbly, a whetstone or kindling box (as in *Caesar;* see Anson, and Kaufmann and Ronan). The association of fire with constancy—a strong motif in Shakespeare's *Caesar,* Jonson's *Sejanus,*

Chapman's *Caesar and Pompey,* and Marston's *Sophonisba*—has a long history and may well reflect Stoic physics (Caputi 74). In Stoicism (and Lucretian Epicureanism represented in *Aeneid* 6.724–32), fire is a standard part of man's, nature's, and the gods' soul-stuff. All contain *pneuma,* hot breath: fire and air in a state of dichotomous tension between inwardness and outerness, "a compound of self-unity and multiple connectedness" (Long 157). When purified of its baser watery element, the pneuma becomes ready for the process of instellation, transfer into the starry heavens. All of this may well make one think also of that Romanized "eastern star," who feels herself to be all "fire and air" (*Antony* V.ii.289, 308), or of the Romanized princes in *Cymbeline,* "worthy / To inlay heaven with stars" (V.v.351–52; cf. Walker).

Among the images of fiery constancy in *Wounds* are the forge, oven, and volcano, each yoking stasis with activity. Scilla boasts of being "fire," possessing noble "metal," and having "*sparkling* eyes" more fiery than furies (II.i.10, 14, 78). Soon after, foundry imagery is applied to his vengeful assertiveness, and he is termed someone with "a rash revenging *hammer* in his brain" (84). This image is emphatically reiterated by the hero himself: "I hammer in my head / With every thought of honor some revenge" (II.i.187–88). Later, in a parallel commonplace image probably inspired by impeccably Roman authors like Vergil (*Aeneid* 3.570–87) and Seneca (*Medea* 410, 639), Scilla is likened to stony-fiery Mount Aetna, "vomiting . . . fire" (V.iii.72).

In *Titus* fiery constancy is again pictured by "hot Aetna" (III.i.241), as well as by an oven with movable apertures. "O that I knew" Lavinia's rapist, the protagonist exclaims,

> That I might rail at him to ease my mind!
> Sorrow concealed, like an oven stopp'd,
> Doth burn the heart to cinders where it is.
> (II.iv.35–37)

These images are augmented with references to mettlesome horses (as already mentioned) and to wind-tossed rocks (implicitly in III.i.220ff.) and trees. Cedars, like oaks, are traditional symbols of strength and greatness—constancy and royal power. Yet the noble Andronicus sometimes views the family as "but shrubs, no cedars" (IV.iii.46). When the play opens, the audience is fittingly treated to a sight of Titus's recently re-edified family tomb of stone. This constitutes a symbol not only of his majestic family pride and *constantia* but also of his savagery. For in front of this stone, he shows himself stonily cruel toward both his own and Tamora's offspring. Appropriately, too, he finds that Rome's tribunes can prove stonier than the city's streets (III.i.29–47).

In Marston's *Sophonisba* we find a heroine who seems the ultimate product of the Great Machine Shop of Virtue (Caputi 74):

> Thou . . . like *sparkling steele* the strokes of Chance
> Made hard and firme; and like wild fier turnd
> The more cold fate, more bright thy vertue burnd,
> And in whole seas of miseries didst flame.
>
> (V.iii.164–67)

Chapman's *Caesar and Pompey* uses a less conceited and more intellectually striking image for the continuity between celestial fire and human stoical resolution. In II.ii he first has Caesar note that his sacrificial fire "burns . . . eternal and sincere" toward heaven "right and upright" to its "proper sphere" (25–26). Then the soothsayer submits that the flame also has a mystical downward (Hebraic?) direction: "Heaven's pure flame flew down and ravish'd up / Your offering's blaze in that religious instate" (28–29). This interpretation is immediately confirmed by the "miraculous" appearance, over the camp, of a "sacred blaze . . . like a torch enlighten'd" (34–36). The subsequent sixty lines are then devoted to the proposition that Caesar's "great and fiery virtue" (78) is living in the "graceful" astral "sign" of "power divine." Yet success depends still on how each Stoic Roman soldier is himself "*resolv'd* for fight," allowing the "*resolv'd* addres[s]" awakened by the "spirit to act enflam'd in" him.

In Jonson's *Sejanus* Arruntius and the rest cannot make the sparks of old Roman greatness still blaze. In IV.142–61, Sejanus's spy Latiaris mimics the old Republican fiery constancy:

> Methinks the genius of the Roman race
> Should not be so extinct, but that *bright flame*
> Of liberty might be revived again.
>
> (IV.142–44)

The old ways supposedly kept Romans horselike (not asses) and gave them a flame, a spark, genial warmth, and life, permitting the Republicans to light and heat the world they conquered. Now, instead, Romans puff "in the dark at one poor *coal,* / Held on by hope till the last *spark* is out."

> This ass's fortitude doth tire us all.
> It must be active valor must redeem
> Our loss, or none. The rock and our hard steel
> Should meet t'enforce those glorious fires again
> Whose splendor cheered the world and heat gave life
> No less than doth the sun's.
> (IV.156–61)

An old Roman was a flinty kindler, or a "ready sword" sharpened on whetstonelike opponents. His fortitude, valor, and constancy were active, virile, heat- and life-giving.

The titular hero of *Sejanus* is less an Aetna than a sputtering flame. Appropriately, with no prompting from his sources, Jonson pictures the favorite's ominously smoking statue—symbolic image of the inner man himself—as a "furnace, black and dreadful" (V.30), but finally not dangerous. What is constant, cruel, and "dreadful" is not Sejanus himself, but his empty likenesses. All along, in the days of Sejanus's power, the Romans are said to have worshipped him like an "idol" (I.550, V.451). The man's empty constancy parodies the statuesque Stoic, a fact beyond the mental capacity of the foolish mob, who act like dogs "biting stones," attacking his statues as if they were "sensive grown" (V.767–68), and clustering about his corpse by the "thousand[s]" and "ten thousand[s]" as if he were a fallen colossus (or saint) and could afford them all a view, a touch, a fragment (V.811–12).

Here and in the other dozens of dramas, there is a contrasting variety of tone, attitude, and image in the playwrights' depiction of the active and passive sides of Roman constancy. Too, there is continual emphasis on histrionic and pedagogic suicidal gestures—fairly often expressed through tropes of hardness, coolness, and stable flame. Together, these motifs all help link the idea of Roman *constantia* not only with that of Roman *majestas* but also with the subjects of the next two chapters: pride and savagery, *superbia* and *saevitia*.

CHAPTER FIVE

Superbia: Insulting, Aquiline, Overmounting Pride

> How many ages hence
> Shall this our lofty scene be acted over.
>
> SHAKESPEARE
> *Julius Caesar*

Noble/royal Romans sporadically pursue what Shakespeare's Prince Malcolm defines as the "king-beseeming graces": "concord," "all unity on earth," "universal peace," "temp'rance, stableness, / Bounty," "fortitude" (*Macbeth* IV.iii.91–100). But when Malcolm adds "*low*liness" to the list, he and the stage Roman part company. Of all the secular lords known to the Renaissance, none seemed more able to be male, lordly, powerful, majestic, but not lowly. In fact, he is oftener the antic "proud man / Dress'd in a little brief authority," "Play[ing] like an angry ape" (*Measure for Measure* II.ii.117–21)

> such *fantastic tricks* before high heaven
> As makes the angels weep; who, with our spleens,
> Would all themselves laugh mortal.
>
> (121–23)

The Renaissance stage Roman has just enough dignity to be a noble dramatic subject and just enough bifold indeterminacy to be an interesting theme. Incomplete in his self-control, with "too much weakness for the Stoic's pride," the Roman is like the rest of us,

> Created half to rise, and half to fall;
> Great lord of all things, yet a prey to all.
> (Pope, "Essay on Man," 2.15–16)

Lofty aspiration was the chief Roman urge, a characteristic near allied to pride, which under the Latin term *super*bia suggests height, aboveness, and overness.

Insulting Aspiration

When Lodge's old dictator Scilla finally resigns his tyrant's/king's/god's ability to humiliate underlings, he defines all men as natural climbers and humiliators:

> kings are gods and make the proudest stoop,
> Yet but themselves are still pursu'd with hate;
> And men were made to mount and then to droop.
> (*Wounds* V.v.92–94)

Even a man who can "mount" and make others "stoop" will eventually himself "droop": an image suggestive of fortune's wheel, of a coasting eaglelike bird, and of a phallus—the coarsest image for overness (even if the one closest to "pride" in the sense of sexual excitement). But Tamburlaine, Hamlet (Ronan, "Multiplex"), and others would agree that it is truly human to be blasphemously soaring. Nature itself "doth teach us all to have aspiring minds"; man is most man when he most resembles scrambling "mighty Jove," full of "thirst of reign" (*libido dominandi*) and lunging upward toward the Hesperidean "fruition of an earthly crown" (*1 Tamburlaine* II.vii.123–29). To be truly human is, arguably, to live like a god or king. Or so the historical Nero thought when, after leveling central Rome to accommodate his new palace, gardens, and two artificial lakes, he exclaimed that 'at last' he had a place 'fit for a human being to live!' ("quasi hominem tandem habitare"; Suetonius, 6.31).

In a work associated with Britain as much as Rome, Tacitus has a noble Briton term Romans "lords . . . whose intollerable pride [*superbiam*]" is such that colonials cannot placate or "avoide by service and humble behaviour" (*Agricola* 30). In Vergil's great national epic, the central issue of Roman *superbia* is problematized. In the opening lines the goddess Juno condemns for its pride the whole bellicose imperial nation—"populum late regem belloque *superbum*" (1.21). Her phrase, richly ambiguous itself through its word order, literally means 'a people ruling (*king*ing it) widely and in war proud': a line that Milton elegantly renders as "An old and haughty nation, proud in arms" (*Comus* 33, qtd. in Greenough 1.21.3 n.). A little later in Vergil's poem, Anchises explains that it is Rome's aptitude and mission to assert kingly rule (*regere*) and crush the proud, "debellare superbos" (*Aeneid* 6.851–53). But the poet calls into question the eulogistic judgment upon Romans by prefacing this remark with a passage (6.817–19) about the savage pride of the Republic's founder, son-executing Lucius Junius Brutus ("animamque *superbam* . . . *saeva*sque securis," 'proud spirit,' with his 'wildly harsh juridical axes'). Vergil's pattern of references to *superbia* thus seems to sully where it praises.

References to Roman pride, crushing and triumphing over opposition, are omnipresent in English drama. We hear in Kyd that the "pryde" of Rome, the "world's Queene," "over-peare[s] / The worthiest citties in the conquered world" (*Cornelia* IV.ii.1–2, III.ii.1), though now Caesar has yoked the "proud neck" of "proud Rome" (III.ii.6, 31). "Romes imperiall crowne" has always been "*haut* . . . Ambition" (*Messallina* II.i, 1163), while the three sources of her greatness are "Lawes, Armes, and *Pride*" (*Caesar's Revenge,* Chorus, 38). Pride, according to the latter play, brought about the civil wars, undermining "proud Rome" when she had "growne proud, with her unconquered strength" and had "waxen proud with peace and soveraine raigne" (i, 44; Chorus, 33; iii, 311). This play's eponymous hero is a Titan "of high aspiring thoughtes, / And uncontrould ambitious Majesty" (II.iv, 1028–29; cf. "imperious Caesar," *Hamlet* V.i.213; also *As You Like It* V.ii.31, *2 Henry IV* IV.iii.41). And megalomaniacally he brags that "all the world was but a *Charyot* / Wherein I rode Triumphing in my pride (III.i, 2002–3).

In Brito-Roman plays, we hear of Julius Caesar's swelling "ambition" (*Cymbeline* III.i.48–50), Rome's "avarice and pride" (*Fuimus Troes* II.vii, 482), her army of "proud thieves" (*Bonduca* IV.ii.30), dedicated to fulfill "the pride of Romane Caesar" (*Welshman* III.i.76)—"proud" aquiline "Roman Caesar" (*Shoemaker* III.iii.16–17). Similar charges are found in plays about Rome's ravaging forays into Sabine territory (*Faithful Friends* II.iii, 244), Armenia (*Tiberius* 1834), Egypt (Daniel's *Cleopatra,* 1599 ed., IV, 876–77), elsewhere in North Africa (*Hannibal* II.v.225), and the Levant, where King Antiochus fears that if his nation's captive virgins escape the lust of the "prowde insultinge Roman" soldiers (IV.iv.46), the newly enslaved women may yet be "spurned and trod on / By their prowde mistresses, the Roman matrons" (I.i.61–62).

But even though the accusation of Rome's *superbia* is basically dyslogistic, mastery itself is essential to governments and individuals. There is an acceptable sort of overness, needful for managing the self and outside reality. To engage in the Vergilian task of sparing the *subjectis,* or 'people thrust [*ject-*] down [*sub-*],' some Romans must do the putting down. Early Modern audiences knew that the Bible identifies man as ruler *over* God's creation.

> God said, Let us make man in our image according to our likenes: and let them *rule over* the fish of the sea, and *over* the foule of the heaven, and *over* the beastes, & *over* all the earth, and *over* every creeping thing that creepeth upon the earth. . . . and God said to [men], Bring forth frute, and fil the earth, and *sub*due it, and *rule over* [its creatures]. (Genesis 1:26–28)

Similarly, the Psalmist writes that the Lord has given man "dominion" and has "put all things under his fete" (8:6). A male was thought to have the destiny, spiritual as well as physiological, to surmount and "cover" (OED I.6) his mate. According to one Renaissance understanding of Genesis, it was more the privilege of the man than the woman to rule over lesser creatures, just as it was the task of the males in these lesser species to be the "lords" and "masters to their females" (*Comedy of Errors* II.i.24).

Ambivalence about Rome's pride and its claims to majesty and constancy encouraged the Renaissance to associate it with the horse (discussed in the previous chapter) and another flawed but heraldically prestigious icon, the soaring eagle, symbol of "the eagle-winged pride / Of sky-aspiring and ambitious thoughts, / With rival-hating envy" (*Richard II* I.iii.129–31). The tendency to visualize noble Romans as eagles cannot have but been furthered by the national use of that bird as a totem—apt symbol of envious factiousness, cruelty, mastery, and pride as well as of more Stoical and royal qualities. Another source of the tendency was the stereotypical Roman nose: aquiline, that is, 'eagle-beaked', a shape regarded as aristocratic since Hellenic times (Plato, *Phaedrus* 34/254D).

No image of Roman pride is better than the eagle at combining Rome's reprehensible tyrannical and savage side with a glimpse of her more admirable aspects. Because this bird lives "on mangled prey," it thus becomes, in Erasmus's anti-imperial view, a dubious model for governors and governments (*Christian Prince* 166). In that it mounts above the rest of earthly life, the eagle connotes aspirations at once lofty and blasphemous. Iconologists such as Valeriano Bolzani, Ripa, and Tervarent speak of the former sort, of the eagle's staring unblinkingly at the sun and causing its progeny to do the like. Traditionally, this painful testing and curative process certifies the offspring's noble descent while renewing the parent's own eyesight and strength. Power, majesty, prudence, constancy, immunity to change—all these aquiline qualities obviously relate to the private and public goals of Romans.

Verbal and/or presentational reference to the national royal bird is explicit in a dozen Roman plays. Given the conservative nature of theatrical property departments, eagle insignia may well have been standard in dozens more of the Roman plays. In Shakespeare's *Caesar* the titular hero "soar[s]" above his fellow Romans (I.i.79). Later in the play Cassius says he has had two live eagles perch upon his ensign (V.i.80), and their ominous departure is simultaneous with the disintegration of the conspirators' military power. *Coriolanus* (III.i.139, V.v.114) and *Cymbeline* (V.v.470–76) also have crucial eagle allusions, suggesting, in the first instance, that Martius typifies the national royal predator, and, in the second instance, that James's infant British empire is establishing a *traditio imperii* from old Rome.

The eagle can serve as metonym for a Roman's career, army, party, or country. As Alexander's Juno says, Romans are "ravenous Eagles soaring o're all lands" in search of "mighty prey" (*Julius Caesar* 129–30). Lodge's factious Marius threatens the deadly "t[h]rote of war" (*Wounds* Q IV.i,104–09) when he waves his "Imperial Ensign." And Jonson's Catilinarians appropriate the silver eagle of the deceased Marius to solemnize their treasonous oaths. Rowley's Dioclesian enters with "Eagle borne before," calling his Vandal opponents "base Ravens" near whom he will not "nessell" except to "peck out their eyes" (*Shoemaker* III.iii.7–58, iv.11). The eagle *is* proud Rome.

In several passages cited above, characters in *Caesar's Revenge* and *Believe As You List* have spoken arrestingly of Roman victors as insulting, spurning triumphers. We should be on our guard against dismissing these phrases as mere figures of speech for proud Overness. A harsh image would immediately present itself to the Early Modern imagination, where proud Romans were recalled as preeminently victors, accustomed to the supposedly archetypal honor of the *triumphus* and to subjecting victims to pedal humiliation. Triumph scenes appear in fully a third of the Roman plays—just about as great a fraction as contain that other allegedly archetypal national pastime, the suicide.

The *Romanitas* of the triumph is established in, among many other works, Ovid's *Amores* 1.15.26, which is imitated in *Catiline* III.ii.46 and *Sejanus* I.69. Petrarch had aided in the resurrection of the custom, and Bacon praises Roman triumphs as no gimrack "Gauderie" like modern ones but "the Wisest and Noblest Institutions, that ever was," conferring "Honour" upon generals, "Riches to the Treasury," and "Donatives to the Army" ("Greatness of Kingdoms," *Essays*). A more representative Early Modern view is that of Milton's Christ, who berates Rome for its sudden and decadent ambition "of triumph, that insulting vanity" (*Paradise Regained* 4.137–38). Two centuries before Milton, a quattrocento Italian, Duke Francesco Sforza, had also rejected the custom as impious, calling it a monarchical blasphemy ("superstitione de' Re"; J. Burckhardt 416–17). Sforza's implications are developed along Massingerian lines in the early 1620s (McDonald 88, 114 n.6), in a passage already cited in connection with allegedly Roman clemency:

> The Lordly Roman, who held it the height
> Of humane happinesse, to have kings and Queenes
> To wait by his triumphant chariot wheeles,
> In his insulting pride depriv'd himselfe
> Of drawing neare the nature of the gods,
> Best known for such, in being mercifull.
> (*Maid of Honour* IV.iv.3–8)

This whole issue had been a lively one in England since at least the time of *Gorboduc*, and one that would gain increasing topicality with Charles's purchase of Mantegna's stunning *Triumph of Caesar* in 1629 and Rubens's analogous *Apotheosis of James* in the same year. By the time of the Christmas festivities of 1631/32, Charles himself was playing Caesar, and he led in the captive kings appearing in Aurelian Townshend's *Albion's Triumph* (Butler 152).

Late Medieval and Renaissance princes all over Europe were continually complimented and diverted with formal entries and civic triumphs, as well as with pageant wagons, masques, and graphic portrayals of *trionfi* designed around Petrarchan abstractions. In London civic life, triumphs were frequent. According to George Puttenham, by 1589 the "triumphal" had become a standard subspecies of poetic *laudatio* at Elizabeth's court (Carnicelli 55–56). But onstage, triumphs were unusual, except in Roman plays.

What would the Roman triumphal ritual on the Elizabethan stage be designed to say to an audience? Dialogue and stage directions establish that triumphs employ simulated crowns, metal eagles, regalia, gold-encrusted scarlet/purple garments, and often banners, soldiers, captives, and carts. Every acting troupe, even at the universities, must have had access to a "Triumphal Chariot" that could serve in Petrarchan entertainments. Doubtless these rivaled in elegance and beauty the many surviving Renaissance carriages and barges of state, with their elaborately sculpted and gilded surfaces. Two of the earlier plays make clear how elaborate and potentially kingly most of such scenes are. The stage directions in *Wounds of Civil War* specify three triumphs. One of these involves a mere lieutenant, who enters "in royalty" (IV.iv.SD1), while elsewhere Scilla himself is said to wear a crown (II.i.16–17), to ride a chariot ("chair") "triumphant of gold," and to be accompanied by "colors," a crest (probably golden, IV.i.412), and captives bearing "crowns of gold" (III.iii.SD1). John Marston's *Sophonisba* V.iii requires that Scipio appear "in full state, triumphal ornamentes carried before him" (115.3–4). He wears the "roabe of triumph," and he bears a scepter, and a triumpher's "conquests wreath" or "crowne" (159–61). Stage directions in such later plays as *The Prophetess* (1622) and *The Roman Actor* (1626) tell the same story: "Enter, in Triumph with Roman Ensigns [and "triumphant Robes,"] Guard, Dioclesian" (*Prophetess* IV.vi, 374–75); "Enter . . . Captaines with Lawrels, Domitian, in his Triumphant Chariot" (*Roman Actor* I.iv.SD14).

Renaissance antiquarians could easily determine the nature of a Roman *triumphus* from the graphic arts and from standard authors like Appian and

Plutarch (Versnel 71–92). The historical ancient *triumphator* in Republican Rome wore kingly reddish-purple garments. These, since the abolition of the monarchy, had been dedicated to the king of the gods in his Capitoline temple. Like the face of Jove's regal/divine statue, that of the triumpher was covered with red powder. This redness is probably to be understood in the way that George Sandys did the scarlet gowns: as a sign of the juridical power to take human lives—a proud mark of deadly *majestas* tinged with a potential for cruelty. On the *triumphator*'s head was a crown of green laurel. Over it was suspended the larger-than-life gold crown of oak leaves that normally resided on the head of Jupiter's statue. The triumpher thus symbolically approached the regality and dark divinity of Jove, as symbolized in his sacred idol. During the passage of the triumphal train through the Eternal City, the eponymous cry rose up of "Triumpe!" an expression reserved for the epiphany of a god. At the conclusion of the triumphal procession, animal and human blood was spilled in sacrifice to the god, some of it just outside the temple itself. Thereupon the triumpher returned the vesture and crown to the deity. It is not too difficult to see that the blood magic was to transform the triumpher into a conduit for the energies inherent in the godhead and the now defunct kingship. *Titus Andronicus* I.i, with its triumpher's human sacrifices, suggests that the Renaissance sensed remarkably well the dynamics of the Roman victory rite.

The association of triumphs with Rome must have been strong, or the custom would not be alluded to or mimicked in so many non-Roman plays. Marlowe's Conqueror Play, though set in the late Medieval Middle East, is conceived in partially Roman terms: specifically, the play's Scythian hero promises Theridamas that both of them "will triumph over all the world," "reign as consuls of the earth," and have "mighty kings" "our senators" (*1 Tamburlaine* I.ii.173–98). In *Edward II* Gaveston is so much the master of the king's love that he deems himself a "Caesar riding in the Roman street / With captive kings in his triumphant car" (I.173–74). Marlowe's notion of captives in the cart may be anachronistic but is an Early Modern convention. A verbal link of triumphs with things Roman appears also in *As You Like It* (IV.ii.3) and *Measure for Measure* (III.ii.43–68). So strong is Shakespeare's linking of triumphs with Rome, he seems to make orthographical slips between *triumph* and *triumvir*. In *Love's Labor's Lost* (Q IV.iii.51), near a reference to an "empress" (54), there appears the spelling "triumphery" in place of *triumviry*. A similar slip survives in *Antony and Cleopatra* III.vi.28, where "triumpherate" appears instead of *triumvirate* (ed. Wilson, III.vi).

In a historically authentic Roman triumph, some prisoners would be in chains and, admittedly, could finally be slain. But no victim, living or dead, would undergo the Marlovian cruelty so often depicted on the Elizabethan stage. Historically, the victor rode or sat in his chariot above the crowd, above and behind the marching prisoners (R. Payne 128/129). But little or nothing is made of this superior-inferior placement in ancient art or literature. How very different this is from the Renaissance view of a victory procession or tableau!

About 1430 Donatello sculpted a *David* that more than one critic has deemed erotically charged. The smiling nude youth rests his foot by old Goliath's severed head, still wearing a helmet decorated with a Roman triumph (fig. 11). Subsequent art is full of pedal humiliation, as if it had been a universal Ancient custom. An armed Roman conqueror with naked dead or dying abjectly below him is displayed in Rubens's quite typical *Victors* in Stockholm and Vienna (Kunsthistorisches) and his *Triumph of Rome* in London (Dulwich; cf. DuBon pl. 69; Lucie-Smith 247).[1] In Bartolomeo Ammannati's *Triumph* (Bargello, Florence; Avery, fig. 164), a work of the later sixteenth century, a clothed Lady Victory uses both foot and knee to humiliate one of the Vices, aptly personified as a naked male.

Scenes of the Victor were obviously intended to recall Roman Antiquity. The sixteenth-century iconologist Valeriano Bolzani writes that 'it is the custom of kings who are in a triumph to tread under foot the bodies of prisoners as a token of the victims' subjection—a motif illustrated by many Roman insignias or representations where there is a person in triumph who has disposed his foot in this fashion' (*Les hiéroglyphiques* [1615] 2.QQ4r).[2]

Caligula fantasized how lovely it would be if all Rome had one neck so that he might set his foot upon it (Suetonius 4.30), and surviving Roman art is full of battle, victory, and triumph scenes. But I nowhere have seen in Ancient art or literature the insistence upon the personal desecration that is standard in a Renaissance victory (contrast *Triumph of Galerius*, Payne 128/129; Bianchi Bandinelli pl. 254–56, 341, 343, 356). Nor have I found any modern art-historical confirmation of Bolzani's view. Like English, the Latin language has foot images within phrases for the crushing and squashing of opposition, and grinding it/them with one's heel into the dirt (e.g., *tero, calco*). But as in English, these are largely dead metaphors. I know of no Ancient Latin author except Prudentius who shows much interest in trying to bring them back to life (e.g., *Psychomachia* 33–34; Mahoney 76). If the topos of pedal humiliation is at all Ancient, it is from Prudentius, the cult of Mithras, and the Bible—Asiatic origins rather than Graeco-Roman.³

What can such a deeply engrained Renaissance misconception indicate about Early Modern Europe except a strange need to believe that Roman majesty naturally pushed onward beyond hubristic pride into sadistic, even inhuman, cruelty?

Shakespeare seems especially ready to associate these cruel expressions of power with upper-class Romans or Romanized characters. This is most evident in *Cymbeline*, where, as T. W. Baldwin explains (*Small Latine* 2: 159–60), a new label is coined for these acts: "insul[t]ment" (III.v.140). This term, suggestive of *insolence* and *insult*, is etymologically derived from the Latin word *jump upon: in* (on) and *-sult* ("jump," as in "somersault" and the French *sauter*). One connotation of statements about *insult* is seen developing as early as *1 Henry VI* (whether or not entirely Shakespeare's). There the Roman hauteur of young Julius Caesar is recalled in a reference to the tossing of his "proud insulting ship" (I.ii.138). In a well-known moment of danger at sea, Caesar had recklessly and blasphemously argued that the Powers would never sink a vessel in which he sailed. Sure enough, the boat went through the storm, dipping up and down in triumph—and insult—over the elements themselves.

Another connotation of *insulto* in Latin is sexual, referring to any genital act, particularly aggressive and humiliating ones (Adams 200). In *Cymbeline* the abusive Cloten, living on a Romanized fringe of the empire, dreams of defeating Imogen's husband, wearing his clothes, raping his wife, and then concluding his "insul[t]ment" by a "foot[ing]." With Posthumus's "suit upon my back will I ravish [his wife]. . . . He on the ground, my speech of insul[t]ment ended *on* his dead body, and when my lust hath din'd . . . , to the court I'll knock her back, *foot her* home again" (III.v.137–44). This play's Roman eagle is also ready to "foot" the fractious (V.iv.116), and Posthumus's two royal brothers-in-law are taught a similar action in their Romanized sylvan *paideia*. Their tutor, trained in fighting Romans, describes the British princes as method-acting their way through triumph and insultment. When the elder prince listens to "The warlike feats I have done, his spirits fly out / Into my story"; and when he says,

> "Thus mine enemy fell,
> And thus I set my *foot on's neck*," even then
> The princely blood flows in his cheek, he sweats,
> Strains his young nerves, and puts himself in posture
> That acts my words.
> (III.iii.90–95)

The younger brother too learns the pedal Roman lesson, the old tutor says, and "strikes life into my speech... much more" (97).

For at least two decades before *Cymbeline*, insultment and triumph had been closely associated with stage Rome. Under the probable stimulus of Marlowe's *Tamburlaine,* Lodge introduces pedal humiliation that is contrary to Roman history but more in keeping with Marlowe's play about a classicized Middle East. Lodge has Scilla, like Marlowe's Scythian tyrant, use the neck of a defeated prince (the consul Carbo) for a footstool (V.i.53). More authentically, the Clown in Shakespeare's *Titus* is supposed to kneel at the "foot" of the emperor (IV.iii.111). In William Rowley's *Shoemaker,* the "Insulting Tyrant" Dioclesian boasts that it is "Europa's proud throat we tread on" (III.iii.21, 47). In *Catiline* (1611) a rebel wishes to tread Cicero into the ground like a "worm" (V.viii.6). In Jonson's earlier Roman tragedy, the eponymous hero is disgusted at the thought of bearing the print of "barefoot Hebrews" on his face and body (*Sejanus* II.141–42), and his successor, Macro, plans to "tread his [rival's] brains / Into the earth" (V.678–79). Fletcher's Cleopatra "scorn[s] to tread on" mere material riches (*False One* IV.ii, 346). In May's *Cleopatra* Agrippa tells Caesar that Cleopatra has long had "A Soveraignety ore halfe the Roman world, [and] / Trodd on the necks of humbled kings" (III.ii.73–74). More spectacularly dramatized is the triumphant insultment in Heywood's *Rape of Lucrece,* a play that reflects semihistorical sources but may also inspire, or be inspired by, the ending of the contemporaneous tragedy of *Coriolanus*. Heywood's Queen Tullia shows total exhilaration when she literally runs her chariot over, and stands "tread[ing] on," her father's corpse (341).

In *Caesar* a suppliant lies prostrate at the foot of the dictator, who himself soon dies at the foot of a statue of Pompey, over whose blood Julius is triumphing at the play's start. Shakespeare's Cassius is especially disgusted at having to live and die vilely under the "huge legs" of a colossal Caesar (*Caesar* I.ii.137). In a play with a nonclassical setting, *Twelfth Night,* Shakespeare's Sir Toby expects his conquering Amazonian Scyth Penthesilea to command him to follow her in triumph to the gates of Tartary and to let her "set [her] foot o' my neck" (II.iii.177; v.188, 205). In *King John,* where the papal invasion replicates an Ancient pagan Roman conquest (Knight, *Crown* 137) down to the matter of tribute, we hear that only civil war could make England "lie at the proud foot of a conqueror" (V.vii.113).

The story of Antony and Octavius seeps oddly up into the semi-Medieval world of *Macbeth,* suggesting to most scholars that the latter play immediately preceded *Antony.* Similarly, Shakespeare seems to have been planning *Julius Caesar* while he wrote the second Henriad, for Rome keeps emerging throughout. Perhaps he sensed that contests of pride in fourteenth- and fifteenth-century England, Ancient Rome, and an Elizabethan England about to face a dynastic crisis could mutually reflect and re-present one another. In any case, Bullingbrook is cast as an "ingrate" who has "downtrod" the more legitimate ruler (*1 Henry IV* I.iii.135–37). This locution gains deeper Roman coloration when action or talk presents Hal straddling various fallen figures on the battlefield (Hotspur, Falstaff, the king). Henry IV indeed requires protection from several Roman-like warriors: Douglas with his "insulting hand" (V.iv.54); Hotspur, who "triumph'd upon" this Scot (V.iii.15); and the other rebels who dreamed of living to "tread on kings" (V.ii.85). In *Henry V* Hal is likened to a triumphant Caesar (V.Chorus.28), and Pistol humiliates a kneeling captive. In *2 Henry IV* the old king recalls Northumberland's laying "his love and life under my foot" (III.i.63), Falstaff reenacts on Sir John Colevile the rapid conquest made by "hook-nos'd" Caesar, and old Jack intends to have the deed memorialized in a picture of the victim "kissing [the] foot" of this pseudo-Roman conqueror (IV.iii.40–54).

A mutual contamination of lust with violence is evident in references to insultment not just in *Cymbeline* but also in Shakespeare's "Lucrece," *Titus Andronicus, Coriolanus,* and a Romanized section of *Othello.* Playfully, the amorist Ovid spelled out a preexisting equation of love with war, seduction with conquest, the phallus with the sword. The Renaissance's archetypal Romans are not only overwhelmingly male but military. Thus it is not surprising to find their *Romanitas* to include what we now call male sadism: he who dominates with his plunging steel will do the same, presumably, with his plunging phallus, for each is a ready substitute for the other.

When we read Shakespeare's epillion, our awareness of the stereotype of Roman insultment complicates and enriches our response to the savage "insulting falchion" of the son of Tarquin Superbus. What emerges is a picture of a sadistic, imperialistic conqueror and factious "usurper"—and an anticipation of the aquiline piercer of the wall of Corioli. Proud in his savage predatory overness, Tarquin hovers above the foreign "wall," "land," and "worlds" of the body to which he longs to give "the hot charge" and make subject to "death and ravishment":

> he shakes aloft his Roman blade
> Which like a falcon tow'ring in the skies,
> Coucheth the fowl below with his wings shade,
> Whose crooked beak threats, if he mount, he dies:
> So under his *insulting* falchion lies
> Harmless Lucretia.
> ("Rape of Lucrece" 505–10)

Swooping Tarquin's "insulting" blade is held aloft, waiting for the repeated "mount[ing]" and plunging of murder/intercourse. Appropriately, the extinguishing of Lucrece's (cf. *lux*) pure light is both facilitated and symbolized by Tarquin's stomping his foot on the burning candle in the victim's bedchamber (672–73).

Titus shows similar associations among aggression, conquest, *Romanitas*, and intercourse. In III.ii mad Titus affectingly rejoices that his brother has stabbed a black fly that resembles the lascivious foreigner over whom the Andronici wish to triumph. Vengefully, the general grabs for his brother's "knife" so as to "insult on" the dark insect. As he plunges the weapon up and down, he shouts, "There's for thyself, and that's for Tamora"—a likely hint that sexuality and a conqueror's violence have merged in this Roman's imagination.

In *Othello* Cassio is a Florentine (I.i.20) but to the protagonist resembles a laughing *Roman* antic and winning, triumphing conqueror. "Do you triumph, Roman? Do you triumph? . . . they laugh that wins" (Q IV.i.118–22). The proud womanizer is apparently hook-nosed. And the husband, whose wife Cassio has allegedly "topp'd," wants to feed his enemy's nose to the dogs because he feels that he is Cassio's inferior in race, in nose, and in another organ for which "nose" is a metonym—the phallus. The context, then, encourages the Renaissance auditor to picture "Roman" Cassio not merely as the lascivious antic and "exultant fellow" described in the glosses of the Riverside edition, but also as a haughty Ancient conqueror who indulges in proud, leaping insultments.

The fact that sadism suffuses *Coriolanus* is a critical platitude, easily illustrated by pointing to such evidence as the erotic battle dream of Aufidius (V.v.106–35) or Volumnia's views of heroism. Appropriately, there are over four references to insultment in this Roman play (I.i.155–57, 261–62, iii.46–47; V.iii.116–26), culminating emphatically with a fifth in an episode too frequently omitted from productions (Halstead 9, "*Cor.* V.vi"). This is Aufidius's dishonorably "tread[ing] . . . upon" the hero's "most noble corse" (V.vi.133–43), an action that the antagonist instantly regrets in what more than one critic has seen as a sadistic postcoital *tristitia*. For this or any other hint of a desecration of Coriolanus's corpse, the histories give Shakespeare absolutely no precedent. Furthermore, the theatrical company must have experienced difficulties in playing the scene so as to protect the leading actor from genuine physical danger. Shakespeare's use of this treading (a sexually loaded term) is manifestly intentional, an effort to privilege a very special set of decadent meanings in this Roman play.

Proud Tyranny

Like other representatives of humanity on the Early Modern stage, Romans often forget that "lords" who "rightly . . . inherit heaven's graces" and favor must "have pow'r to hurt," yet "do none" (Shakespeare, Sonnet 94). Through the sheer weight of horrifying example, the Early Modern spectator is focused on the perilous proximity of barbarity to all that is civilized in Rome. And if descent into barbarism was Rome's ever-present threat, so too it threatens the audience's England as centralism and imperialism continue to grow.

Complexity and ambivalence were inevitable in the portrayal of stage

Rome. After all, the Renaissance inherited the Herodian tyrant of the Middle Ages: a figure of fun as well as of horror. Mystery plays emphasize the blood-engorged savagery of Rome, to judge from the red-masked Roman emperor painted in the late Medieval parish church at Little Missenden, Buckinghamshire. Stage tyranny, as Marlowe knew, gratifies an audience's desire to be outraged and yet to be fed with power fantasies. Thus, Shakespeare's death-dealing *Mart*ius, whose eye can pierce a corslet as he sits absorbed in thoughts of the "[forge]-fire / Of burning Rome," is a manifestation not just of the pagan red-eyed god Mars but also of the demonized Romans of the Medieval stage (*Coriolanus* V.iv.20, i.14–15, 64).

Jonson's parody of the swaggerer in *Poetaster* III.iv presents a benign example of the Renaissance marriage of the Medieval Herod and the classical antic *miles gloriosus*:

> *Tucca*. Now the horrible fierce soldier, you, sirrah.
> 2 *Pyrgus*. What will I brave thee? Ay and beard thee too.
>   A *Roman spirit scorns* to bear a brain
>   So full of base pusillanimity.
>
>   (1338–41)

In tragedies particularly, however, the Roman is torn by the stresses of his role as tyrannic king, and he comes to resemble Walter Benjamin's archetypal postclassical tragic hero, as described by George Steiner in his introduction to *Origins of German Tragic Drama*. The Roman fits Benjamin's view of the hero-king as a "Janus-faced composite of tyrant and martyr"; straddling history and myth, this "sovereign . . . incarnates the mystery of absolute will and of its victim (so often himself). Royal purple and the carmine of blood mingle in the same emblematic persona" (17–18). Indeed, tyranny and other public acts of high *superbia* are at the heart of tragedy. The antitheatricalist John Greene scarcely exaggerates when he says, "The matter of tragedies is haughtiness, arrogancy, ambition, pride, injury, anger, wrath, envy, hatred, contention, warre, murther, cruelty, rapine, incest, rovings, depradations, piracyes, spoyles, roberies, rebellions, treasons, . . . and all kind of heroyick evils whatsoever" (*A Refutation of the Apology for Actors* [1615], qtd. in Hunter, "Seneca" 23). Himself an admirer of theater, Scaliger classifies the first two tragic subjects ("Res tragicae grandes") as "atroces" and "jussa Regum" (Hunter, "Seneca" 23):

the rather Senecan duo of atrocities and royal commands. (Other tragic subjects Scaliger lists include "desperationes," suggestive of the suicides we considered in chapter 4, and "parricidia," which will be discussed in chapter 6.) In England lessons in the tyrannical abuse of great power are chief among the conventional topoi of Renaissance tragedy. A modern critic (Moretti 17–18) demonstrates this point with evidence from three representative and influential sources: tragedies make a man "execrate and abhorre the intollerable life of tyrantes" (Thomas Elyot); "Tragedy . . . maketh Kinges feare to be Tyrants, and Tyrants manifest their tirannicall humours" (Philip Sidney); and "playes and pageants" can show princes their "infamous life and tyrannies," predicting punishment and/or prescribing amendment (George Puttenham).

In view of the alliance of *Romanitas* with both tragedy and tyrannically "heroyick evil," it is little wonder that Tudor-Stuart drama associates Rome with tyrants and calls Romans "tyrannical" almost interchangeably with "proud." God may be the fountainhead of all power, but he seemed always to have been giving a putative tyrant to Rome, a view amusingly expressed by a character in *Every Woman in Her Humor,* who remarks that there never went by a "yeare" but some "great Tyrant raigned in Rome" (II.i, C4v). This idea may further encourage us to emphasize the word *greatest* in the subtitle of another Stuart Roman play, *Tiberius, Rome's Greatest Tyrant.* "Roman," then, came to subsume the paradigm of "tyranny," and Richard Peterson finds that even into the later seventeenth century, the Stuarts were being damned by allusion to Roman tyrants like Tiberius and Nero.

Respect *and* taint, justifiable or not, devolve on those who possess or assert control: control over space, time, knowledge, other people, and/or themselves. Since the most prominent of Romans were in government and the army, two traditionally male pursuits, the Renaissance tended to regard Romans as quintessentially male, participating in the stereotypically ambiguous aboveness that has been conventionally appropriate for males during countless centuries in Europe and the Middle East. In literature as in life, our moral nature is always of a mixed yarn. Good and bad *superbia* inevitably merge, and aspirations to majesty and divine status can tumble into their opposites or into mere meaninglessness. Roman *superbia* can be as admirably royal a trait as the king's treatment of traitors in *Henry V,* or even his bluff threatening of future English atrocities (a threat that effectively makes Harfleur surrender to him). There is a time for war, and a time for peace; a time for truth, and a time for Machiavellian dissimulation. No matter what the *Homilies* say, the distinction between king and tyrant is a fluid one. And so too is that between royal and tyrannical *superbia* of Romans.

CHAPTER SIX

Saevitia: Wolves, Demons, Parricides, and Self-Corrosion

> Everything evil, terrible, tyrannical in man,
> everything in him that is kin to beasts of prey and
> serpents, serves the enhancement of the species
> "man" as much as its opposite does.
>
> NIETZSCHE

In aspiring to be aquiline gods, many stage Romans emerge as part-tyrants, blood-sucking furies, treacherous snakes, devilish dragons. Patriots slip into being actors (*Caesar*) or brigands (*Antony*) or mere machines (*Believe*), and family defenders lose their *pietas* and change into parricides (*Titus, Appius*). It is almost as if the monarchically governed Renaissance was secretly as disgusted with kings as with their supposed opposites, tyrants. Indeed the cynical maxim ascribed to Cato was widely diffused: "That kinges be fierce and tirauntes naturally, what humanitie so ever their pretende" (Ferrarius, *De rege,* trans. William Bavande; qtd. in Bushnell 44). And the connotation of *rex* is sometimes as abhorrent as it was during the late Republic, when both species of rulers were said to operate through "*vis, superbia, libido,* and *crudelitas*" (Dunkle 151)—force, pride, obsessive desire (especially what Augustine terms *libido dominandi*), and cruelty.

Tyranny and Anti-Romanism

In chapter 1 we observed the intentionally anachronistic blurring of the distinctions between Ancient pagan Rome and a supposedly superstitious papal Rome. The mention of relics in Shakespeare's *Caesar,* for instance, blurs and modulates the English Protestant sense of the otherness of the Antique city. Protestantism also connected Rome with both pagan and papal cruelty. The "skarlet coloured beast" of Revelation 17:3 "signifieth the ancient Rome; the woman that sitteth thereon, the new Rome" (Geneva gloss). The pope was successor to the hydra-headed Roman mob (De Luna 247–49), and since the days of Romulus and Numa, the city had been full of murderers, magicians, and thieves, laying "hands on others King-domes" (pamphlet of 1591, cited in Praz, *Flaming Heart* 91–92). Rome had been "infamous for cruelty ever since Romulus kylde his brother: but specially in the Persecutors and the Popes," whose salient traits are indicated by their fondness for "purple coloure" (Broughton G4v). In the Markham-Sampson *Herod*, Augustus's comic slave attests, from personal experience, that the English Catholic seminaries on the Continent are "*colledges* where letchery and murder are *pue*-mates" (I.v.97). Shakespeare's Iachimo, another example of the linking of Ancient and papal evil, is a parodic "Tarquin" of old Rome as well as a Renaissance Siennese poisoner, a "false Italian / (. . . poisonous tongu'd as handed)" (*Cymbeline* II.ii.12, III.ii.4–5). In *Messallina* the spies of the Emperor Claudius are men of "*machiavillian* darkenesse" (V.i, 1735); and in *Shoemaker* the bloody "hands" of Antiquity are quibblingly equated with the italic/roman hands of humanist penmanship (II.ii.53, 115–16). In Protestant England, to link Ancient Romans with modern Italian Roman Catholics would be to see them as "beyond" civilized mankind: violent, superstitious, and barbaric creatures, devil worshippers, outside good citizenship and fellowship.

Writing at the start of the Augustan Age, Livy describes the immediate past of his self-destructive nation as so filled with greed, self-indulgence, and "sensual excess" that it seemed that Rome was "in love with death both individual and collective" (1.1., trans. de Sélincourt). A few Tudor-Stuart Roman scripts begin to convey such a mood (and perhaps more would if we knew what gestures, obscene or otherwise, actors inserted into texts). *Valentinian* surely has a dirty-minded bully for emperor, and he terrorizes his courtiers, saying:

> Your wives are Fencers [gladiators'] whores, and shall be Footmens,
> Though sometimes my nyce will, or rather *anger*,

> Have made ye Cuckolds for variety,
>
> . . . .
>
> Thou Licinius,
> Hast such a Messalina, such a Lais,
> The backs of bulls cannot content, nor Stallions;
> The sweat off fifty men anight do's nothing.
> (IV.i.43–56)

This "anger" is more witty and whimsical than sadistic, and the effect is largely Juvenalian (e.g., *Satires* 6), with little of the pain to be found in Livy's lament of an earlier century.

Today's cultural historians focus more seriously on the casual violence and sexual abuse that slavery, empire, and tyranny fostered in Rome: the condemnation of a slave boy to a pool of flesh-eating lampreys when he broke one of a family's crystal cups (L. Seneca, *De ira* 3.40.2–5); the night-long contest in prostitution between the lascivious Empress Messalina and a professional woman (Pliny 10.172; Juvenal 6.115–32); the custom of this or that monarch to witness an execution as a daily aperitif before dinner. The Emperor Tiberius was just unluckier than most other powerful Romans in having his peccadillos widely exposed: his crushing a boy's or youth's skull as easily as if it were an apple; his culling unweened babies to perform fellatio on him; his schooling a band of little boys to swim and nibble between his legs; and his hurrying through a religious sacrifice so as to rape the aristocratic lad who was the acolyte, and then punishing the youth's complaints, and his raped brother's too, by ordering their legs broken (Suetonius 3.44, 68). When a character in *The Prophetess* refers to an innate or "native Cruelty" in Roman behavior (IV.iv, 369), many authors, Ancient and Early Modern, would agree. Montaigne does not expressly connect Roman recourse to suicide with any Roman appetite for violence, but in "De la cruauté" (*Essays* 2.11) he imagines Cato ripping up his own bowels, not in Stoic self-restraint but with a 'feeling of pleasure and voluptuousness [sentit du plaisir et de la volupté].' More important statistically is the existence of forced labor, which must have encouraged Romans to engage in innumerable unchronicled acts of extreme inhumanity. Too, from earliest times, habituation to "continuall warfare," Livy states, made Romans' hearts . . . grow "wild and savage" (trans. Holland, qtd. in Barton, "Livy"

120). Vergil, Horace, and the author of *Octavia* suggest that Romans sadistically delighted ("gaudent," Vergil, *Georgics* 2.510; "gaudet," *Octavia* 983) in civil bloodshed, a trait plausibly inherited by the race since the time of Romulus's slaying of Remus (Vergil, *Eclogues* 4.13; Horace, *Epodes* 7). Plutarch is especially shocked at the parricidal Triumvirs, whose actions "shewed that no *brute or savage beast* is so cruell as man, if with his licentiousnes he have liberty to execute his will" ("Cicero," *Lives,* ed. Bullough, 5.362). Under the Empire familial murder ran rampant in the highest circles, and among impatient heirs to large properties.

Writing in this age, Seneca distinguishes between *crudelitas* ('cruelty') of an excessively harsh punishment and the *saevitia* of, in effect, sadism. *Saevitia* sounds a little like *savag*-ery, to which it is semantically allied, the probable root of the Latin word being *s[c]aev-*, a term for an enraged wild beast (Lewis and Short, s.v. *saevitia*). A certain kind and amount of rage is, of course, not out of place in a true king (Seneca, *De clementia* 1.11.4), but *pleasure* in a surrender to rage is: 'A tyrant differs from a king . . . only in the fact that tyrants rage [saeviunt] for the pleasure of it [*voluptatem*], while kings do so for a reason and out of necessity [*ex causa ac necessitate*]' (cf. Velz, "Clemency"). In *De clementia* 1.12.1, 1.25.2, and *De ira* 3.18.2, Seneca applies *saevitia* to people who would vary and prolong human suffering, cruelly suspending the sufferer between an excruciating life and tantalizing death. Such actions, he says, express a perverse, sick, insane delight ("morbis," "insaniam," "delectatur") and pleasure ("voluptatem")—a definition that closely anticipates the modern clinical definition of sadism.

Sejanus and *Catiline* constitute brilliant attempts to deal with Roman voluptuary cruelty. The mob of women and old men that tears apart the protagonist's corpse in the earlier tragedy is incapable of literal rape; yet Jonson goes beyond his sources and employs diction indicative of sexual violation. The crowd is "transported with cruelty": "virgins" and the rest start "digging out [Sejanus's] eyes, mounting" at his head and face; they "ravish" his limbs and distribute a thigh and other "pieces of the flesh for favors" (V.814–23). In *Catiline* I.504–12 Jonson invents a sardonic side effect at the hero's blood rite: the sexual arousal of bestial Bestia, the pederast. A moment after he drinks of the brimming bowl by which "each man [is] strengthned," Bestia starts to seek the "throat" of one of Catiline's pretty "boys."

A Roman rapist in *The Valiant Welshman* is revealingly likened to a "bloudy Tarquin," rather than simply to a lecherous one (V.i.14). Additional authors also attempt Jonson's sadomasochistic themes. Richards's Empress enhances her sexual charms by carrying a loaded "pistoll" (*Messallina* 197), an anachronistic item that fills her lover, Silius, with both lust and obedience. "Ravisht" and "panting," he bounces off to murder his wife, his two arms waving like excited sexual partners in a high-leaping "Lavolto," his "ambitious blood" "point[ing his] actions" (944–50). But here, unlike in Jonson, the effect is merely *antic*.

The most deeply upsetting dramatic analysis of Roman sadistic *saevitia* is, for most readers and viewers, *Coriolanus*. There, the borderlines between erotic love, bloodletting, and humiliation (not to mention between erotic and mother-son relationships) keep dissolving for the hero, his mother, and his martial associates. A warrior's greeting to, and fighting with, a fellow male are taken as equivalent gestures and equated with love embraces in bed. Battlefield activities are like the action of a mechanical phallus—"a *thing* of blood, whose every motion / Was tim'd with *dying* cries."

Beyond and Below Humanity

Whatever *saevitia* is, it is like *clementia* and *constantia:* beyond the ordinarily human, though of course in an opposite direction. It can partake of occult, animalistic bloodlust, like that of the heart-based *saevitia* ("tyrannis saevitia cordis") that Seneca assigns to the tyrant Sulla, who thirsted after the blood of seven thousand fellow Romans: "What Tyrant hath there ever beene that so greedily drunke up humane bloud, then [Sulla] who commanded seven thousand Romane Citizens to be slaine?" (L. Seneca, "A Discourse of Clemencie," in *Workes,* trans. Lodge, 593). Like far better qualities such as *clementia* and *constantia, saevitia* exceeds the normal hierarchical bounds of humanity. Typically, *saevitia* is a 'going beyond the bounds both of custom [*fines . . . solitos*] and of civilized human community [*humanos*]' (*De clementia* 1.25.2). If the most godlike activity for a ruler is to save citizens, Seneca proleptically tells the future incendiary Nero, the worst is to act like a fire. 'To save life in masses and universally, this is a godlike use of power; but to kill in multitudes and without distinction is the power of conflagration and of ruin' (*De clementia* 1.26.5).

Horrible though *saevitia* may be, the Ancients and their Early Modern dramatic followers are sometimes ready to see it as Nietzsche does, as a measure of panache or *virtù:* "With every degree of a man's growth towards greatness and loftiness, he also grows downwards into the depths and into the terrible" (*Will to Power,* sec. 1027). Even Vergil, when he writes of the consular axes of Brutus, says, as we have seen, that they were "saevas" for slaying his kinsmen (*Aeneid* 6.817–20).

Since the time of Plato, the wild tyrant had been associated with the other, with what is beyond or below civilized, God-fearing man. He is like a wolf or serpent (*Republic* 8.565D–66A), a hawk or kite (*Phaedo* 82a). Or he is like the barbarous parricide and cannibal King Lycaon, who slew a kinsman, ate his flesh, and (like Webster's Aragonian duke) turned wolf (*Republic* 8.565D–66A). Repeating these Ancient imagistic motifs, the humanist Ferrarius speaks of a prince as forfeiting his title of king by becoming a parricidal wolf and (Herodian) "slaughter[er] of innocents": "A woulfe ... bloodieth his handes with the slaughter of innocents, devoureth up with his unclean wrath the nexte blood of his kind" (qtd. in Bushnell 50). Erasmus visualizes a tyrant as a "lion, bear, wolfe, or eagle, all of which live on their mangled prey," or as some mad tigress, lioness, insatiable wolf, or composite "frightful, loathsome beast, formed of a dragon, wolf, lion, viper, bear and like creatures; . . . with never satiated hunger, fattened on human vitals, and reeking with human blood" (163, 166). This, then, is the hierarchical beast tradition that helps fill out the imagery of most Roman tyrant plays, as might be seen from an inspection of *Coriolanus,* where the stormy, self-indulgent killer-hero is likened to no fewer than six of Erasmus's beasts.

Although the standard Ancient historical view was of a once-pristine city corrupted through conquest of Carthage, another long set of writers from the time of pagan Antiquity till the Renaissance viewed Rome as a chronically immoral and unjust state ever since its founding. Augustine and Orosius collect an immense brief of charges, including the murder of Remus, the Sabine rape, the suicide of Lucretia, Lucius Junius Brutus's condemning his kinsmen (including her guiltless husband, the consul Collatinus), the nation's shabby ingratitude toward its savior Camillus (Augustine, *City* 3.16–17), the existence of only one full year of peace in the seven centuries from Romulus to Augustus (Orosius 4.12), the attempts to deny freedom to the conquered and food to the poor (Augustine, *City* 2.20, 3.17), and the plagues not just of factionaries but also of tyrants.

Shakespeare, like many other writers, would add the charge of "cruel irreligious piety," more "barbarous" than the Goths', Scyths', or Moors' (*Titus* I.i.130–31, 378; II.iii.78): Andronicus, we recall, sacrifices a Gothic prince to placate the spirit of his own dead son. Renaissance readers could easily determine that Rome engaged in human sacrifice (for instance, after the Battle of Cannae in 216 B.C.; Wilkinson 21) and for centuries killed prisoners at the end of a triumph (Dio 43.19.4–23; Ralegh, *History of the World* 5.6; Appian, *Auncient Historie* 205; Zonaras, *Epitome* 7:21 [all cited in R. Payne 71]; cf. Versnel 95). The occasion for a bloody triumph, Valerius Maximus and Orosius attest, was any victory in which at least five thousand enemy had been slain (Versnel 380). Human sacrifice was long a Roman custom, as Plutarch maintains in his *Questions* (despite contrary statements in his "Life of Publicola"); and it was "verie absurd" that late Republican Rome should lecture some other supposedly "barbarous nation" on the need to eliminate human sacrifice when the Romans themselves had just recently buried four foreigners alive (*Questions* 83, 124–26; R. Payne 61).

Renaissance dramatists fully grasped the extent of mere gore in Rome when referring to her maimings, suicides, slayings, triumphs, and gladiatorial games. Historically, these last events were identified as *munera*, rites to placate the gods and the dead, and occasional attempts were made (by Cicero, for instance; cited in Carcopino 229) to praise this institution for exemplifying a Stoic contempt of pain and death. Rightly, the plays are less enthusiastic, to judge from the disparaging references to Roman *sworders* (*Antony* III.xiii.31 and *2 Henry VI* IV.i.135; *gladius* means "sword") and *fencers* (*Valentinian* IV.i.43, *Shoemaker* III.iv.17). Onstage, numerous devices like bloodshed, "bloody" flags (*Caesar* V.i.140), and eagle standards contributed to Rome's "savage spectacle[s]" (*Caesar* III.i.223).

Barbaric sanguinary images, prominent in Homer and Euripides, are also unmistakable in Vergil, Ovid, Claudian, Prudentius, and perhaps most significantly, Seneca and Lucan. In the time of Lucan's Marius and Sulla, Rome's pavements are "slippery / . . . with slaughter," and the Tiber becomes a "streme of blood" (*Lucan's "Pharsalia"* 2, B7v, C2v). Like a typical tyrant, Lucan's Caesar is accused of being more "barbarous" and beastlike

132 "Antike Roman"

(*saevus* and *ferus*) than his troops, even those who practice human sacrifice (1. 444–84), and the dictator's sanguinary tastes are thought to prevent him from bringing the Battle of Pharsalus to a close until he sees that "the feild with Roman blood / Was overflow'd enough" (8, N5v). Pompey is charged with being a "barbarous" tiger, ever athirst since the time when he "lickt / Warm goare from Syllas sword" (1. 330–31). And in Lucan's translator's independent work, we read:

> Many will talk of title to a crown:
> What right had Caesar to the empery?
> Might first made kings, and laws were then most sure
> When, like the Draco's, they were writ in blood.
> (Marlowe, *Jew of Malta*, Prologue 18–21)

Most of the Judaeo-Christian commentators whom the playwrights read excuse even less of this bloodshed than pagan authors do. Citing Lucan, Augustine (*City* 15.5) voices sentiments like the Goths' in *Titus*, adding that Rome has long been peopled by persons bestial and demonic. He that "glories in dominion" (15.5) or "dotes on domination is worse than a beast. . . . Such men Rome has had: . . . nay Rome (says history) had many such. . . . Nero Caesar was . . . [at] the top turret of this enormity" (5.19). The Civil Wars, Augustine states, were antic "devils' revels" and resembled "banquets for the infernal spirits" (3.18). Examining the Book of Daniel, the humanist Juan Vives and his translator suggest that the whole tyrannical Roman Empire was a horned predatory iron "beast," unnatural (and implicitly demonic): a bloody, barbaric parricide, ruining its "own breeding": "the strangest, strongest, bloodiest of all, and such was the Roman Empire, that exceeded barbarism in cruelty, filling all the world with the rust of her own breeding, with bones of her massacring, with ruins of her causing" (Vives, qtd. by Healey in Augustine, *City* 2.442).

Renaissance anthologists, schoolteachers, playwrights, and casual browsers might be expected to notice the final choral lines of Rome's model *fabula praetexta*, the pseudo-Senecan *Octavia*:

> urbe est nostra mitior Aulis
> et Maurarum [*alternatively* Taurarum] barbara tellus
> hospitis illic caede litatur

> numen superum;
> civis gaudet Roma cruore.
> (979–83)
>
> The barbarous Moores to rudenesse bent
> The Prynces Courtes in Rome forlorne.
> Have farre more Cyvile curtesie:
> For there doth straungers death appease
> The angry Gods in heavens on hie,
> But Romayne bloude our Rome must please.
> (*Octavia,* trans. Nuce, 190)

'Rome is more barbarous [*barbara*] than the land of the Moors or the Central European Scyths'—and Goths (Tauris is in the Caucusus)—'who content their gods with the slaughter of a foreigner, not of a fellow citizen as the parricidal Romans do.'

Unmistakable allusions to this passage appear in the opening, already cited, to *Titus Andronicus* and to the anonymous *Nero:*

> The Inhospitable Caucusus is milde:
> The More, that in the boyling desert, seekes
> With blood of stranger to imbrue his jawes
> Upbraides the Roman now with barbarousnesse.
> (I.iv.127–30)

Similarly, likely allusions also appear at the start of May's *Agrippina* (I.i.236), *Shoemaker* (I.i.97), *Caesar and Pompey* (I.i.6), Alexander's *Caesar* (138), *Wounds* (V.i.245), *The False One* (II.i, 315–16), *Coriolanus* (III.i.237), *Prophetess* (IV.iv, 370), and, after the Restoration, Lee's *Sophonisba* (IV.i. 370–73). Doubtless, Early Modern England was obsessed with the irony of civilized Rome's barbarity.

The stage Roman exhibits an unmistakable urge to touch blood. According to *A Shoemaker, a Gentleman,* "true Romans" are accustomed to wade and "swim in a st[r]eame of blood"; "bloud" too is the "theame" they boldly write and "treate in Roman hand" across any invaded country (II.ii.53, 115–16). One Antony verifies his courage by bathing in consuls' blood (*Anto-

nius III, 950). One Caesar laments that he has opened the "dear Veins" of Mother Rome—

> And sail'd upon the torrents that flow'd from her,
> The bloody streams, that in their confluence
> Carried before 'em thousand desolations.
> (*False One* II.iii, p. 325)

And in Shakespeare's *Antony and Cleopatra,* the conspirators against Julius Caesar are described as having "drench[ed]" the Capitol in blood (II.vi.18). Garnier's characters find that Romans are crazed by an urge to massacre during each successive generation ("de race de race / Massacrer eternellement," *Marc Antoine* [IV, 1718–19]).

In the Early Modern view, Romans had an almost physical appetite for human gore—an insatiable urge that variously demonizes them, wraps them in pathos, or makes caricatures of them. Their ravenous "faim glouttone" (*Cornélie* I, 98) moves them "Nero"-like to want to "drink hot blood" (*Hamlet* III.ii.390–94) in ceremonies often dense with allusion to barbaric practice and supposedly superstitious papal doctrine. By inversion of Romish transubstantiation, blood is wine. The titular hero of *Catiline* formalizes his conspiracy in Act I with a communal bowl of human blood—an event whose historical counterpart was denied in Jonson's sources. Metaphoric blood-bibbing is evident in a long line of descendants of the pseudo-Senecan *Octavia.* Besides the Romans who "imbrue" their jaws in *Nero* I.iv.129, there are those who supposedly "quaffe the blood of Christians" in *Shoemaker* IV.ii.50, "dra[w] tuns" of enemy blood in *Coriolanus* IV.v.99, and "carouse" in order to get "drunk" upon plebeian "blod" in *Appius* II.ii.54.

The perverted sacraments of stage Rome include bodily ingestion as well, a motif that often gives rise to bathos, intentionally or not. Besides the Thyestean banquet in *Titus Andronicus* and the convict's sentence to devour his own flesh in *Cicero,* there is the scene in *Tiberius* of the "loving Romane Canibals," imprisoned and starving imperial nephews who seek to save one another on a diet of their own flesh (3090–103). Less literal are the crimes of Shakespeare's "Sylla"-like Duke of Suffolk, who is accused of eating "gobbets" of his Mother England's "bleeding heart" and who feels himself worse beset than "Roman" Cicero (*2 Henry VI* IV.i.84–86,

135–381). In *Coriolanus,* the offspring of Mother "dam" Rome is in effect "devour'd" by her surrogates (III.i.292–93, IV.v.76), a fate that the plebs think threatens them as well (I.i.85). *Appius* II.ii depicts a similar suggestion that the Roman plutocracy is taking to the "canibal trick," themselves "devour[ing]" the "flesh" of the starving plebeian soldiers metaphorically while teaching them to do the like literally (45, 53). Paradoxical phrases like "Roman Cannibal" (*Cicero* V, E2v; *Tiberius,* 3090–103) or quibbles on the same (*Coriolanus* IV.v.188, *2 Henry IV* II.iv.166, Brandon's *Octavia* 114–22) were of obvious interest and ironic amusement to spectators of the time. Doubtless, the subject of cannibalism, both figurative and actual, was especially fascinating in an age when anthropophagy had acquired a new transatlantic name and evoked fresh comment from Hakluyt (*Voyages* 8.5), Las Casas, and Montaigne.

The Roman predilection for blood is a universal Renaissance stereotype. Durantinus writes that Catiline intended (Circe-like) to use the eagle oath and communion of blood to transform his co-conspirators into "wylde beastes," craving the "taste of mannes bloud" (10v, cf. Duffy 25). The chief counterpart of whom the medieval Scottish regicide thinks when he contemplates his "bloody business" is a Roman (a bit surprisingly, Tarquin; *Macbeth* II.i.45–56).

It is platitudinous that the church grows from the blood of her martyrs, an idea with numerous analogues in Renaissance analyses of Rome. Du Bellay explains the rise and fall of old Rome in terms of magic: Romulus's shedding of Remus's blood created "ferme fondement" for Rome's walls—a foundation whose demonic firmness was eventually dissolved by an outraged and vengeful God ("Antiquitez" 34.12–14). This Romulus was he who, the dramatists say, "bath'd" in brother's blood (Alexander's *Caesar* I, 1390) and "built his Monarchy in bloud" (*Cicero* Dr-v), "cement[ing]" with it the walls of his capital and "manur[ing]" his growing empire (*False One* V.ii, 359–60).

Early Modern dramatists insist on Roman blood magic in several ways. Prologues of bloodthirsty spirits, coming straight from hell, open the scene in *Catiline, Caesar's Revenge,* and *Agrippina.* In *Messallina* there is an antimasque of Furies. In *Virgin Martyr* a devil attacks the heroine, and in *Caesar and Pompey* a character conjures a devil. That "Roman fight like devils" (*Shoemaker* III.iv.1) is no mere figure of speech in some plays: in

Caesar's Revenge (III.v, 1577–88), Cassius promises to let a fury literally drink Caesar's blood if she will guide the knife, while in *Appius and Virginia* the "fury" of the hero is said to have been "arme[d]" by a "divel" (V.i.112–13). Finally, in *Herod* Augustus's foreign slave protests "I'm no Italian" and cannot be easily turned into the national model of a murdering "divell" by the ministration of any "dull bloody Romans" (71–76).

As Jonson was to do in *Catiline,* Shakespeare does not let mere historicity or decorum prevent the introduction of references to Roman bloodrites. In *Caesar,* Shakespeare invents, or greatly exaggerates, Roman interest in hunterlike blooding, ritualistic bloody handshakes (Sterling 40–54), necromantic name-conjuring, and exorcism. And of course equally missing from Shakespeare's source are the Satanic affinities of the hero of *Coriolanus:* a "red"-eyed, bloody "dragon-like" figure, nursing "injury" as "The jailer to his pity."

The chief Latin antagonist of Aeneas in Vergil's epic resembles, significantly, a wolf whose throat is parched for blood (*Aeneid* 9.68). Canines, with their human-looking frontal eyes (and bears, close relatives of canines) have long served not just as models for marginal humans but also as alleged sources of, and receptacles for, their souls. Warlike Rome, like many subsequent powerful civilizations, was originally populated by marginal and wild men: discards, fugitives, outlaws of other cities.

In view of the Renaissance association of wolves with otherness in general and tyrannical *saevitia* in particular, it is inevitable that imperial Rome should have seemed especially well symbolized by its oldest tutelary deity, the wolf. In Western emblemology, wolves and werewolves like King Lykaon stand for tyranny, parricide, and cannibalism, but also for fraud (Dante, *Inferno* 1), "greediness" (*Lear* III.iv.93), the demonic (Rowland 163, 165), sexual pride or appetite (*Othello* III.iii.404), and thievish "voracità" (Ripa; cf. Valeriano Bolzani, *Les hiéroglyphiques,* trans. Montlyard, 11.4).

Once again, as with the rest of Romans' mixed reputation, the trait of wolfishness was not totally negative. Most important, the *pater patriae* "Romulus / Was fed by a she wolf" (*Appius* II.ii.51–52) when his mother discarded him. Too, in the old bestiaries, wolves are said to whelp only in May and during thunderstorms (Rowland 163)—details that suggest vegetation gods and complicity with the heavens and future events, and may help explain the presence of prophetic storms in *Julius Caesar, Caesar and Pompey,* and *Wounds*. In Germanic countries "wolf" is used as a first name to suggest laudable aggressiveness, while in mythologies more likely to be known to Tudor-Stuart playwrights, the wolf was associated not just with destroyers like Mars (and Lok) but also more positively with Zeus (Rowland 161–62) and the sun/Apollo (Valeriano Bolzani 11.2). In hagiography the wolf can also symbolize the misunderstood sinner, as in the tale of St. Francis's encounter with the wolf of Gubbio. And an easy inference from the Romulan myth is implicit in numerous English Roman plays: the idea that wolfishness nurtures Rome, providing a tyrannical savagery without which her greedy urge to acquire and dominate other lands would be doomed to failure—as would her fabled urbanity, with its basis in immense imperial wealth and human cultural resources.

Historically, Etruscan and Latin peoples regarded wolves with special reverence (Tervarent 86, 251). In *Aeneid* 1.295 Vergil ambivalently describes Romulus as taking joy in (*laetus*) the hide of the wolf. Later, in 8.634, we read that the (metaliterary) tongue of this wolf (like, implicitly, the legendary tongue of the mother bear) licks the twins (cf. *Bestiary* 45; Aelian 2.19): this we are meant to understand as an act of *shaping* the offspring. The physical survival of an Archaic bronze she-wolf in Rome occasioned a famous late-fifteenth-century re-edification (as Shakespeare might have put it; cf. *Titus* I.i.381). Antonio del Pollaiuolo (Macadam 62; Haskell and Penny, 335–37) added the two suckling cherubic figures in his lush quattrocento style. The resulting configuration is richly suggestive of nurturance as well as of predation, of community as well as of marginality—altogether a creative Renaissance reshaping of Roman Antiquity for new symbolic functions.

With the other two major canines—the fox and the dog—the wolf has a reputation of hypersexuality. Reciprocally, *lupus* meant not just 'wolf' but also 'prostitute' (Plutarch, *Lives* 1.72; Livy 1.4–5). The latter sense is on the vulgar minds of the British Queen Bonduca's daughters when they would insult the "salt" Roman invaders:

> *1. Daughter.* Ambitious salt-itcht slaves: Romes master sins,
>   The mountain Rams topt your hot mothers.

>   *2. Daughter.*   Dogs,
> To whose brave Founders a salt whore gave suck.
>   (*Bonduca* III.v.48–50)

It is not surprising that Desdemona—ironically deemed as fit as, implicitly, Messalina to "be by an emperor's side"—should be libelously coupled with Romanized Cassio as "wolves," "salt . . . in pride."

Living on the margin of civilization and often subsisting through it, the wolf can represent the outlaw within, able to interbreed with man's companion, the dog (Bodin 144, citing Varro), if not also with the third canine, the fox. Also implicit in lupine symbolism are parricidal factionalism, cannibalism, suicide, and various other forms of attack on the self or one's own group. Traditionally the wolf eats its fellows in the pack until it starves to death (*Troilus,* ed. Baldwin, I.iii.130). Roman ambition tempts toward parricidal factiousness and self-cannibalistic suicide. "Mere oppugnancy" leads "rude son [to] strike his father dead":

> Then every thing includes itself in power,
> Power into will, will into appetite,
> And *appetite, an universal wolf*
> (So doubly seconded with will and power)
> Must make perforce an universal prey,
> And last *eat up himself.*
>   (*Troilus* I.iii.111–24)

Because they swallowed up and retained so much territory, Romans are, in many plays, the implicit archetypal "*universal* wolf."

In most plays a connection between wolves and Rome is strongly felt, even though not expressed by the gestures, costumes, and property lists implicit in the texts as they have come down to us. An association of Romans with canines, especially wolves, is, however, explicit in over a half dozen Roman plays,[1] including, as we have seen, *Appius,* as well as *Wounds, Cicero, False One, Fuimus Troes,* and, most interestingly, Shakespeare's *Caesar* and *Coriolanus*[2] and Jonson's *Sejanus.* Jonson's second Roman play gives us "a world of wolf-turned men," wolvish in their very "hearts" (III.251, II.273); wolvishness is explicitly distributed among several Romans, led by "night-eyed" Tiberius, a tyrant with "wolf's jaws," a howling wolf, who banquets on blood with his bloodhounds (III.347–48, 370–76). A play like *Roman*

Actor employs dog imagery as if in allusion to déclassé or marginal wolves. And in *Cymbeline,* where Caesar's proud "brag" (III.i.23) still lives in memory, no sooner does Posthumus identify himself as a Roman than a British captain calls him a bragging dog (V.iii.89–91). Perhaps, noble Romans are just dogs obeyed in office.

Lupus

Yet another Renaissance meaning of *wolf* is occasionally implicit in Roman plays. Formerly, some kinds of ulcers, cancers, lupus, and other autoimmune diseases went under the name of "the wolf" or "lupus" (*OED;* Gr. *lukos*). In earlier pages we have already taken note of Lucan's referring to the last hope of the Republic, Pompey, as a hollow rotted oak, reverently left to stand by its own huge weight. Obvious Roman concern with outward *dignitas* and *constantia* encourages English dramatists to contrast disease and inner hollowness with outward show, and occasionally to imply that such spiritual malady was the symbolic equivalent of "the wolf." In the language of Renaissance iconography, a stage Roman might therefore belong to a wolf pack not only because of his martial cruelty and overall aggressiveness but also because of his unnatural predator's tendency to "eat up" his own kind (*Troilus*) and, through inordinate ambition or inner insecurity, destroy even himself.

Julius Caesar and *Coriolanus* are two plays with motifs of self-devouring and internal emptiness: Volumnia starves by feeding herself with her own anger; Portia burns, chokes, and is poisoned by the coals she devours; and Caesar's priests find that beasts can live without a heart and entrails. Both dramas brilliantly urge questions of the Romans' canine or specifically lupine identification. Strong hints are also given that Coriolanus resembles the disease of "wolf" and needs cauterization or amputation if the *corpus politicum* is to be saved. To the tribunes in III.i, he seems an "infirmity" (81), a "violent" and "poisonous" "disease" (220–21), "a disease that must be cut away" (294), a "gangren'd" organ whose "infection, being of catching nature," will otherwise "spread further" (305–9).

But Martius is more than a disease. He is a boyish hero, perhaps half-consciously modeled on that legendary Spartan youth who illicitly hid a canine (a fox) in his cloak and suffered mutilation and death from it rather than reveal his theft in a cowardly cry of pain (Plutarch, "Solon"). Shakespeare's mind may be on this legend in the tragedy's closing moments. There Martius denies that he is a "boy" and instead defines himself as the royal/tyrannical Roman predator (eagle): an adult, not a child; a doer, not a victim. The cancerous wolf, inherited from his mother and fed on the anger that she served to the family (IV.ii.50–51; cf. Adelman, "Anger's My Meat"), acts like "hatred's hidden ulcer," eating from within (Marvell, "A Dialogue Between the Soul and Body"). This is what disables his basic instincts for self-preservation. He is a hungry, emotionally licentious wolf: at once a killer and the person killed, both a boy/man of murderous appetite and his own victim, consumed by cancerous emptiness and a doomed attempt at Spartan stoicism.

At any rate, identifying himself as the eagle who wantonly raided the Volscian "dove-cote," he sees himself as killer-devourer, randomly spoiling pigeons, which, like lambs, represent a literal food source and constitute a crucial symbol of peace and sociability. In recalling how he deprived others of these things, he seems to ask to be recognized as a predatory danger to the community, something that deserves to be killed immediately by the "lords" and their guard dog: "Cut me to pieces, Volsces, men and lads, / Stain all your edges on me," "false hound!" (V.vi.111–12, 120). But typical of the early modern ambivalence that marks this scene, at the very moment when Coriolanus is most the sociopathic predator, he paradoxically is made to resemble the ultimate Western victim, the Lamb of God, condemned in a public square by hired agents and a mob yelling, "Let him die" (V.vi.119).

Uncivil Parricide and Self-Destruction

Apparently out of a desire to introduce an explosive topic and appropriate the *Romanitas* that allegedly adhered to it, dramatists sometimes ignore their probable sources in order to fabricate parricidal speeches and incidents. This motivation seems to obtain in the case of Mutius's murder in *Titus* I.i, the mention of Caesar's being able to charm even the offspring of women he killed in *Caesar* (I.ii.274), and the decision to make Sabinus's betrayer a cousin instead of a friend in *Sejanus* (I.22). Explicit allusions to Romulus's archetypal Roman parricide, the slaying of Remus, occur in *Cornelia* I.30–31, II.386–89 (in *Cornélie*, "romuliste" often substitutes for "romain"); Alexander's *Julius Caesar* I.137–40; *The False One* V.ii.12–20; *Cicero* II, C2r, and *Catiline* II.365–67 (mentioned, even if disingenuously denied). Also, explicit references to parricide are made in prologues, opening scenes, and several other dramatically prominent places: for example, the start of *Catiline* (I.32–34, 93–94) and *Agrippina* (62–76). Literal parricide is, in fact, a Roman act occurring in, or just before the start of, 25 percent of Roman plays. And it is mentioned in many more.[3]

Because it figures prominently in a quarter of the Roman plays, parricide has about as good a claim as suicide to the title of the Stage Roman Way of Death. Plutarch's "Life of Publicola" (*Lives,* ed. Perrin, 1.101), however, might temporarily lead one to a different conclusion; there the sainted Romulus is said to have defined *parricida* as any murder because he thought no one would ever be so dastardly as to commit literal parricide—and indeed, Plutarch reports, there was none in Rome for six hundred years until *finally* one evil Roman (Lucius Hostius) slew a relative. (Seneca, on the other hand, criticizes Claudius for prosecuting parricides, saying that for the government to ignore the many offenders would help control and suppress copycat crime; *De clementia* 1.23.) Romulus slew his brother and led the tribe in a war against their wives' Sabine fathers and first husbands; thus he must have been as hypocritical on this subject as his whole nation proved to be. At any rate, the literal term was extended to include acts of treason and the killing of any fellow citizen (Lewis and Short, s.v. *Parricida*). Upon the assassination of the *pater patriae* Caesar, the Ides of March was immediately redesignated as the *Parricidium.*

Early Modern England appears to have seen Roman eagerness for parricide as the result of cruel pride: "As if a man were author of himself / And knew no other kin" (*Coriolanus* V.iii.36–37). René Girard speculates (61–67) that the archetypal mythic fratricides recounted by many societies reflect a human need to establish "difference," a task supposedly completed when one's brother, twin, fellow citizen, or other counterpart lies dead at one's feet. Literal parricide came to be viewed as essentially *factionalism* confined to the family, or as a figurative form of *suicide* extended to the intimate family circle or to the whole *patria*. Lucan's Caesar so inspires his troops that the centurion Laelius (doubtless a fictional person) brags that his personal commitment sets him above social and religious taboos. Laelius is prepared to "rob the god, or sacred temples fire" or "Rome itself" for Caesar's sake; he would commit treason, murder, and parricide out of loving loyalty to his master. "Caesar, he whom I hear thy trumpets charge / I hold no Roman";

> shouldst thou bid me
> Entomb my sword within my brother's bowels;
> Of father's throat; or wom[a]n's groaning womb.
> This hand (albeit unwilling) should perform it.
> (Q 1.366–67, 383–86)

Brother, father, wife (Ronan, "*Pharsalia*"), unborn child, or the goddess Mother Roma herself—all are less important to this fanatic supporter than his leader's wishes.

The strength of the Lucanic model is visible also in the references of the parricidal protagonist in *Catiline,* who has allegedly slain a wife, son, and brother, and now plans to probe the entrails of Mother Rome (I.32–94). The Laelian pattern is even more manifest in Macro's soliloquy about serving *his* Caesar in *Sejanus* III.714–34, a villainous speech looking Janus-wise at both Antique Rome and Stuart England: Macro will sacrifice wife, parent, child, or twin brother at a monarch's demand—for "a prince's power makes all his actions virtue"; "It is the bliss / Of courts to be employed, no matter how." Even *Coriolanus* employs the Laelian motif when Cominius swears that he is willing, for Rome's sake, to surrender his life and his wife's "estimate, her womb's increase / And treasure of my loins" (III.iii.114–15). At this point the tribune Sicinius highlights the Roman conventionality of Cominius's speech by snarling, "We know your drift" (116).

The rhetoric of intestine parricidal *saevitia* is established for all subsequent Western literature by Lucan's account of the war between Pompey and Caesar—former son- and father-in-law—a war with relatives on both sides of the battle line ("cognatasque acies," 1.4). Any good Roman in Lucan is family-centered; any villain is *saevus*. In scenes and descriptions that are likely to have set precedents for Shakespeare's paralleling of Caesar and Brutus in *Julius Caesar,* Lucan stresses the bonds of family love: of Cornelia for her husband Pompey and father Scipio; of Brutus for his father-in-law Cato; and of Cato and his newly returned exwife Marcia for one another (cf. Ahl 348). Lucan's villain, Caesar, by contrast, is not pictured with his family, and his dead daughter's ghost acts as divisive figure, steeped in vengeance against her former husband, Pompey. Caesar's personality is tellingly exposed in a vision that he has before crossing the Rubicon: he sees the aged goddess Roma, clearly a mother figure, failing to stop his destructive advance upon her. He and his former son-in-law turn into bestial predators (a lion and bloodthirsty "barbarous" tiger, 1.206, 329) for want of a peacemaking woman of the Sabine type to reestablish family (1.118).

In the latter half of the sixteenth century, England, like the rest of Early Modern Europe, experienced a craze of infanticides, real or imagined. The numbers approached those of the witch craze (Sharpe 200). To artists and audiences, literal infanticides, whether by the parent or by a Herod figure, were like literal rapes: interesting subjects in themselves and symbols for the breakdown of familial *pietas* and civic mutuality.

Dynastic parricides were also very much on Early Modern European minds. These actions were safely discussed only if they arose from Rome or the Ottoman Empire, but seldom if (as in the Romanized *King John*) they involved political struggles at home. "This is the English, not the Turkish court," where "Harry Harry" "succeeds," thanks to "good brothers" (*2 Henry IV* V.ii.46–49). The government of the Sublime Porte had legally institutionalized routine dynastic assassination of secondary claimants to the throne. Unofficially, however, their many Christian majesties of Europe had been clearing away inconvenient family members for centuries. As Richard Hillman explains, late Medieval and Tudor-Stuart England had a record only marginally better than the sultanate's, a fact that English audiences could recall from the chronicles or from such plays as Shakespeare's *King John, Richard III,* and *Richard II*. Too, there might be fresh memories of more recent supernumerary royalty persecuted and executed: the children of Clarence, Lady Jane Grey, the royal bastard duke of Richmond, the impossible Lord Darnley, the neurotic little Arabella Stuart, and of course the Scottish Mary herself—all victims of their own relatives.

Ancient history gave other good excuses regarding parricide as a stereotypically Romulan crime, not just of the Neroes and Tullias but also of the *patres patriae* themselves. Christian writers grew fond of recalling that Collatinus did not forestall the suicide of his wife, Lucretia; and that Virginius killed his daughter lest she have to suffer Appius to rape her. Romulus slew his grandfather, Orosius stresses, "then his brother," and arranged to marry his subjects to mourning Sabine women, using "the blood of their husbands and parents as dowry" (2.4). Augustine caustically terms "the whole city" of Rome "guilty" of parricide in murdering the reputation for virtue of their *pater patriae:* if Remus was not slain by Romulus, "then is the whole city guilty of the same crime nonetheless, in giving so total an assent unto such a supposition; and instead of killing a brother hath done worse in killing a father" (3.6). Augustine finds Roman parricide everywhere, maintaining that even Rome's early foreign policy was parricidal in its violent absorption of Alba, the land of Romulus's and Remus's birth. This war, says Augustine, in purposeful echo of Lucan, "was worse than civil," "where the daughter city bore arms against the mother. Besides, . . . a sister of the [Roman] Horatii was espoused to one of the [Alban Curiatii], who seeing her brother return with the spoils of her dead husband [whom he had slain], and bursting into tears at this heavy sight, was run through the body of her own brother . . . [, though] there was more true affection in this one poor woman (in my judgment) than in the whole Roman nation besides" (*City* 3.14, trans. Healey). From this appreciation of the slain Horatian girl, one might jump perhaps to thoughts of Shakespeare's Virgilia. Such legends illustrate tensions upon which dramatists can build whole works.

In 1547 the sycophantic Welsh versifier Arthur Kelton developed an especially full account of Romulan parricidal *saevitia* in order to praise the rationality of Englishmen and their beloved peacemaker, Henry VIII. Kelton emphasizes the Roman twins' "savage" lupine upbringing and the fact that their uncle Emilius "his brother slewe, with fraude and treason."

> Thus of Rome was the Antiquitie
> Murdre upon murdre, voyde of all pitie.
> (d2)

Clearly, parricide ran in Rome's—but of course not England's—royal family.

The embrewing of blades in bowels is one of two popular parallel, and intertwined, images in the Early Modern repertoire. Each, though rhetorically apt in personal situations, is usually given a political application. We have glanced, in an earlier chapter, at the lethal family life of the oversexed pit viper. The female devours the head of the male *in flagrante delicto*, and suffers the cannibalistic vengeance of her dead mate's little ones. These matricides tear open her abdomen as they eat toward an independent existence (fig. 1), feeding "on mother's flesh which did them breed" (*Pericles* I.i.65). Theirs is the "serpent's tooth" of an unthankful child (*Lear* I.iv.288).

The other image was popularized by Lucan from a suggestion in Vergil's *Aeneid* (8.833), a suicidal/patricidal figure of speech that the later author emphatically reiterates a half dozen or more times in describing Rome's civil wars. Subsequently, the rhetorical figure was imitated in political contexts throughout Early Modern Europe without cease. To kill one's fellow countrymen is, in effect, to kill one's own family and, ultimately, oneself, as Marlowe, Lucan's translator, suggests in a work of his own:

> sword . . .
> In civill broiles makes kin and country men
> Slaughter themselves in other and their sides
> With their owne weapons gorde.
> (*Edward II* IV.iv.5–8)

As Lodge puts it in a Roman context, when "thou does raze and *wound thy city* Rome," "*murders* makest thou *of thyself*" (*Wounds* I.i.276–81). Civil war is parricide is suicide.

Du Bellay moves toward a sociogenetic explanation for Roman parricidalism. Romans are like not only Hercules's Hydra but also the legendary snake-associated parricidal monsters in the Jason and Cadmus stories. As Spenser's translation puts it ("Ruines of Rome" 10, 136), Romans are raging fratricidal snake men, "ranke seede," who

> Emongst themselves with cruell furie striving,
> Mow'd downe themselves with slaughter mercilesse,
> Renewing in themselves that rage unkinde,
> Which whilom did thou earth born brethren blinde.
> ("Ruines" 10, 137–40)

Roman proclivity to parricidal *saevitia* and "furie"-like "rage unkinde" is stopped by neither "prince," "nor peere, nor kin" (23). Was this self-mutilation punishment?

> some old sinne, unappeased guilt
> Powr'd vengeance forth . . . eternallie?

> Or brothers blood, the which at first was spilt
> Upon your walls . . . ?
>
> (24)

Probably both were the causes is the implication.

Civil war was perceived to be an archetypally Roman institution, and the Early Modern habit of using viper-bitten entrails and allied snake imagery to discuss internal political relations became as strong and "Roman" as the urge to use in the same contexts a Lucanic reference to parricidally incised entrails. It is therefore not surprising to find serpentine references everywhere, almost all suggesting the dangers of fostering potential rebels. In lines anticipating Shakespeare's *Caesar* (II.i.32), Kyd has his Caesar called a "serpent" "waxen warm" and growing dangerous with "unhatched Ambition" (*Cornelia* IV.53) because he is "envenomed with ambitious thoughts" (III.ii.40–43). The allusion is to the Aesopian fable of the farmer who is bitten by an apparently frozen snake that the man has put under his cloak, hoping to nurse it back to life (Velz, "Emblems"). In becoming the giver of life, the poor man lost his—just as the viper mother does.

When Thomas Heywood translates Sallust, he inserts his own viper reference, saying that Romans of Catiline's time were at once both viperously parricidal in public life and suicidal in private. They "*fostered . . . within their owne bowels a viperous consort of fellow-Cittizens,* who rather then they would surcease the obstinacie of their private Humours cared not what became of themselves and their countrey" (*Cateline* 88). Perhaps the most influential Early Modern work to connect vipers with politics and Rome is the anonymous 1579 defense of rebellion by "Junius Brutus," where Caesar serves as a prime example of that "viperous brood which gnaws through the entrails of their mother," abrogating the people's armies "to make themselves masters of the state," according to Languet's or Mornay du Plessis's *Vindiciae contra tyrannos* (183–84).

Political use of references to the parricidal viper appears in at least eight Roman plays. When Young Marius watches his army's disappointing retreat from Scilla's forces, he exclaims:

> Look how these murderous Roman[s], viper-like
> Seek to betray their fellow citizens.
>
> (V.ii.29–30)

Traitors in *Faithful Friends* are a "brood of vipers" (V.ii, 297), and in *Lucrece* the "unnatural" parricidal "monster" Tullia and her "viperous brood" are expelled from Rome (2520, 2526). For his literary sins, a plagiaristic poet in *Poetaster* is a "viper . . . that eat'st thy parents" (V.iii, 2884), while in Jonson's second Roman play, the pro-Republican historian Cordus is slandered as an "ingrateful viper" (*Sejanus* V.678) because he castigated "the present age" that gave him and his fellow citizens birth, and supposedly, he bit "with a viper's tooth" and thus attacked each man's "private" (III.384–94). Grotesquely "Roman" parricidal parallels may well have been felt to be ironically implicit between the legendary viper and the heroes of both *Catiline* and *Coriolanus*. The one is an unnatural son who would plow his Mother Rome, reach her head, and re-create himself in her dead and rocky womb (I.74–95; cf. Roman, "Snakes"). The other, the son of an unnatural mother, is explicitly viewed as a dragon/snake by his friends and as a viper by his enemies (III.i.263, 285). But Coriolanus as much as Catiline ultimately proves a serpentine victim, unfed and smothered in the anger-filled abdomen of his mother.

With or without explicit references to vipers, a linking of Rome, civil war, suicide, and parricide enhance structure and theme. Regarding Shakespeare's *Julius Caesar*, mention has already been made of those citizens who would forgive Caesar even if he stabbed their mothers. A series of additional interesting touches occurs in III.i–IV.iii. In III.i Brutus attempts to show his love of Antony by proffering a bloody hand and a heart "of *brothers'* temper" (165–75). This gesture would be especially rich in irony for an audience familiar with the stereotypical descendants of Romulus. In IV.i Shakespeare intensifies the speed and nonchalance with which the Triumvirs historically bartered for the deaths of a sister's son or a brother. And then the dramatist immediately juxtaposes the conspirators' quarrel (IV.ii–iii), where Brutus and Cassius call one another "brother" six times, despite the fact that they have never used this term themselves before. Brutus so torments his brother-in-law in this scene that Cassius first threatens aggressive violence (IV.iii.63–64). Then, feeling "brav'd by his *brother*" (95), he offers self-immolation, for scarlet fratricide is the "Roman" way:

> There is my dagger,
> And here my naked breast; within, a heart

> Dearer than Pluto's mine, richer than gold.
> *If that thou be'st a Roman, take it forth.*
>
> (100–103)

The reconstructed relationship of Cassius and Brutus, unlike that of the Triumvirs, will be truly fraternal instead of fratricidal—for the short time they have to live.

The trope of the disembowelment of one's native land in civil war rises to the surface everywhere in Early Modern England. The proem to Lucan's epic contains the phrase "populemque *potentum* / In sua victrici conversum viscera dextra" (1.2–3), which classically educated spectators at *Caesar* would realize was being echoed in Brutus's statement that Caesar's spirit is "*mighty* yet! / . . . and turns our swords / In our own proper entrails (V.iii.94–96). Lucan's Stuart translator, Thomas May, ends his *Cleopatra* with Augustus's sheathing the "civill sword; / Whose fatall edge these twenty yeares has ript" Rome's "bleeding entrails" (V.v.114–16.) In *Antonius* (1713–28) the chorus of Roman soldiers lament that their land is "gnaw[ed]" with civil war and that they must pierce and "bath in our owne brest." When Catiline wishes to assert his love of independence, he prays that when he lacks it he may die of some variant of suicidal evisceration, his sword hand ripping "my breast for my lost entrails" (*Catiline* III.iii.251–53). Like Jonson's Catiline, Fletcher and Massinger's Caesar declares, "I have enter'd" "the Womb (that gave me life)" and have "open'd" my country's "veins" (*False One* II.iii, 325). Earlier, Caesar is said to have cut "through [the senators'] bowels" in order to "invade the laws of Rome" (I.i, 309). So too, the Lucanic Caesar in the anonymous *Caesar's Revenge* laments that he has "peerc'd" the "bowels" of the "native" country who "bred and fostered" him in her "lappe" (II.294–303). Similarly, the hero of *Coriolanus* is said to be "pouring war / *Into the bowels* of ungrateful Rome" (IV.v.129–30), "*tearing* / His Country's *bowels out*" (V.iii.102–3). *Titus, King John,* and *Richard III* alike end with the Lucanic topos that civil war is a parricidal, suicidal, self-mutilating plunge into the national bowels.

In many ways the most adroit use of this idea occurs in Shakespeare's *Julius Caesar,* which seems to have been written by a person who has very recently perused or revisited Lucan. Within fewer than sixty lines (V.iii.41–96), Shakespeare reemphasizes the idea of "piercing" the vitals with steel, "thrusting" it into the "bowels," "bosom," "heart," "entrails," and even "ears." Fittingly, the Lucanic sequence that includes the imitation of *Pharsalia* 1.2–3 culminates with the identification of "a Roman's part" as acting with complete loyalty to one's leader—something suggestive of Lucan's Laelian motif.

Just as Shakespeare's cluster of passages about incision is strengthened by extrinsic ties to Lucan, so too it is reinforced by, and lends support to, another of the play's motifs: the unwished-for releasing of some inner reality. Historicity probably demanded mention of the steel by which Caesar and his assassins died. But why the images of incision are so persistent is ultimately mysterious. Possibly some awareness of Julius's own Caesarean birth coalesced in Shakespeare's mind with memories of the historical assassination and suicide, as also with reminiscences of Lucanic imagery of incision.

Declining to reject the strange account in Plutarch and other of the historical sources, Shakespeare decides to make the beast sacrificed for Caesar a hollow one—a motif that possibly owes something to Lucan's description of the hollowness of Pompey and all Rome (1.239). Like the historical sacrificial animal on a previous occasion (an occasion that Suetonius says gave Julius Caesar an irresistible opportunity to satirize the morally exhausted Republic), the play's beast had no entrails, and, in particular, was found to lack a heart (II.ii.39–40).

Calphurnia dreams of a statuary fountain hollowed out, and empty insides are the supposed cause of her barrenness and/or Caesar's sterility (the playwright having decided not to remind us that Cleopatra and their son, Caesarion, were resident at the time in Rome). Images of anatomic and auguring incision are deployed also in another marvelous bit of dialogue unsanctioned by history, when the mob threatens to "pluck" Cinna's name "out of his heart." In this play, breast after Roman breast is opened to attack as a standard device of private and forensic rhetoric. Baring their flesh to blue steel or heaven's blue lightning, Caesar, Cassius, and Antony successively try to affirm their questionable honesty, love, or courage. And Portia actually draws blood as she vainly probes her thigh for proof of her love, and, more dubiously, her manly constancy. But the most central and ironical bit of revelatory surgery is performed on Caesar, whose wounds release voices that the conspirators expected to still. The suicides-by-incision of Cassius and Titinius do more than corroborate a network of personal friendships. They also ironically confirm the void in the Republic and all Rome: for under the tragically emptied name of Rome, all the troops were originally marshaled and the factious, and factitious, acts of violence were commanded. Reverberations of the symbolic motif of hollowness, which echo throughout this tragedy, may also have inspired the later portrayal of self-destructive Coriolanus as a wolfish beast with paradoxical suicidal dreams of being an eaglelike "nothing" (cf. V.i.13; II.ii.77).

Again and again, Romans are like those begnawed "hollow men" of *Caesar,* the devoured "boy" of *Coriolanus,* and the "giant-brethren" of *Catiline* (V.ix.75)—stony, chthonic, serpentine. They are all what we have heard Seneca call 'beyond human bounds and bonds' (*De clementia* 1.25.2). And "like the brethren sprung of dragons' teeth," they "ruin each other" (*Catiline* III.iii.247–48) as if they were so many splintered artifacts crying for our anthropological reassembling.

AFTERWORD

Stage Rome and the Romanized Plays

> Ever seen a Roman, farmer boy? The sun shines out
> of their navels. Two navels. And big, very big men.
> In metal. Whey they walk they clank.
>
> BRENTON
> *The Romans in Britain*

In some ultimate sense it is arguable that there is no transmission of Great Ideas, or even that there are no Great Ideas in the first place. But all socialization, all *paideia* and *communitas,* are based on the commonsense assumption that concepts do have at least a temporary reality. And this is effectually the assumption that Early Modern writers brought to bear on many of their notions, including those of Rome.

Romanitas

The Rome idea of Tudor-Stuart England is a metaphoric cluster of ambivalent motifs that have driven—and complicated—Western life for half a millenium; and they center around a Faustian, Promethean, Icaran, Phaeton-like model for life. At the conquest of Carthage, the victorious Roman general, Scipio, wept, experiencing a melancholy awareness of the transience of his, Rome's, and all victories, as well as the serious costs that they occasion. Rome generates ideas that still are problematic—full of exciting intellectual *play*—even if today we are tempted to misread them as statically patriarchal, gendered, Eurocentric, even Nazi-like. Empire is one central idea, and following from it are the notions of personal superiority and cultural uniformity over vast extents of place and time. The empires abuilding five hundred years ago, as well as the empires that were born later, have experienced retrenchment or dismantling; and the very idea of a thousand-year Reich on either the Roman or Holy Roman model is justly repellent. But a half millennium ago ideas like these had power. To grasp the thrill as well as the horror that Roman settings imparted to English Roman plays, we presently need to enlist a modicum of sympathy, or actual *enthusiasm,* for these ambivalent concepts. Our uneasiness about such ideas will return as it did for the first audiences, automatically.

The foregoing chapters have depicted the Early Modern Roman play as open to multiple chronotopes, and full of circularity, historical irony, and topical anachronism—all serving the audiences' needs for ethical, artistic, and political power. Rome and her citizens represented power, puissance, *rhomé,* though Rome and Romans could also figure forth loss and emptiness. The Roman thus conceived was as much an animal, and devil, as anyone else, but advanced above the rest of mankind by the arts: political, military, Stoical, architectural, verbal. Stage Romans were sovereigns over time as well as space, and were thus tempted to aspire beyond the royal, and tyrannical, to the divine. Like the hero of *Coriolanus,* they knew how to "play the god," enjoying it and doing so half-convincingly, for our delight, instruction, and apprehension (V.iv.24–25). To Early Modern England, the Ancient Roman was sometimes a refined Stoical monarch, sometimes an appetite-driven barbarian, sometimes a superstitious and decadent Latin Roman Catholic. He straddles the Aristotelian distinction between citizen and Other: "he that can not abide to live in companie, or through sufficiencie hath need of nothing is not esteemed a part or member of a Cittie, but is either a beast or a god" (*Politiques* 15, qtd. in Miola, *Shakespeare's Rome* 192). For the Roman is all three: god, man, and beast. And his temptations toward godhead and bestiality derive from his powers as citizen in a polity that owns most of the known world.

Rome had an allegedly endemic "thryst of signiore" (*Cornelia* III.iii.107), or what Augustine terms the *libido dominandi* in the *civitas terrena* (Cochrane 491). This trait led to lordly conquest, wealth, refined leisure, architectural magnificence, widespread and long-lived prestige, with an attendant weakness for factionalism, greed, thoughtless waste, and unjustifiedly proud selfishness and cruelty. Not that this weakness was inevitable: power and material success could bring on fits of the temporary withdrawal and denial that go under the name of Stoicism. Usually, however, riches and a constitutional tradition of shared aristocratic power kept introducing both vigor and bloody division into the state. This fostered traitors, bullying rule by generals, and finally permanent tyranny. Rome's goal of tyrannical absolutism and the processes by which it enforced its will were topical subjects in sixteenth- and seventeenth-century England, easily understood by commoner and monarch alike, and yet dealt with in so unspecific a fashion that Roman plays generally escaped censorship.

Roman plays gave audiences a distanced view of political realities at a time of imperial expansion and monarchical encroachment on upper-class and popular freedoms. Further, these dramas provided an emotional and spiritual education on the rewards—and perils—of ambition, lofty aspiration, and self-assertion. Rome reminded England that man (*male* man, unfortunately, more than all humankind) needs *room* of his own to organize and fulfill his wishes. Rome produced putative giants, who, like their fearsome but doomed prototypes in classical mythology, dared to pledge their lives in challenge to authority. But like the "giant brethren" in Jonson's *Catiline* (V.ix.75), Romans had not just size and power but also potential monstrosity (Estienne, s.v. "Gigantes"), the power to become one of the "prodigies and monsters / That [Rome] hath teem'd with since she first knew Mars" (*Catiline* I.95–96).

The bestiary of Rome—with its obviously ambivalent eagle and horse, its viper, and its incompletely negative wolf—would remind the English of the exhilaration and dangers of independence. Horses and eagles, no matter their respective moral deficiencies, are physically beautiful symbols of aspiration. And the viper, luckier than Coriolanus, does break out of the maternal stomach. As for wolves, they fight well, enjoying their own sexuality and yet nursing the weak. The wolf, which has given its name to the disease of self-corrosion, risks valuing cruelty for its own sake and thinking that it must eat up the whole of its pack—and its very self—to achieve the hollow goal of mere survival.

Roman majesty and Stoic constancy resemble the Antony in the Queen's description: "Though he be painted one way, like a Gorgon, / The other way's a Mars" (*Antony* II.v.116–17). Roman *majestas,* even if the cousin of tyrannical cruelty, is at the heart of many traits that have given meaning to life for twenty centuries: *gravitas, sobrietas, magnanimitas, dignitas, clemen-*

tia, thoughtfulness to one's underlings, enthusiastic patronage of the arts, ability to expand unselfconsciously into a demanding role, *noblesse oblige,* and grace under pressure. Enthusiasm for *constantia* has declined since the Renaissance as the mysterious effects of repression have become more apparent. Admittedly, Stoical self-restraint is like many other actions we engage in: simultaneously self-asserting and self-defeating. But *constantia* is a valuable aid to self-consistency, continuity of self, and a still fashionable wholeness or *integritas,* without which, some would say, we have no being worth worrying about. *Constantia* thrives on an audience, and it manipulates a crowd; but then again, so do preaching and teaching, both of which involve roles that the Stoic also seeks to enact.

The Roman plays and other Early Modern meditations on Rome also help keep alive a concept that, however Christian it may now have come to seem, is really more Roman than Hebraic. Rome bequeathed not just 'tears at the thought of human mortal things' ("sunt lacrimae rerum et mentem mortalia tangunt," Vergil, *Aeneid* 1.462), but also the very rich gift of a sense of *aeternitas,* including terrene immortality. From Roman culture more than from that of Greece, Egypt, or Palestine, the Renaissance inherited a sense of *earthly* dignity that will last. Though Romans believed in a variety of transcendent *cosmoi,* many Latin writers directed a great deal of energy toward earthly eternity: a social world in which permanence of a manageable, if imperfect, sort could be engineered for a manageable, if imperfect, mankind, the "glory, jest, and riddle of the world." Horace offers a heaven more tangible, immediate, and convivial than the Valhalla of the Patriotic in Cicero's *Dream of Scipio.* This lyric poet is one of many Romans who define not just the philosophy of seizing the day but also the goal of a *perennial*ness through in*scribed* literary monuments ("monumentum . . . perennis," *Odes* 3.30) of unaging art and intellect, a goal that has pleased many countries and poets in the past two thousand years.

A typical Renaissance commentator like Sidney would agree that God created the world, and the eternity of the human spirit, but that man plays God by creating a new heaven and new earth in constructions destined to live from age to age. What artists like Horace learned from Greece became totally Roman in Renaissance eyes, including the invention of making artistic creations outlive oneself and never die so long as one's society is remembered. The artist—literary, political, graphic, and so on—makes his or her "own lofty scene [to] be acted over / In states unborn and accents yet unknown!" "ages hence" (*Caesar* III.i.111–13). Sometimes this is in dignity; or sometimes with Poloniuses, in Antike "sport" (114). Rome provided the Renaissance with access to a secular aesthetic human connectedness: an artistic "throne" in which to act and react, a temporary "eternity" in which (like Coriolanus) to play the "god."

According to proto-Adlerians like Guillaume Du Vair, the urge to conquer, control, and dominate is a human universal. Certainly in the English Roman play it generally outpulls every other imaginable appetite—monetary, festive, romantic, sexual, spiritual, intellectual. Among the forty-three English Roman plays of 1585–1635, there are several acute commentaries on Roman power-centered behavior. Some such moments can be found not just in the numerous Roman works of Shakespeare and Jonson but also in those of Fletcher and Massinger, who between them wrote a startling total of seven Roman plays. Other plays in which the portrayal of Roman power warrants our attention include the touchingly dignified *Appius and Virginia* of Webster, the anonymous *Nero* (despite its wooden villain Nimphidius—pace Butler), and the *Sophonisba* of Marston (despite its often obscure and pompous phrases—pace Ure).

Plays interesting for other reasons include *Every Woman in Her Humour*, a spirited romp that has little to say about Rome's political history or cultural power. In Lady Mary Sidney Herbert's and other Garnerians' closet dramas, there are observations of psychological and political interest, though the best passages are frequently attractive only for what they have borrowed from classical sources. Bloody grotesquery brings Antike Rome to life in otherwise slovenly dramas like Heywood's *Lucrece* (where a clownish noble sings bawdy while the heroine is raped), Lodge's bluntly political *Wounds of Civil War*, and the anonymous *Faithful Friends* (with its alleged impersonation of James's homosexual postures (D. Adler 25–26; Dyce 205; Goldberg 143).

If Roman plays were more accessible onstage or in film, it would be easier to make a fair judgment of the stage quality of these and other works, and their ability to comment on Roman power. In the study a reader may find what is apparently bad verse, a meaninglessly tasteless episode, or a fatal oversimplification of a conflict or character. Most readers keep needing good groups of actors and directors to determine whether a text has vitality and resonance.

The Romanized Play

A knowledge of the stereotype of the Roman in Early Modern Roman plays alerts modern readers to the polysemous intertextuality in many of the best works. Such knowledge also can provide a sharper focus on the way several non-Roman plays work. Beginning at least as early as the fifteenth century Coventry Welcome, English dramatic material has been enriched by Ancient, particularly Roman, subtexts. Sixteenth-century non-Roman works in this category include *Gorboduc* and *Tancred,* the latter a tragedy with a Medieval Italian setting but dialogue that evokes Seneca and the entire pagan pantheon. Other non-Roman plays with unmistakable Roman strands include *The Revenger's Tragedy,* Thomas Hughes's Lucanic *Misfortunes of Arthur* (Jones, *Origins* 123), the *Bussy* and *Revenge of Bussy* of Chapman, Marlowe's works, and Shakespeare's *Hamlet, Othello, Macbeth,* and the histories.

No author's plays are more Romanized than Marlowe's, a corpus marked by what Knoll calls "Caesarism" (30, 36, 106), a theme we have noted above in the prologue to *The Jew of Malta. Tamburlaine,* despite its overtly Medieval Moslem setting, summons up the power-hungry worlds of both Renaissance European Christians and Ancient Mediterranean pagans—alike heroic, vicious, magnificent, and megalomaniacal. *Tamburlaine* bombards us with a host of Roman-tinged references, including the pagan gods of old, humiliating triumphal procession (as, earlier, in Antiquish *Jocasta* of 1566; cf. Whitworth), pedal humiliation, filicides worthy of Roman parents, suicide (including by a Stoic classically named Olympia), and a royalizing and divinizing *libido dominandi:*

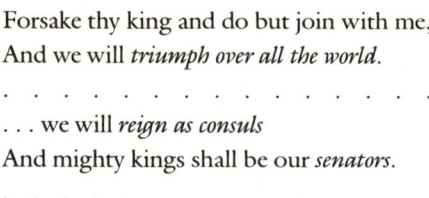

> And by those steps that [Jove] hath scaled the heavens,
> May we become *immortal like the gods*.
> (*1 Tamburlaine* I.ii.170–71, 196–200)

In Marlowe's *Massacre at Paris* there is a series of obvious references to ancient Rome and quotations from Roman Lucan and others. As in Caron's painting (fig. 3), the religious wars of sixteenth-century France re-present Roman reigns of terror. The Romanist duke of Guise and Medician Queen Catherine plot an urban massacre implicitly recalling those of Marius and Sulla. In welcoming home her Henry III, Queen Catherine refers to his "warlike" nation as equipped with a "watchful Senate for ordaining laws" (xi.6). In King Henry III's eyes, the Guise is a "haughty," "insolen[t]" self-appointed "dictator" who expects the king to serve in some lower Republican role, voting by crying "*placet*, like a senator" (xvi. 56–58). The Catholic leader explicitly likens himself repeatedly to pagan Caesar in statecraft and ability to face death fearlessly (ii.98); and he plans to lead his erotically obsessed king in a Roman triumph:

> As ancient Romans o'er their captive lords,
> So will I triumph o'er this wanton king;
> And he shall follow my proud chariot's wheels.
> (xviii.51–53)

In Marlowe's *Edward II*, as we have seen, Queen Isabella applies the opening lines of Lucan's epic to her own era in England—

> In civill broiles . . . kin and country men
> Slaughter themselves in others and their sides
> With their owne weapons gorde.
> (IV.iv.6–8)

Too, she refers to the Low Countries anachronistically by their Roman name of Belgia (IV.iv.3). In this play the English king is for a moment a Renaissance champion of Protestantism, visualizing the quasi-pedal humiliation and Lucanic Roman proscription that he would visit upon papal Babylon:

> Proud Rome, that hatchest such imperiall groomes
> For these thy superstitious taperlights

> Wherewith thy antichristian churches blaze,
> Ile fire thy crased buildings, and enforce
> The papall towers, to kisse the lowlie ground,
> With slaughtered priests make Tibers channell swell,
> And bankes raisd higher with their sepulchers.
> (I.iv.97–103)

And when Edward reflects on Mortimer's power and says, "Two kings in England cannot reign at once," many spectators would know that he is echoing Lucan's line about Romulus and Remus and two of their counterparts, Caesar and Pompey (1.92–93).

This play treats the homoeroticism of Edward II and Gaveston as a feature belonging simultaneously to divers cultures: those of Renaissance Italy and the Ancient pagan world, as well as Medieval and Renaissance England. In Gaveston's first speech this supposedly Medieval Frenchman defines himself as a trendy Italianate Elizabethan waterfly, modishly affecting the Italian word *tanti* ("so many"). And he plans Italian masques and woodsy erotic tableaux on Ancient pagan themes and Italian masques to entertain his Edward (I.i.51–71). Then we are told that Edward's love for Gaveston is classical, resembling the affection of "the mightiest *kings*" for "their minions" (I.iv.391–97): Alexander for Hephaestion, Hercules for Hylas, Achilles for Patroclus, and, absurdly, "grave Socrates" and "wilde Alcibiades," and "Romaine Tullie" and Octavius. The last two pairs of analogues deconstruct themselves, detract from the force of the foregoing ones, and mock the speaker. (For history records that the only service that the thoroughly republican and heterosexual Cicero did for the young Octavius was to help with his political and oratorical education. Of course, neither Socrates nor Alcibiades was a king, and the most memorable aspect of their "affair" as recorded in the *Symposium* is the sexual forebearance of the philosopher.) By being emptied of difference, life Ancient, Medieval, and Early Modern become simultaneously disempowered of signification.

Ancient Roman associations, mixed with those of Italianate Elizabethans, emerge in another (Medieval) history of about the same date, Shakespeare's *2 Henry VI*. As mentioned earlier, the Duke of Suffolk is accused of being another parricidal and "ambitious Sylla, overgorg'd / With gobbets of thy Mother-bleeding [F1] heart" (IV.i.84–85). He himself boasts of his "imperial tongue" and "true nobility . . . exempt from fear" (121–29), likening himself to a quasi-Jovial princely eagle:

> O that I were a god, to shoot forth thunder
> Upon these paltry, servile, abject drudges!
> . . . .
> Drones suck not eagles' blood, but rob beehives.
> It is impossible that I should die
> By such a lowly vassal.
>
> (104–11)

Further, he makes a revealingly inflated parallel between his fate and those of "Tully," Julius Caesar, and Pompey the Great (136–38). Suffolk is thus self-defined as a powerful Roman while the dramatist is actually disclosing that he is merely a bombastic Italianate Englishman. Interestingly, the duke names Cicero's murderer a "bandetto" (135), a term that conjures Italian rather than Roman associations, just as the exclamation "Tanti!" did for Marlowe's Gaveston. Considering that the duke bears the same family name and Suffolk title as the family of the sixteenth-century Cardinal Reginald de la Pole, there is a chance that Shakespeare is making his Medieval duke become a victim of the same bad press that plagued the cardinal, an adherent of Mary Tudor and therefore anathema in Protestant Elizabethan England.

Chapman's Bussy plays postdate *2 Henry VI* and, almost certainly, the works of Marlowe (Tricomi, "Dates"). Chapman's *Bussy* and *The Revenge of Bussy D'Ambois* illustrate a court circle just as given to factious intrigue as Marlowe's and Shakespeare's; and in Chapman's *Revenge* the potentially Antiquish theme of homosexuality is almost as prominent as in Marlowe's *Edward II*. Both Chapman plays have further affinities to Roman Stoicism in their concern with suicide and the inherent kingship of self-restrained men. In the *Revenge* the Senecal man Clermont is termed "Rome's Brutus . . . reviv'd" (II.i.103), a man ranking "with the best of th'ancient Romans (259). The swashbuckling bastard-hero of *Bussy* repeatedly tells the French king, Henry III, that he himself possesses inner royalty, (cf. III.i):

> Let me be *king* myself (*as man was made*),
> And do a justice that exceeds the law;

> . . . .
> *Who to himself is law,* no law doth need,
> Offends no law, and *is a king indeed.*
> (II.i.198–204)

Somewhat as Elizabeth Tudor sought to meet death sitting upright, Bussy actually dies standing, self-defined as a statuesque Stoic monarch:

> if Vespasian thought in *majesty*
> An *emperor* might die standing, why not I?
> Nay, without help, in which I will exceed him;
> For he died splinted with his chamber grooms.
> Prop me, true sword, as thou hast ever done;
> . . . .
> Here like a Roman statue I will stand
> Till death hath made me marble.
> (V.iv.89–97)

Around the collapsing actor in the earliest text (1607) float the memories not only of Vespasian, Elizabeth, and Seneca's kingly Wise Man, but of Shakespeare's "marble-constant" Cleopatra as well.

It is interesting to note that the stiffening buckram of *Romanitas* is also used in the Italianate Grand Guignol of *Revenger's Tragedy*. Overall, as Christopher Ricks rightly remarks (320), the work is given its seemingly "closest affinities . . . with the satires of Juvenal." We can also note that the play, while wittily eschewing every sign of true Roman *dignitas,* is marked by incidents, imagery (especially of fire and stone), and thematic motifs that are mutually supportive of a sense of Ancient Rome. The work is full of parricide, incest, suicidal recklessness, and voracious *libido dominandi.* The dying duke is *"stamp[ed] on"* in insultment in Act III (v.154/155), an event implicitly recalled when the royal son pretends to have treated the disguised Vendice with matching *superbia:*

> *Vendice.* What did your Honour?
> *Lussurioso.*   In rage pushed him from me,
>   *Trampled beneath his throat, spurned* him, and bruised.
>   Indeed, I was too cruel.
> (IV.ii.157–59)

Thereupon Vendice bursts out in an aside, instigating a sequence of civil war topoi suggestive of Lucan (7.447ff.; Ronan, "Omens"): "Has not heaven an ear? Is all the lightning wasted?" Here there is, as in *Thyestes* (and *Wounds, Caesar, Caesar and Pompey,* and *Catiline*), a Divinity shaping the sound effects, and he hears Vendice's cue:

> O thou Almighty patience! 'tis my wonder
> That such a fellow, impudent and wicked,
> Should not be cloven as he stood.
> . . . .
> Is there no thunder left, or is't kept up
> In stock for heavier vengeance? [*Thunders*]
>   There it goes!
>   (201–6)

More obviously Roman still is the drama's framing story of Antonio. The work starts soon after the rape of his wife and ends the minute that the crime has been avenged. The lady is violated Lucrece-style, by a counterpart to Tarquin: a haughtily lascivious cadet of the ruling family. In her suicide she is wrapped in Stoical language with likely Roman affinities—references to fire in the soul and to the majesty of an empress:

> A wondrous lady, of rare fire compact;
> Sh'as made her name an empress by that act.
>   (I.iv.48–49)

Antonio, like Collatine in the Lucrece story, has himself acceded to the sovereign power which his royal enemies have been forced to surrender. As in the story of Brutus, Collatinus, and Lucretia, the friends of the violated woman's husband take an oath to avenge her, and they actually do topple the dynasty. No matter that this fall is accompanied by that of the self-incriminating Vindice! The incompleteness with which this giggling Aaron- or Barabas-like antic resembles Lucius Junius Brutus is all a part of the play's tragic parody of centuries of power exchanges on the Italian peninsula.

In earlier chapters we have also examined *Romanitas* in such non-Roman histories as *Henry IV* and *Henry V*. Each emphasizes wolfishness, triumphing, Caesarism, and pedal humiliation. Many of the same motifs appear too in *Othello*, a play the ending of which combines elements of both "Lucrece" and *Romeo and Juliet* (cf. Cheney). Another of Shakespeare's plays set in the capital of imperial Venice is also explicitly Romanized, at least by terms applied to the heroine and titular antagonist (*Merchant of Venice* I.i.166, III.ii.295). The choice of the rich Venetian republic, with its traditional political independence, is not entirely unexpected. In his *History of Italy* of 1575, William Thomas describes Venetians as ambitious at sea and in trade as the Romans were with their land armies. The nation is led by magnificos, whom he describes as other Renaissance writers did the Ancient Romans: each aristocrat prided himself on being "a prince, and no subject," and as a result the city contained "over two hundred palaces . . . , all able to lodge any king" (qtd. in Einstein 144–46).

Additional Romanized Shakespearean plays make papal Rome and pagan Antiquity coalesce. Medieval, Renaissance, and Antique chronotopes become one in *King John*, where papal invasions suggest Caesar's. The hero of *Henry V* is an interestingly Romanized power figure. In lines adapted from *Pharsalia* 5.357–73, he imitates Lucan's "conqu'ring Caesar," but supposedly is "free from vainness and self-glorious pride" (V.Chorus, 20–28). Quite rightly, critical debate still rages over the humility and morality, for example, of the king's Tamburlainean bluster at Harfleur, where he threatens rape and invokes the Antique precedent of Herod for the licentious "liberty of bloody hand" (III.iii.12–41).

Hamlet, too, is a Romanized play (Montgomerie; Miola, "Aeneas"; Ronan, "Sallust's Beasts"). The references to Caesar are among the most crucial allusions in the entire tragedy, buttressing the prince's sense that fame can outlast the absurd fate of the body. Vergil's story of the fall of Troy also lies in the background (Wright), and numerous other Latin works make their presence felt intermittently throughout the play—Juvenal's *Satires,* the drama of Plautus and Terence, the philosophizing of Cicero and Sallust, and probably Lucan's epic (Jones, *Origins* 275–77). Other likely aspects of this play's *Romanitas* include the fact that several characters have Latin names. That of the monarch belongs, for instance, to a Roman emperor who also was killed by his nephew, as Montgomerie notes. Too, the protagonist gains a bit of Senecal egalitarianism from his best friend, resists his own Neronic parricidal *saevitia* with the Stoically "firm" *constantia* of an actor/"hypocrite," and asserts a power over his own and Horatio's "Antike Roman" suicidal inclinations.

In *Timon* a feeling of Rome is evoked by the use of Latin names for several characters, by the senatorial form of government, and by the society's triple obsession with ingratitude, superiority, and conquest. In Shakespeare's semihistorical tragedy of Medieval Scotland, *Macbeth,* there is an especially sustained concern with implicit or explicit Roman motifs—ingratitudes, tyrannies, an "imperial theme" of *libido dominandi,* murderous slaughter of friends and kinsmen, breakdown of family ties, Senecan and Lucanic rhetoric of gore, awareness of the option of suicide, and even the hero's sense of replaying the fateful rivalry of Antony with Octavius.

The devices that identify a play as Romanized are like all the other tension-manipulating devices of mannerism: they establish both difference and connection—here specifically between the ever-shifting inferiority and superiority of past and present. In terms of Nietzschean historiography (*The Uses of History*), they function in both a "monumental" and a "critical" way, at once celebrating and scrutinizing. And the resulting intellectual and emotional tensions help render many of these works of continued interest today.

This survey of quasi-Roman plays could be vastly extended to embrace non-Roman plays of Webster, Ford, and numerous others. The source studies that were fashionable in Tudor-Stuart scholarship of past decades, and centuries, point the way toward Roman subtexts recognized by original audiences. They show us how to treasure our Roman legacy for its power to explore the coexistence of lofty and antic powers in human nature—and to try to adapt for our own time whatever is helpful and salvageable in Roman *superbia, majestas, constantia, integritas, dominatio, securitas, clementia, virtus, humanitas, castitas, gloria, dignitas.*

APPENDIX A

Short-title Descriptive List of Extant Secular Roman Plays in English, 1497–1651

Agrippina　　　　　Thomas May, *Julia Agrippina* (1628). Subject: Nero's assassination of his mother, Agrippina.

Antonius　　　　　Mary Sidney Herbert, Countess of Pembroke, *Antonie*, or *Antonius*. A translation (1590; rev. 1595) of Robert Garnier, *Marc Antoine* (1578). Closet drama. Subject: Antony, Cleopatra, Octavius—until her suicide.

Antony　　　　　William Shakespeare, *Antony and Cleopatra* (1607). Subject: Antony, Octavius, Cleopatra—until her suicide.

Apius　　　　　R.B., *Apius and Virginia* (pub. 1575). Subject: (naive) dramatization of Appius and Virginia—until her death.

Appius　　　　　John Webster, *Appius and Virginia* (1624). Subject: Appius and Virginia—until her death.

Believe　　　　　Philip Massinger, *Believe As You List* (1631). A revision of his censored lost *Don Sebastian of Portugal*. Subject: largely fictitious story of Seleucid king Antiochus the Great, persecuted by a Republican Roman ambassador as Hannibal had been.

Bonduca　　　　　John Fletcher, *Bonduca* (1613). Subject: fairly historical account of Britons Caratacus, Boadicea, and her family—until he is sent to Rome to grace Claudius's triumph.

Caesar　　　　　William Shakespeare, *Julius Caesar* (1599). Subject: Caesar, Antony, Octavius—until Brutus's suicide.

Caesar　　　　　Sir William Alexander, Earl of Sterling, *Julius Caesar* (1607). Closet drama. Subject: Caesar's assassination.

Caesar and Pompey　　George Chapman, *Caesar and Pompey* (1605). Subject: Pompey, Cato, Caesar—until the death of Cato.

Caesar's Revenge　　Anonymous, *Caesar and Pompey; or, Caesar's Revenge* (1595). Academic play. Subject: Pompey, Caesar,

	Cleopatra, Antony, Cato, Brutus, Cassius, Titinius, Octavius—until the defeat of the conspirators.
Catiline	Ben Jonson, *Catiline's Conspiracy* (1611). Subject: Catiline, Caesar, Cato, Cicero—until the defeat of Catiline.
Cicero	Anonymous, *The Tragedy of That Famous Orator Marcus Tullius Cicero* (1635? pub. 1651). Subject: Cicero, Antony, Fulvia—until after the mutilation of Cicero's corpse.
Cleopatra	Samuel Daniel, *Cleopatra* (1593, and often revised). Closet drama. Subject: Cleopatra—after Antony's and until her own suicide.
Cleopatra	Thomas May, *Cleopatra* (1626). Subject: Antony, Octavius, Cleopatra—until her suicide.
Coriolanus	William Shakespeare, *Coriolanus* (1608). Subject: Coriolanus, from after Tarquin's until his own defeat.
Cornelia	Thomas Kyd, *Tragedy of Pompey's Cornelia* (1594). A translation of Robert Garnier, *Cornélie* (pub. 1574). Intended use unclear. Subject: Cicero's consoling Cornelia, the widow of Pompey—from his death until the suicide of her father, a Scipio.
Cymbeline	William Shakespeare, *Cymbeline* (1609). Subject: semihistorical Roman invasion of Britain, Cymbeline's and Augustus's time.
Every Woman	Lewis Machin, *Every Woman in Her Humour* (1607). Subject: fictitious comedy in friar-ridden reign of Augustus, when Cicero was in love.
Faithful Friends	Anonymous, *The Faithful Friends* (1614). Subject: a fiction of when kings of Rome battled the Sabines—but after the times of Nero and John of Gaunt.
False One	Philip Massinger and John Fletcher, *The False One* (1620). Subject: Caesar and Cleopatra—until the assassination of Pompey.
Fuimus Troes	Jasper Fisher, *Fuimus Troes; or, the True Trojans* (1624). Academic play. Subject: Cassibelanus and Caesar's invasion of Britain, some years before Christ's Nativity.
Fulgens	Thomas Medwall, *Fulgens and Lucres* (1497). Interlude for a banquet. Subject: in self-consciously half-Christian but Republican Rome, a fictional wooing contest

between a stalwart and pious *novus homo* and an immoral patrician snob.

Hannibal — Thomas Nabbes, *Hannibal and Scipio* (1635). Subject: Sophonisba, Massinissa, and Scipio—until Hannibal's death.

Herod — Gervase Markham and William Sampson, *Herod and Antipater* (1622). Subject: Augustus, Herod the Great—until the latter's death and the ascension of his grandson.

Jews' Tragedy — William Hemming (Heminges), *The Jewes Tragedy* (1626). Subject: Josephus's story of Nero, Vespasian, Titus, and the siege and destruction of the Temple in Jerusalem.

Julius Caesar — See *Caesar*.

Lucrece — Thomas Heywood, *Rape of Lucrece* (1607). Subject: rape of Lucretia and aftermath—until deaths of Sextus Tarquinius and Lucius Junius Brutus.

Messallina — Nathaniel Richards, *Messal(l)ina* (1635). Subject: Claudius and Messalina—until her death.

Nero — Anonymous, *Nero* (1624). Subject: Nero, Piso, Lucan, Seneca, Petronius, Poppaea—until the emperor's defeat and suicide.

Octavia — Thomas Nuce's translation (1561) of the pseudo-Senecan *Octavia* (A.D. 50). Translation for, probably, reading. Subject: Seneca, the divorcing of Octavia, Nero's remarriage to Poppaea.

Octavia — Samuel Brandon, *The Virtuous Octavia* (1598). Closet drama. Subject: lament of Octavius's sister for her brother's attack on her philandering Antony and for Antony's suicide.

Poetaster — Ben Jonson, *The Poetaster* (1601). Subject: largely fictitious handling of a romance between Ovid and the daughter of Augustus, all within a context of examination of Roman poetic circles for their relevance to English ones.

Princess — Thomas Killigrew, *The Princess* (1636). Subject: fiction concerning a "Virgilius," supposed son of Julius Caesar, and a princess of Sicily.

168   Appendix A

Prophetess	John Fletcher and Philip Massinger, *The Prophetess* (1622). Subject: almost totally fictitious romance about Diocletian, Maximinian, and a wonder-working witch.
Roman Actor	Philip Massinger, *The Roman Actor* (1626). Subject: basically a fiction of court of Domitian—until his historical fall.
Satiromastix	Thomas Dekker (and John Marston?), *Satiromastix* (1601). Subject: how King William Rufus oversees the untrussing of Jonson through having his Augustan Roman characters out of *Poetaster* appear in the king's Anglo-Norman court.
Sejanus	Ben Jonson, *Sejanus* (1603). Subject: Tiberius and the fall of Sejanus.
Shoemaker	William Rowley, *A Shoemaker, a Gentleman* (1608). Subject: fictitious romance on Maximinus, Diocletian, Saint Hugh, and British princes of the gentle craft of shoemaker.
Sophonisba	John Marston, *Wonder of Women: The Tragedy of Sophonisba* (1605). Subject: Massinissa, Syphax, Carthaginians, Scipio—until the suicide of Sophonisba.
Tiberius	Anonymous, *Claudius Tiberius Nero* (1607). Possibly an academic drama. Subject: Tiberius's mother, Sejanus, Macro, the family of Germanicus—until Caligula kills Tiberius.
Titus	William Shakespeare, *Titus Andronicus* (1593). Subject: a story of the late Empire in the West—probably understood by the author, but not necessarily the audience, as a fiction.
Two Noble Ladies	Anonymous, *Two Noble Ladies* (1622). Subject: fiction of general Claudius of "great Rome" and how he pacifies the half-Christianized dynastic families of Antioch, "the" Egyptian sultan, and "the" caliph of Babylon.
Valentinian	John Fletcher, *Valentinian* (1611). Subject: fairly historical account of Western emperor Valentinian III.
Valiant Welshman	See *Welshman*.
Virgin Martyr	Thomas Dekker and Philip Massinger, *The Virgin Martyr* (1620). Subject: Diocletian, Maximinus, and the miracles of Saint Dorothea.

Virtuous Octavia	See *Octavia*.
Welshman	R.A. [Robert Armin?], *The Valiant Welshman* (1612). Subject: fairly historical romance on Roman invasion of Britain in the time(s) of Caradoc/Caratacus, Boadicea, Cymbeline's son Guiderius, and Claudius Caesar.
Wounds	Thomas Lodge, *The Wounds of Civil War* (1587). Subject: the rivalry of Marius, Sulla, and their supporters—until the death of Sulla.

Note: Unless otherwise specified, all listed plays seem intended for the London stage.

APPENDIX B

The Tudor-Stuart Roman Play: A Survey

Scholarly analyses that compare even a half-dozen Roman plays are rare, and perhaps the fullest of them, Felix Schelling's *Elizabethan Drama,* dates from 1908 and confusingly distributes the subject over several chapters. An interesting dissertation of 1963 by Mathew Joseph Ahern, Jr., omits Shakespeare and reaches a tally of twenty-nine Tudor-Stuart Roman works (implicitly thirty-four with Shakespeare's). Ahern includes two Byzantine plays, *Emperor of the East* and *Martyred Soldier,* neither of which makes any effort to supply local Roman color or other unmistakable signs of *Romanitas.*

Four more recent articles have also examined records of Roman history plays, though not of quite the same period. In the half century 1562–1612, Paul Dean finds nineteen extant works; Vanna Gentili, twenty-five; and George K. Hunter ("Roman Thought"), about twenty. Hunter also reaches a count of forty-three Roman *history* plays from the vague period 1564–65 until "after 1611" (until when? 1642?). Of these forty-three, he leaves unnamed "eleven known plays on Roman history" written after 1611. Further, he takes the perilous step of listing some twelve lost plays among his forty-three "historical" ones. We would probably be right to surmise that Hunter has in mind a total of no more than thirty extant Roman history plays from the period 1564–1642. By underestimating the numbers of Tudor-Stuart Roman plays and overestimating the importance of their historicity instead of their "mythic" dimension, most earlier studies have created impressions in need of selective correction.

Working with what they gleaned of the surviving evidence of the development of the Roman play in England, T. J. B. Spencer and J. W. Lever have stressed that Shakespeare's Plutarchan vision of Rome was less gory and sensational than that of most other dramatists of the age, who generally dwelt on "garboils" and factiousness, in the manner of *Titus Andronicus*. Spencer, G. K. Hunter, Mathew Ahern, and Martin Butler tend to see an accelerating interest in decadent Tacitean imperial stories near the end of the sixteenth century, and a concurrent turning away from more morally inspiring tales taken from Livy's account of the early Republic. Criticism has generally endorsed this supposed development and sees it as a parallel to the transition from the Elizabethan mind-set to the Jacobean, with its greater pessimism, Jonsonian realism, Fletcherian decadence, and sensitivity to the new English awareness of the skeptical traditions of historiography (Rackin; P. Burke) in Tacitus, Machiavelli, and Bodin.

I find this account both appealing and in part true. Onstage, Jacobean sin *is* more contortedly sniggling in its decadence than Elizabethan sin is; Marlowe's Gaveston seems the conventional picture of moral health beside Webster's Prince Ferdinand. So too it is with Roman plays. The Jacobean *Sejanus* is more unrelievedly satiric than the Elizabethan *Caesar;* other Stuart works like *Valentinian* (c. 1611) and *The Roman Actor* (c. 1626) depict worlds whose palace intrigues and neurotic characterizations are more disgusting than the tyrannical rant and blood-slick scenes in the Elizabethan *Wounds of Civil War* (c. 1586).

A play's tone is affected not just by the life of the playwright and by the era of the drama's composition but also by factors that *can* be substantially independent of the zeitgeist of the era: genre and sources, the tenor of the epoch being described, and the temperament of the author of the source. Though Stuart Roman plays tend to be more politically skeptical than Elizabethan ones, it is easy to be too knowing about why authors abandon one source, one genre, or one tone for another. Except in its Jovial apotheosis, the witty tragicomedy *Cymbeline* is as historical as the far more somber reflection on British history in *Lear,* written perhaps two or three years earlier. In shifting from Ovid and a chapbook to Plutarch's *Lives,* Shakespeare came up with a *Caesar* understandably different in kind from his *Titus*—but to what extent does Shakespeare's choice of sources or eras explain why *Caesar* is very different from each of his other three Plutarchan plays: *Antony, Timon,* and *Coriolanus?*

Hunter (and, to a certain extent, implicitly Spencer and Ahern) believes that the surviving titles show a sixteenth-century proclivity toward historical plays about Rome's Republican era, especially the early Republic, Livy's special interest. One difficulty with this view is that if we divide the early and late Republic in the ordinary way at the defeat of Carthage (146 B.C.) or conquest of Spain (133 B.C.), we find, as table 2 (p. 177) suggests, that the early Livyesque period is not particularly more popular in the sixteenth century than in any other period.

Besides this, there is the issue of whether we ever can safely plot the course of the Tudor-Stuart Roman play on the basis of several lost plays. Titles tell us very little about a play's historicity, kind, treatment of subject, or even the subject itself. Geoffrey Bullough points out that a play named *Constantine* need not be about the Christianizing Roman emperor from York but could refer to any of several late classical Britons ("Pre-Conquest" 303). Besides, a true list of lost Roman plays would include titles that do not promise anything at all Roman, at least to judge from the titles of surviving Roman plays. Who, for instance, would have guessed the Roman content of a third of the extant Roman plays: plays with titles like *Wounds of Civil War, Satiromastix, Every Woman in Her Humour, The Poetaster, The Valiant Welshman, A Shoemaker, a Gentleman, The False One, The Jewes Tragedy, Two Noble Ladies, The Princess, The Virgin Martyr, The Prophetess, Believe As You List,* or *Wonder of Women* (the main title of *Sophonisba*)?

All we can begin to be sure of is a text or performance that we can examine. A generically unified series begins with two works published in 1594 but probably written a half dozen years earlier, Lodge's *Wounds* and Shakespeare's *Titus*. What we do see in surviving Tudor texts are rapes, political treachery, gory mutilation, heroism, sentiment—practically everything that we continue to find in Stuart plays, though probably in shifting proportions. Except for out-and-out comedies like *Every Woman in Her Humour,* the various plays are surprisingly consistent in their methods and goals. No matter whether they are closet dramas, academic works, pieces for the private theaters, or plays for the public theaters, they do most of the following: employ similar rhetoric, including a frequent use of the words *Rome, Roman,* and *noble;* have many battle and quarrel scenes; use red costumes and eagle (and red) insignia; and present for discussion the issue of Rome's reputation for (1) factious and imperialistic *saevitia,* (2) *superbia,* (3) the *dignitas, urbanitas,* and *clementia* of true *majestas,* and (4) suicidal Stoic *constantia.* And many of the plays do this well.

Harbage's *Annals of English Drama, 975–1700* (rev. Schoenbaum) lists all kinds of plays and quasi-dramatic entertainments, extant and lost, vernacular and not, from throughout the British Isles and wherever English writers traveled. If a collection of items likely to be in some way connected with ancient Roman life is made from Harbage's list, we obtain something like the material I have assembled in table 4 (p. 180). A major reason for compiling such a list would be to establish the sustained and accelerating interest in Rome over six centuries of English play-writing. And large as table 4 now is, it might have been greater still if I had included classicized masques, or Romanized scripts like Lady Cary's *Mariam,* where there are no Romans onstage, but a bustle about how Rome has changed Judaea's history—and how Judaea might have changed Rome's if a Jewish princess had slept with Antony.

Harbage devotes 148 pages to listing Renaissance and Restoration dramatic works, 1497–1700. If we count the Roman plays on these pages, we can calculate that by 1589 secular vernacular Roman plays were appearing about once a year (table 3, p. 180). To gain a further sense of what that incidence means in terms of the total output of plays, we can examine the entire secular vernacular dramatic output for a brief typical cluster of years, taken from the center of the time span under consideration. Table 5 (p. 185) shows that there is good reason to believe that during most years in the Renaissance, the output of Roman plays was at least 10 percent of the total.

A look at Harbage's *Annals* further suggests that plays with ancient Roman settings or characters are at least as frequent in England as plays of any other nationality, except for ones with English settings. I cannot establish the truth of that surmise very easily, but if we examine the plays surveyed in table 5 we find that the more serious of them use Roman settings more often than those of other lands. Of the works listed in Harbage for 1608–12, there are forty-one plays, excluding moralities, masques, entertainments, and Heywood's five extravaganzas depicting classical myth and legend. Of these forty-one, 12 percent (five plays) have at least semihistorical Roman settings or characters: the relatively historical *Coriolanus* and *Catiline*, and the progressively more romantic *Cymbeline, Valiant Welshman*, and *A Shoemaker, a Gentleman*. Since tragedy, romance, and historically tinged plays were often regarded in the Renaissance as somehow more serious than comedies, one can rightly conclude that a playwright's recourse to a Roman setting was often part of a strategy to dignify the fable.

The thirty-six non-Roman plays, by contrast, are basically comic (though including what we must admit are such spirited works as *Epicene, Alchemist, Roaring Girl*, and *Chaste Maid in Cheapside*).[1] Significantly, most of the twenty comedies have English settings. Among the sixteen noncomic plays that remain,[2] many are set abroad, as are the romances of Shakespeare and Fletcher, or the more or less historical tragedies of Webster, Chapman, or Fletcher. But neither France, Spain, Italy, nor England welcomes the sober muse with the frequency that Rome had done. And because a dramatist's bow in the direction of historicity is a tentative sign of artistic and/or thematic seriousness, Roman plays can be deemed not only a numerically substantial part of the dramatic total but significant enough intellectually to warrant a series of book-length analyses.

TABLES

Table 1. Comparative Frequency of References to Nationality in English Roman Plays

Author	Title	Number of References to Chief Nationality/Place		
		Roman	English/British	Other
Medwall	*Fulgens*	7		
R.B.	*Apius*			
Nuce	*Octavia*	14		
Lodge	*Wounds*	224		
Kyd	*Cornelia*	63		
Kyd	*Spanish Tragedy*			12 (Spain)
(Garnier	*Cornélie*	31		)
Anon.	*Caesar's Revenge*	117		
Marlowe	*Edward II*		38	
Marlowe	*Jew of Malta*			46 (Malta)
Shakespeare	*Titus Andronicus*	124		
(Shakespeare	"Lucrece"	15		)
Shakespeare	*Henry VI, Pt. 2*		48	
Shakespeare	*Comedy of Errors*			21[a]
Shakespeare	*Romeo and Juliet*			12 (Verona)
Shakespeare	*Midsummer Night's Dream*			36 (Athens)
Shakespeare	*Richard III*		22	
Shakespeare	*Henry IV, Pt. 2*		13	
Shakespeare	*Merchant of Venice*			18 (Venice)
Shakespeare	*Henry V*		93	
Shakespeare	*Julius Caesar*	68		
Shakespeare	*Twelfth Night*			9 (Illyria)

Table 1. continued

		Number of References to Chief Nationality/Place		
Author	Title	Roman	English/British	Other
Shakespeare	*Troilus*			84 (Troy)
Shakespeare	*Hamlet*			53 [b]
Shakespeare	*Othello*			46 [c]
Shakespeare	*Lear*		3	
Shakespeare	*Timon*			37 (Athens)
Shakespeare	*Macbeth*			10 (Scotland)
Shakespeare	*Antony*	38		
Shakespeare	*Coriolanus*	106		
Shakespeare	*Pericles*			41 [d]
Shakespeare	*Cymbeline*	42	40	
Shakespeare	*Winter's Tale*			38 [e]
Shakespeare	*Two Noble Kinsmen*			18 [f]
Shakespeare	*Henry VIII*		18	
Alexander	*Julius Caesar*	63		
Alexander	*Darius*			11 (Asia/Persia)
Marston	*Sophonisba*	34		
Marston	*Antonio*			8 (Venice)
Marston	*Antonio's Revenge*			8 (Venice)
Jonson	*Poetaster*	35		
Jonson	*Alchemist*		4 (+London)	
Jonson	*Sejanus*	58		
Jonson	*Volpone*			10 (Venice)
Jonson	*Catiline*	97		
Chapman	*Caesar and Pompey*	48		
Chapman	*Byron's Conspiracy*			9 (France)
Chapman	*Bussy D'Amboys*			2 (France)
Rowley	*Shoemaker*	39	30	
Rowley	*All's Lost*			23 (Spain)
Fletcher	*Bonduca*	99	18	
Fletcher	*Queen of Corinth*			5 (Corinth)
Fletcher	*Rollo of Normandy*			4 [g]
Fletcher	*Valentinian*	24		
Nabbes	*Hannibal and Scipio*	70		
Nabbes	*Unfortunate Mother*			3 (Italy/Ferrara)
Lee	*Sophonisba*	63		

Table 1. continued

Author	Title	Number of References to Chief Nationality/Place		
		Roman	English/British	Other
Lee	*Rival Queens*			11 (Persia, etc.)
Addison	*Cato*	61		

a 14 Syracuse
b 34 Denmark, 10 other
c 23 Venice, 23 Cyprus
d 25 Tyre, 16 Tarsus
e 14 Sicily, 24 Bohemia
f 13 Thebes, 5 Athens
g 2 Normandy, 2 Sparta

Table 2. **The Span of Roman History in Secular English Roman Drama, 1550–1650, Plays Extant and Lost**

Historical Period	Short Title of Play	Approximate Date of Composition
Origins	"Dido"	1563
	"Dido"	1564
	"Dido"	1598
	Dido and Aeneas	1590
	Faithful Friends	1614
Early Republic	"Lucrece"	1596
	Lucrece	1607
	"Mutius Scaevola"	1577
	Coriolanus	1608
	Apius and Virginia	1561
	Appius and Virginia	1624
	"Quintus Fabius"	1574
	"The Four Sons of Fabius"	1580
	"Cenocephalis"	1575
	"Alucius"	1577
Later Republic	"Scipio Africanus"	1580
	"Hannibal and Hermes, Pt. 1"	1598
	"Hannibal and Scipio"	1601
	Hannibal and Scipio	1635

Table 2. continued

Historical Period	Short Title of Play	Approximate Date of Composition
	"Massinissa and Sophonisba"	1565
	Sophonisba	1605
	"Jugurtha"	1600
	Believe As You List	1631
	"Titus and Gisippus"	1550
	"Titus and Gisippus"	1565
	"Titus and Gisippus"	1572
	Wounds of Civil War	1587
	"Sulla Dictator"	1589
	"Catiline"	1570
	"Catiline's Conspiracies"	1578
	"Catiline's Conspiracy"	1598
	Catiline	1611
	"Tooly" ["Tully"?]	1576
	Cicero	1635–51
	Every Woman in Her Humor	1607
	"Pompey"	1581
	"Caesar and Pompey"	1581
	Caesar's Revenge	1595
	Caesar and Pompey	1605
	"Caesar and Pompey, Pt. 1"	1594
	"Caesar [and Pompey], Pt. 2"	1595
	"Julius Caesar"	1562
	Cornelia	1594
	The False One	1620
	"Ptolomy"	1578
	"Telemo"	1583
	Julius Caesar	1599
	Julius Caesar	1607
	"Portia" [only projected?]	1595
Transition to Empire	*Antonius*	1590
	"Antony"	1601
	Antony and Cleopatra	1607
	Cleopatra	1593
	Cleopatra	1626
	"Octavia"	1590
	Virtuous Octavia	1598

Table 2. continued

Historical Period	Short Title of Play	Approximate Date of Composition
Empire	*Princess*	1636
	Poetaster	1601
	Satiromastix	1605
	Sejanus	1603
	Claudius Tiberius Nero	1607
	"Pontius Pilate"	1602
	Nero	1624
	Agrippina	1635
	Octavia	1560
	Herod and Antipater	1622
	Cymbeline	1609
	Messallina	1635
	Fuimus Troes	1625
	Bonduca	1613
	"Caratach"	1594
	Valiant Welshman	1612
	"Titus and Vespasian"	1592
	"Destruction of Jerusalem"	1584
	"Marcus Geminus"	1566
	Roman Actor	1626
	"Zenobia"	1592
	"Mad Priest of the Sun"	1588
	"Heliogabalus"	1594
	"Diocletian"	1594
	Virgin Martyr	1620
	"Constantine"	1599
	"Fair Constance of Rome, I, II"	1600
	"Julian the Apostate"	1550
	"Julian the Apostate"	1596

Note: The titles of the lost plays (in quotation marks) have been taken largely from Harbage and Schoenbaum's *Annals,* interpreted in the light of Hunter's "Roman Thought" and Schelling's discussions in his *Elizabethan Drama.* Unfortunately, we can never assemble a complete list of lost plays. Nor do we have any way of telling whether a given title is not a variant of another one and actually refers to a separate Roman play—or any Roman play at all. In compiling the above list, I have tended toward excessive inclusiveness rather than to its opposite.

Table 3. Incidence of English Roman Plays per Year, 1497–1700

Period	Number of Years in Period	Number of Plays Extant	Approximate Number of Plays Lost	Average Total per Year
1497–1588	92	4	22	0.3
1589–1642	54	41	18	1.1
1643–1700	57	37	4	0.8
Total	203	82	44	—

Source: Compiled from Harbage's *Annals,* rev. Schoenbaum.

Table 4. Annals of English Roman Plays, 1100–1700

Date	Author, Title, and/or Other Information
1090–1110	Dunstable school, "Saint Catherine"
1170–82	London martyr plays
1100–1300	Several Passions and Resurrections
1175	Anglo-Norman *Resureccion*
1200–1600	Saints' plays, cycles, etc., in 100 towns
1343	London, "Saint Catherine"
1300–1500	Chester, York, N-Town, Cornish, Wakefield plays
1441–42	Lincoln, "Saint Lawrence"
1400–1500	Bodl. Ashmole. 750, *Caesar Augustus*(?) fragment
1490–91	Magdalene College, Oxford, "Saint Catherine"
1480–1520	Digby MS, *St. Mary Magdalene*
1497	Medwall, *Fulgens and Lucres*
1504	Cornish, *St. Meriasek*
1522–32	Ritwise, "Dido" (academic)
1546–55	Radcliffe, "Titus and Gisippus"
1556–66	Ashton, "Julian the Apostate" (Shrewsbury School)
1559–67	R.B., *Apius and Virginia*
1561	Nuce, *Octavia* (translation of pseudo-Seneca's *Octavia*)
1562	"Julius Caesar" (at court)
1563	"History of Aeneas and Queen Dido" (at court)
1563	"Dido," Chester town

Table 4. continued

Date	Author, Title, and/or Other Information
1564	"Dido," King's College, Cambridge
1565	"Massinissa and Sophonisba" (at court)
1565	"Titus and Gisippus"
1566	"Marcus Geminus," Oxford
1570	Wilson, "Catiline"
1572	"Titus and Gisippus"
1574	"Quint Fabius," Children of Windsor
1576	"Mutius Scaevola," Children of Windsor
1577	"Alucius"
1577	"History of Cenocephalis," Sussex's Men
1578	E. Campion, "Nectar et Ambrosia," Prague
1578	Wilson, "Catiline"
1578	"Ptolome," Bull Inn
by 1578	Gosson, "Catiline's Conspiracies"
1580	"The Four Sons of Fabius"
1580	"Scipio Africanus," Children of Paul's
by 1580	"The History of Caesar and Pompey"
1581	"Caesar and Pompey"
1580–92	"Zenobia," Henslowe's
1580–92	"Constantine," Henslowe's
1581	"Story of Pompey," Children of Paul's
1582	Geddes/Eedes, "Caesar Interfectus" (Latin), Oxford
1583, 1592	Gager, *Dido,* Latin fragment
1583	"Telemo" ("Ptolome"?), Leicester's Men
1584	Smythe, "Destruction of Jerusalem," Coventry
1586	Lodge, *Wounds of Civil War*
1587–93	Marlowe and Nash, *Dido, Queen of Carthage*
1588	"Dominus de Purpoole" feast, Gray's Inn (Sulla)
1588	"Mad Priest of the Sun" ("Heliogabalus"?)
1589	"Sulla Dictator"
1590	"Octavia," Christ Church, Oxford
1590	Pembroke, *Antonius* (translation of Garnier's *Marc Antoine*)
1590	Shakespeare, *Titus Andronicus*
1591	"Titus and Vespacia," Henslowe's
1594	"Diocletian," Henslowe's
1594	"Caesar and Pompey, Pt. 1," Henslowe's
1594	Kyd, *Cornelia* (translation of Garnier's *Cornélie*)

Table 4. continued

Date	Author, Title, and/or Other Information
1594	Daniel, *Cleopatra* (1st ed.)
1595	"Caratach," Henslowe's
1594	"Life and Death of Heliogabalus," Stationer's Reg.
1595	*Tragedy of Caesar and Pompey/Caesar's Revenge*
1595	Kyd, Garnier's "Portia" [only projected?]
1595	"2nd Part of Caesar," Henslowe's
1596	"Lucrece"
1596	"Julian the Apostate," Henslowe's
1597–1602	Dekker, prologue and epilogue to "Pontius Pilate," Henslowe's
1598	Brandon, *The Virtuous Octavia*
1598	Wilson and Chettle, "Catiline's Conspiracy," Henslowe's
1598	Drayton, Dekker and Wilson, "Hannibal and Hermes, 1"
1598	"Dido," Henslowe's
1599	Shakespeare, *Julius Caesar*
1600	Daniel, *Cleopatra* (2nd ed.)
1600–1601	Greville, "Antony and Cleopatra"
1600	Boyle, "Jugurtha"
1600	Munday, Hathway, Dekker, et al., "Constance, 1"
1600	Hathway, "Fair Constance of Rome, Part 2"
1600	["Tartarian Cripple, Emperor of Constantinople," Stationers' Reg.]
1601	Hathway and Rankins, "Hannibal and Scipio," Henslowe's
1601	Jonson, *Poetaster*
1601	Dekker, *Satiromastix*
1601	Machin, *Every Woman in Her Humor*
1602	Webster, Drayton, Dekker, Munday, and Hathway, "Caesar's Fall"
1603	Gwinne, *Nero Tragoedia Nova* (Latin, Oxford)
1603	Jonson, *Sejanus His Fall*
1603–8	Heywood, *Rape of Lucrece*
1604	Alexander, *Julius Caesar*
1605–9	A droll, "Julius Caesar"
1605	Marston, *Sophonisba*
1604–11	Chapman, *Wars of Caesar and Pompey*
1607–8	Shakespeare, *Antony and Cleopatra*
1607	*Tiberius*
1607–9	Shakespeare, *Coriolanus*

Table 4. continued

Date	Author, Title, and/or Other Information
1610	Rowley, *A Shoemaker, a Gentleman*
1611	Shakespeare, *Cymbeline*
1611	Jonson, *Catiline His Conspiracy*
1610–14	Fletcher, *Valentinian*
1613	Fletcher(?), *Faithful Friends*
by 1614	R.A. [Robert Armin], *Valiant Welshman*
1616	Fletcher, *Bonduca*
1618	[Bernard, *Alexius Imperator/Andronicus* (Latin), Magdalen College, Oxford]
1618–19	*Nero*
1600–1700	*Caracalla* (Latin, academic)
1619	W.S., *Petronius Maximus* (19th-century forgery?)
1619–22	Fletcher, *The False One*
1619–22	*Two Noble Ladies*
1620	Massinger, *The Virgin Martyr*
1622	Fletcher, *The Prophetess*
1622	Markham and Sampson, *Herod and Antipater*
1623–64	Saint Omers Latin saints' plays, by English Jesuits
1624	Webster, *Appius and Virginia*
1625–33	Fisher, *Fuimus Troes* (Magdalen College, Oxford)
1626	May, *Cleopatra*
1626	Massinger, *Roman Actor*
1628	May, *Agrippina*
1628–33	Heming, *The Jews' Tragedy*
1613–30	May, *Julius Caesar* (Latin)
by 1630	Massinger, *Believe As You List*
by 1631	[Massinger, *Emperor of the East*]
1631	[Simons, *Zeno*, Saint Omers]
after 1631	[Simons, *Leo Armenius*, Saint Omers]
1635	Nabbes, *Hannibal and Scipio*
1637	Richards, *Messallina*
1638	[H. Shirley, *Martyred Soldier* (under Emperor "Hubert")]
by 1642	"Romanus" (design only), Kings' Men
1644	Killigrew, *The Princess*
1644	*Titus: Palm of Christian Courage*, Kilkenny Jesuits' School
by 1651	*Marcus Tullius Cicero*
after 1660	Cockayne, *Ovid's Tragedy*

Table 4. *continued*

Date	Author, Title, and/or Other Information
1655	Lowrer, *Polyeuctes* (translation of Corneille's *Polyeuctes*)
1656	Lowrer, *Horatius* (translation of Corneille's *Horace*)
1661, 1662, 1663, 1668	Revival of Massinger, *Virgin Martyr*
1663	K. Philips, *Pompey* (translation of Corneille's *Pompé*)
1663	Waller, Sackville, et al., *Pompey* (translation of Corneille's *Pompé*)
1664	R. Howard, *Vestal Virgin*
1664	[L. Carlell, *Heraclius, Emperor of the East* (unacted)]
1664	"Heraclius" (Duke's Theater, Pepys's *Diary*)
1665–71	Cotton, Corneille's *Horace*
1667	Dover, *Roman Generals/Distressed Ladies* (unacted)
by 1668	Revival of Massinger's *Roman Actor*
1668	Revival of Jonson's *Catiline*
1668	[J. Wilson, *Andronicus Comnenius* (unacted; 11th century)]
1668	Denham and Philips, *Horace* (translation of Corneille's *Horace*)
1669	Betterton, *Roman Virgin* (revision of Webster's *Appius*)
1669	[Killigrew, *Imperial Tragedy* (revision of Simons's *Zeno*?)]
1669	Dryden, *Tyrannick Love* (Saint Catherine)
1670	Dauncer, *Nicomedes* (translation of Corneille's *Nicomede*, Dublin)
1671	Joyner, *The Roman Empress*
1674	Lee, *Nero*
1674	A droll(?), "Mock Pompey"
1675	Lee, *Sophonisba; or, Hannibal's Overthrow*
1676	Lee, *Gloriana: Court of Augustus Caesar*
1677	Crowne, *Destruction of Jerusalem*, pts. 1 and 2 (adapted from French)
1677	Otway, *Berenice* (translation of Racine's *Titus and Berenice*)
1677	Sedley, *Antony and Cleopatra*
1677	Dryden, *All for Love*
1678	Lee, *Mithridates*
1678	Ravenscroft, *Rape of Lavinia* (revision of Shakespeare's *Titus*)
1679	Bancroft, *Sertorius* (translation of Corneille's *Sertorius*)
1678–79, 1686	Rochester, *Lucina's Rape* (revision of Fletcher's *Valentinian*)
1680	[Lee, *Theodosius*]
1680	Otway, *Caius Marius*
1680	Lee, *Lucius Junius Brutus*
1680	S. Butler, *Nero* (incomplete)
1682	Revival of Jonson's *Sejanus*
1682	*Romulus and Hersilia*

Table 4. continued

Date	Author, Title, and/or Other Information
1682	Tate, *Ingratitude of a Commonwealth* (revision of Shakespeare's *Coriolanus*)
1682	D'Urfey, *Injured Princess* (revision of Shakespeare's *Cymbeline*)
1683	Lee, *Constantine the Great*
1687	"Augustus Caesar II" (lost?)
1689	Tate(-Purcell), *Dido and Aeneas* (opera)
1690	Sheffield, *Caesar* (revision of Shakespeare's *Caesar*)
1690	Sheffield, *Brutus*
1690	Betterton, *Diocletian* (revision of Fletcher's *Prophetess*)
1692	Crowne, *Regulus*
1695	Powell, *British Heroine* (revision of Fletcher's *Bonduca*)
1696	Gildon, *Roman Bride's Revenge*
1696	Hopkins, *Boadicea*
1698	Crowne, *Caligula*
1702	Sedley, *Beauty the Conqueror* (revision of Sedley's *Antony*, 1677)
1708	Dennis, *Appius and Virginia*
1712	Addison, *Cato* (1st draft 1700?)

Note: Titles of lost works are in quotation marks; works on Byzantine subjects appear in brackets. Knotty questions of dates and authorship are avoided; yet it is hoped that enough information will be provided to let the nonspecialist find more precise references—and the texts—elsewhere. All works whose authors are not supplied are anonymous. Extra notations after a title indicate type of play, provenance or auspices or subject, or the chief source of information about the work.

Table 5. **Percentages of Roman Dramas Among Extant London Plays, 1608–12**

Year	Number of Roman Plays	Number of All Plays	Roman as % of Total
1608	2	13	15
1609	1	8	13
1610	0	7	0
1611	1	10	10
1612	1	3	33
Total	5	41	12

NOTES

Introduction: "Antike" Rome and the Renascent *Fabula Praetexta*

1. Crucial to my understanding of this and other aspects of the many plays discussed have been essays and books too numerous to name, but I would, nevertheless, single out a few: for political indeterminacy in drama, the studies by Norman Rabkin, Annabel Patterson, Paul Yachnin, and Theodore Leinwand; for Shakespeare's *Titus Andronicus,* the essays of Eugene Waith ("Metamorphosis of Violence"), Alan Sommers, and Albert Tricomi ("Aesthetics of Mutilation" and "Mutilated Garden"); for Jonson's *Poetaster,* Anne Barton's *Ben Jonson, Dramatist;* for Jonson's *Sejanus,* Barton (*Ben Jonson, Dramatist*), Geoffrey Hill, and Jonas A. Barish; for Jonson's *Catiline,* Whitney Bolton and Jane Gardner's edition; for Shakespeare's *Coriolanus,* Janet Adelman ("Anger's My Meat") and Stanley Cavell; for Massinger's *Believe As You List,* A. D. Hogan and Douglas Howard; and for Shakespeare's *Cymbeline,* Glynne Wickham, and (even when I violently disagree with him) G. Wilson Knight.

Additionally, there are the wider studies that compare and contrast clusters of Roman, or sometimes Roman and non-Roman, plays by various dramatists. Especially worthwhile in this category are J. W. Lever's analyses of *Sejanus* and *Caesar and Pompey* (along with non-Roman "tragedies of state") and more recent volumes such as Rebecca Weld Bushnell's on tyrant plays like *Caesar, Sejanus, Valentinian,* and *Roman Actor;* Jonathan Goldberg's on Roman theatricality in Shakespeare, Jonson, *Roman Actor,* and *Bussy;* and Gail Kern Paster's on the city in *Titus, Caesar, Coriolanus, Sejanus, Catiline.* Two or more dramatists are also compared by George K. Hunter, Martin Butler, William Dinsmore Briggs, and M. W. MacCallum, among others. And clusters of a few Roman plays are treated in a revealing way by students of single dramatists: of Shakespeare (especially by Robert Miola, Hunter, James Simmons, John Velz, Reuben Brower, Maurice Charney, Derek Traversi, Paul Cantor, John Alvis, James Phillips, Michael Platt, Michael Payne, and Charles Martindale and Michelle Martindale); of Jonson (by Herford, Simpson, and Simpson; Barish; and Barton); of Massinger (by Butler and Howard).

Essential background is provided for the cultural context by J. Leeds Barroll, Roy Walker, Hunter, and foremost, T. J. B. Spencer. Of great help have also been the image studies of Knight, Traversi, and Charney (and Adelman, *The Common Liar*) and the guides to Renaissance iconography (Cesare Ripa, G. Bolzani Valeriano, Guy de Tervarent), and emblemology (Henkel and Schöne). I am especially grateful for the analyses of symbols by Charney and by R. A. Yoder (on metal), Albert Caputi (on fire), J. Philip Brockbank (on dragons), and Knight (on buildings, birds, and horses). For invaluable help with background and source studies of Shakespeare and others, I acknowledge MacCallum, Kenneth Muir, Geoffrey Bullough, Gilbert Highet, T. W. Baldwin, and J. A. K. Thompson. For Jonson studies, I am greatly indebted to Ellen M. T. Duffy, Lynn Harold Harris, Briggs, Barish, Bolton and Gardner, and of course, Herford, Simpson, and Simpson. For my sense of Massinger, I am beholden to his editors, Philip Edwards and Colin Gibson, to Doris Adler, and to the contributors to the Howard and Butler anthology. Indispensable for Webster has been the work of F. L. Lucas; for Chapman, that of T. M. Parrott (in his edition of *The Plays of George Chapman*); and for Fletcher, that of Clifford Leech and Michael Taylor. My use of various other local studies, especially of anachronism and suicide, will be acknowledged below, but I cannot here omit my admiration for studies of Senecanism: by John Anson, on the background of Shakespeare's *Julius Caesar,* and by Gordon Braden on a wide range of texts, both Continental and English. Finally, as models of how to pay close attention to word choice and meaning, I have tried to follow as best I could the examples in Harry Levin's remarks on charactonyms ("Shakespeare's Nomenclatures"), and in William Empson's, Eric Partridge's, and Stephen Booth's several discussions of multiplicity of word senses.

2. *Rumpitur ingratos pariendo Vipera foetus,*
   Prolis & ad vitam suscipit illa necem:
Pectoris arcanum dum profert garrula lingua,
   Dat vitam verbis, interitumque sibi.

Quand le serpent de la Vipere sort,
La mere meurt, & il vit par son aage:
Qui parle trop se prepare à la mort,
Et donne vie à son parler volage.

3. Lodge intensifies, rather than evades, what ironies history records regarding the actions of Marius's and Scilla's gods. Marius dies a friend of Heaven, expiring soon after he is granted the sight of seven eagles, which are auspiciously crossing the sky in honor of his seven consulships. Scilla then returns to Rome, slays thousands, abolishes the tribunate, and situates himself cruelly, blasphemously, and

amusingly(!) in tyrannical power. Hearing of the courageous suicide by which Marius's heir has taken himself out of political competition, Scilla laughs, then reflects on the transitoriness of life, and retires from the political scenes. Act V of the play ends with his apotheosis: a Latin-speaking spirit dubs Scilla "foelix" and summons him—like another Oedipus at Colonus—to join "innumeros . . . heroas" in Elysium. Fate or providence is silent. Apparently, the Antike gods love powerful men, whether good or bad.

In the background of Lodge's antic theodicy is intermittently found a more coherent classical tradition. When Seneca's Atreus slays his nephews and prepares their blood for their father Thyestes' dinner, the skies darken and the earth shakes. Most noncomic plays, Roman or otherwise, follow suit. Except for *Titus, Coriolanus,* and *Believe As You List,* Roman tragedies and romances have at least as much of the supernatural as their sources authorize. Typical are *The Prophetess,* with its storms and celestial music; *Antony,* with its departure of Hercules; *Cymbeline,* with its Jupiter's tablet; Jonson's *Sejanus,* with the omens of the snake and smoking statue, and *Catiline,* with its storm; Chapman's *Caesar and Pompey,* again with a storm; and Massinger's *Roman Actor,* with its astounding dog pack; and, of course, *Caesar,* with its ghost, augurs, omens, storm.

Chapter 2. *Rhomé:* Power, Place, Politics

1. Puns on *puissance* and *rhomé* may also have been felt to float to the surface in several other works, including English Roman plays. In a 1544 poem of Thomas Berthelet's, Hannibal challenges his "puissant enemies," the Romans, with "worthy stomach and courage valiant" (Hunter, "Roman" 98). In *Agrippina* Caligula's ghost brags of being "obey'd by all the Romane power" (I.42). Perhaps audiences at Shakespeare's *Caesar* would have found Cassius's attacks on Julius's physical strength less obviously irrelevant than we do. One has to be puissant and strong to be Roman, and ill-swimming Caesar is not unassailably so.

2. Literal motifs of rape occur in *Titus, Lucrece, Virgin Martyr, Cymbeline, Bonduca, Valiant Welshman, Appius, Catiline, Valentinian, Roman Actor, Two Noble Friends,* and *Messallina.*

Chapter 3. *Nobilitas* and *Majestas:* Munificence, Clemency, and Sensitivity to Slight

1. Eagle insignia appear in the dialogue or stage directions in, at very least, the Admiral's Company's *Wounds* of about 1587 (IV.i.106ff.); the Trinity College, Oxford, *Caesar's Revenge* of about 1595 (III.ii.1288–89); the King's Men's *Catiline*

of about 1611 (III.iii); and the Red Bull's *Shoemaker, a Gentleman* of about 1608 (III.iii.44). Eagle insignia seem also to be implied in the King's Men's *Bonduca* (II.i.62) of about 1613 and probably their *Cymbeline* of about 1608 (V.v.470–81), in the Red Bull's *Virgin Martyr* of about 1620 (II.ii.29) and their *Two Noble Ladies* of about the same year (1643ff.), in the Queen's Revels' *Sophonisba* of 1605 (I.ii.75–76), and in the Magdalen College, Oxford, *Fuimus Troes* of about 1625 (I.i.451). In these last two plays and maybe more, the eagle referred to is black and/or binecked and is likely to have anachronistically suggested the Habsburgian Holy Roman Empire as well as the Ancient one.

2. Heywood's melodramatic *Lucrece* opens with Tarquin and Tullia's deposing her royal father, murdering him, and mutilating his corpse: a fate he has arguably attracted to himself by ungratefully dispossessing the Tarquinian dynasty, which earlier had befriended and adopted him. Webster's *Appius* sounds a similar note: Virginius, who feels he must kill his own daughter to save her from Rome's lustful ruler, is a loyal Roman general with grounds for boasting of a "life so oft ingag'd for *ingrateful* Rome" (IV.ii.143). So too his starving soldiers have cause to complain that Rome's refusal to send them supplies proves that the city in turn is "a most unnaturall mother" to the very soldiers/children who have preserved it "from sinking into ruine" (II.ii.49–51). Gratitude, or its absence, becomes good theater in *The Roman Actor* too, when Domitian expects that none of his hangers-on will be "so ungrateful" as not to extend to the emperor on demand the use of a "jewel"—or a wife (I.iv.46–48). Indeed, when the actor Paris is found to have succumbed to the advances of Domitian's "ingratefull" wife (IV.ii.120), Paris is sorriest not for adultery but for his betrayal of imperial trust and favor:

O dread Caesar!
To hope for my life, or plead in the defence
Of my *ingratitude,* were again to wrong you.
I know I have deserv'd death.
(IV.ii.185–92)

Shakespeare's interest in the theme of Roman thanklessness, along with political touchiness about prestige, commences early in his career. *Titus Andronicus,* for instance, is emotionally centered on the vengefulness and ingratitude of the Emperor Saturninus and his party. And verbal repetition underlines this theme. The Andronicans' supporters speak in outrage not just against the dynasty and government but also against all "ungrateful Rome" (IV.iii.17), that "ungrateful country" (IV.i.111), that "ingrateful Rome" (V.i.12). Hence Lucius swears "with revengeful war [to] / Take wreak on Rome for this ingratitude" (IV.iii.33–34). When Lucius grows furious at the way his family has been treated, though they have been so stalwart in Rome's defense, he decides to join the bellicose Goths, hurling the cry "Farewell, proud Rome" (III.i.290), where *proud* is a mere synonym for *ungrateful*. Even before the first scene is over, the audience has heard the wily Gothic queen urge attention to public relations, admonishing the emperor to avoid the reputation for "ingratitude, which Rome reputes to be a heinous sin" (I.i.448). Audiences would quickly sense that she, like more modern Machiavels, is merely burnishing a public image, not correcting an ingrained reality.

Rome is a city threatening or delivering ingratitude, as is easy to see from *Tiberius* xvi.2050; *Cicero* IV.D2v, *Hannibal* IV.ii.248 (and IV.iv.252; V.Argument, 258), and Nahum Tate's subtitle for his revision of *Coriolanus* (*The Ingratitude of a Commonwealth*). Ingratitude is what Lucius suspects in *Cymbeline* (V.v.105–7) and what the plebs would avoid a reputation for in *Coriolanus* (II.iii.9). Too, that is allegedly Brutus's crime and sin in *Caesar* (III.ii.189; cf. *Caesar Interfectus*, qtd. in Bullough, *Narrative and Dramatic Sources* 5: 194).

3. The passage (mis-?)ascribed to *De oratore* 1 reads "Nihil est tam regium, tam liberale, tamque munificum, quam opem terre suppliciibus, excitare afflictos, dare salutem, liberare pericolis homines" ('Nothing is so *kingly,* so worthy of a free and liberally educated person, and so munificent as to grant supplicants the riches of the earth, to uplift the afflicted, to confer safety and salvation, and to liberate men from dangers').

4. In a line of reasoning that has upset many critics, Renaissance and modern (Augustine, Erasmus, Muller 221, Goldberg 283 n. 27, Braden 16), the great Seneca prefers the word *clementia* to *misericordia,* 'clemency' to 'mercy,' though he admits that there is an element of arbitrary semantics in his preference (*De clementia* 2.7.4). What Seneca is getting at—and what his critics object to—is the suppression of emotional sympathy (possibly quirky, he thinks; possibly God-sent and more humane, some of his critics think) in the conferring of prudent, measured aid to one's fellow man.

Chapter 4. Suicide and the Dynamics of Stoical *Constantia*

1. Several scholars have written revealingly on suicide in Elizabethan drama: Rowland Wymer, James H. Hanford, John E. Hankins, Cora Eiland Hicks, Bernard Paulin, Samuel E. Sprott, and perhaps most important, Theodore Spencer.

2. The *Antony* citations in this paragraph are *seriatum* V.ii.308, 289, 6, 240, 240; II.vi.122; III.iii.21; III.xiii.121.

3. Sugden also cites, e.g., *Cruel Brother* V.i, *Woman-Hater* III.ii.128ff., and *Humorous Courtier* II.i.

4. The newly naturalized word *constancy* (OED) was modish in the late sixteenth century, selling books and play tickets. The title page of R.B.'s *Apius and Virginia* (c. 1560; pub. 1575) announces that the work will illustrate the heroine's "constancy" in choosing to die at her father's hand.

In addition to the plays cited in the text, the code words of suicidal Stoicism appear in, for instance, *Caesar's Revenge* III.v.1523–24, I.i.1040–59; *Catiline* III.iii.2–8, IV.iii.6–8, IV.i.38; *False One* V.iv, p. 365; *Messallina* 2575, 737; *Roman Actor* I.iii.19; *Believe As You List* 2019–20; *Jews' Tragedy* 3097–98; *Virgin Martyr* I.i.176–77, II.iii. 75–176, IV.iii.68, V.ii.213–14, 235; *Sophonisba* V.iii.91, 96; Alexander's *Caesar* 847; *Faithful Friends* III.ii, p. 252; *Valentinian* III.i.266, I.i.75–76, 92, IV.iv.294–95; *Titus* III.i.238; *Hannibal* III.iv.233, *Lucrece* 2903; *Cornelia* V.321.

5. Underestimating the complexity of dramatic interest in several Jacobean plays, Wymer (156) finds that their "fully tragic" stage suicides are few because they must balance "dignity with despair," a feat that Wymer finds difficult because he believes that suicide was generally employed "as an *unambiguous* label" and "*definitive* theatrical image for female virtue, passionate love, or the honour of 'an antique Roman.'"

Chapter 5. *Superbia*: Insulting, Aquiline, Overmounting Pride

1. Alert to the air of erotically charged sadism in the *Victor*, Lucie-Smith points out that the triumpher's dagger is pointed at a vulvalike fold in Victoria's dress, while one half-naked victim lies dead under the Victor's feet and another leans weakly by his knee.

2. "C'estoit *la coustûme des Rois* qui triumphoyent de *fouler aux pieds les corps* des prisonniers, en signe de subjections, plusieurs enseignes des Romains *signifient un personnage qui triumphe* quand il a le pied comme cela."

3. I might add that the pseudo-Senecan *Octavia* reports that the Roman mobs were trampling on the head of the statue of Nero's consort, Poppaea (Nuce trans. 183). Too, Vergil speaks of putting inferiors "sub pedibus" (*Aeneid* 7.100) and he provides elementary raw material for Prudentius's exaggerated pedal humiliations.

In Psalm 110:1 and repeatedly in the New Testament (e.g., Matthew 22:44), reference is made also to using a vanquished person as one's footstool. In Daniel 7:23, the Beast of Empire will not only devour "the whole earth" but also will "*treade it down* and breake it in pieces." Psalm 91 speaks of a good man's treading on asps, and Genesis refers to grinding one's heel into the head of the serpentine figure of evil (3:15), a figure that in Revelation is to be hurled down (12:7).

Seemingly, when Rome and Jerusalem joined forces, they bequeathed to the

Middle Ages a redoubled tradition. Throughout the Middle Ages scenes of pedal humiliation signify inferiority, as in the victory of good angels over bad, Virtues over Vices, or saints and heroes over human or serpentine enemies (Freccero; Ross, "Wingless Victory"). Prudentius, in particular, apparently encouraged numerous medieval illustrators with their images of foot squashing (Weinberger 1: 143), partly because he invented pedal humiliations and other indignities that do not appear in his Vergilian source (Mahoney 76). When Vergil's Hercules crushes Cacus, for instance, the beast is throttled till his eyes pop out and the throat has no blood: "elisos oculos et siccum sanguine guttur" (*Aeneid* 8.261). Into this sufficiently shocking account, Prudentius adds the idea that the victim's mouth hits the dust and his eyes are trampled on—all the time echoing the vocabulary of the original classical epic (cf. "elisos" and "gutturis," *Psychomachia* 33–34).

Chapter 6. *Saevitia:* Wolves, Demons, Parricides, and Self-Corrosion

1. Fellow Roman enemies are "brawling wolves" (*Wounds* V.i.20); plutocratic Roman governors are rapacious "wolves" who devour soldiers' flesh "instead of feeding" them as "Romulus / Was fed by a she wolfe" (*Appius* II.ii.51–53); and Rome's Triumvirs are said to reincarnate the original werewolf, King Lycaon; and if Jove should call on the Triumvirs as once he visited that Greek tyrant, they

> would with more unheard of *savageness*
> Feast his divinity; not with some poor infant
> But even their *Mothers flesh*, I mean their countreys,
> And 'stead of Nectar give him *bloud to drink*.
> (*Cicero* V, E2v)

Pompey's Roman betrayer is a "bloody wolf" (*False One* III.ii, 338), and a hint of Roman wolfishness is made in *Poetaster* through the charactonym of one of the foolish literati, Asinius ('asslike') Lupus, whom Rome's emperor is nevertheless able to control. In *Fuimus Troes,* which proclaims the islanders' kinship with Rome and Troy, Britons share alike the martial wolfishness of their cousins: though the Britons at first decry the invasion of the Roman army as a "ravenous wolf" (II.i.467), these Celtic (and "Gothic"; cf. Kliger) descendants of Brut soon redefine themselves as barbaric "Scythian wolves midst of a bleating fold" (IV.iv.514). They conclude that if given slightly better fortune, they would have been able to invade Italy and "make Romulus' wolf / Howl horror in their streets, and Rome look pale" (IV.iv.515). In yet another variation on the theme, the *loving* brothers in *Tiberius* give each other their own arm meat to keep away the "hungry woolfe" of appetite (3091).

Roman Actor makes more prominent and surprising mention of canines than

Massinger's source does. Whereas Suetonius, Massinger's authority, specifies that some dogs ate a prophet's corpse before it could be cremated (ed. Sandidge 8), the playwright describes an epic battle of "all the Dogs of Rome / Howling, and yelling like famish'd wolves." The slain among Massinger's "eager fang[ed]" beasts amounted to thousands (V.ii.256–60). Certainly, with his prodigious amplification of the historical account, the dramatist is symbolically suggesting that all the Romans are currish foragers, wandering like wolves amidst the ostensible *urbanitas* of civilized Rome, and waiting to devour the play's equally brutal Roman, Domitian. Additionally, the play's eponymous hero himself prompts English audiences to remember Rome's wolves, when, in a play-within-the-play, the actor describes "man" as by nature merciful—someone who will not act as if he "did . . . *sucke the milke / Of Wolves,* and Tigres, or a mother of / A rougher temper" (III.i.22–23). By this definition, archetypal Romans would, of course, not qualify as men.

2. In Caesar's and Coriolanus's worlds characters ask, Who are the sheep, the shepherds, the wolves? The inciting incident in *Caesar* occurs during a festival that, as any student of Latin could immediately guess, has something to do with wolves. Caesar is celebrating the Lupercal, a festival fashioned by the *luperci* (priests of Pan Lupercus, 'wolf-involved Pan') to keep wolves from the flock. Though the ostensible purpose of Caesar's association with this fertility festival (Fowler 310–21) is to regularize and intensify the differentiation between male and female, a covert function, surely, is to flush out Cassius: a "spare," "lean and hungry" wolf, whose peaceful disguise Caesar rightly suspects. Cassius admits to being a carnivore (and no sheep) when he states that he has fed on the same "meat" as Caesar, and that Julius "would not be a wolf, / But that he sees the Romans are but sheep." Extending the motif further, Shakespeare elsewhere has Brutus tell Cassius to "chew" on political issues.

Antony terms Casca's attack on Caesar that of a "cur" (V.i.43), but the Triumvir himself successfully unleashes on the conspirators the "dogs of war" in III.i, 273. In IV.iii Brutus associates canine imagery with himself, for the first time adopting a nonhuman animate image to define his identity positively or negatively. Hitherto he has spoken of himself in terms of *people,* human identities he does or does not share: a son of Rome, rude villager, old man, coward, superstitious priest, actor, butcher, bastard, murderer, slave. Yet now he likens himself not only to a victimized lamb but also to a moon-baying dog (109, 25–28). This little change in rhetoric may well quibblingly underline a hint of the brute in his family name.

The hero of *Coriolanus* hopes finally to evade being "dogg'd" with an eternally bad name (V.iii.144), though in almost the opening speech of the play he is termed "a very dog to the commonalty" (I.i.28). Secondary characters are also termed canines. Titus Lartius is Rome's "greyhound" (I.vi.38); the plebs are cast as "dogs on sheep" (II.i.257); Aufidius is a "hound" and "cur" (V.vi.106, 112); and there are many other "curs" as well (I.i.168, II.iii.216, III.iii.120). A highlighting of Coriolanus's canine identity is seen in II.i.6–11, when Menenius and the tribunes wrangle about the identity of Martius and the plebs. Each disputant characterizes his friend(s) as lamblike and likens the opposition to a wolf, as well as to a bear. The presence of the lamb simile puts more stress on that of the wolf, the traditional antonym of the lamb. A tentative resolution of Coriolanus's identity seems about to be forthcoming when he complains of having to follow Roman custom and appear in a "woolvish tongue" (F II.iii.110). No matter whether the form of this last phrase should be emended to "wolvish toge" or sheep's "woolyish toge," almost any of the suggested readings situates Coriolanus more solidly within the lamb-wolf dichotomy, thus problematizing his identity in antithetical fashion.

3. In *Virgin Martyr*, the emperor's agents sentence their own children to death, with one agent expressing his beastlike and compulsively bloodthirsty parricidal *saevitia* as follows: "Aetna is in my brest, wildfire burnes heere, / Which onely bloud must quench"; "with mine owne hand I take that life / Which I gave to you" (III.ii.103–4, 114–15). One of the models for *Virgin Martyr*, *Titus*, opens with the Romulan clash of the royal brothers Saturninus and Bassianus at Rome's walls (cf. Paster 59–61); and at the end of Webster's *Appius*, the mourning fiancé calls the murdering Virginius "a noble Roman / But an unnatural Father" (V.i.110–11)—a verdict that would be equally appropriate also to the *paterfamilias* of the Horatii and to Lucius Junius Brutus.

Heywood's *Rape of Lucrece* depicts several of the earliest parricides in Roman history, the most obvious involving the fact that Tarquin and his "monster" wife, Tullia, slay her father (his adoptive father) and run over the corpse in her chariot. In Jonson's treatment of the Julia story, we hear the Emperor Augustus threaten to kill his daughter; *Catiline* relates three of the protagonist's literal parricides, and in *Sejanus* the number of parricides recorded, promised, or threatened is about a dozen. In *Caesar's Revenge,* two unwilling parricides, a father and son, lie dead on the field of Pharsalus; in *Claudius Tiberius Nero,* the heir apparent, Caligula, chokes to death his kinsman Tiberius Caesar. The lover of Claudius's wife in Richards's *Messallina* plans to slay his own wife in order to live with the empress, pleading for these actions the powerful Roman precedent of Catiline: "Did Lucius Cataline / Spare wife nor Childe, for Orestillas love[?]" (d913–14). The archetypal parricide, Nero, slays his wife in the anonymous 1624 play of the same name; and his mother in May's *Agrippina* of the same year. In Fletcher's *Valentinian* a wife kills a husband, and another husband orders his spouse, the play's heroine/victim, to commit suicide.

In Massinger's *Roman Actor* (1626) Domitian falls victim to his kinswomen. Dioclesian is attacked by a nephew in *The Prophetess*. Marginal examples of a parricide motif in Roman plays would include also Volumnia's treatment of Coriolanus and, in *Caesar and Pompey* (II.i.70–71), the fratricidal accomplishments of Chapman's Fronto.

Appendix B

1. The other sixteen comedies are *Amends for Ladies, Birth of Merlin, Captain, City Gallant, Coxcomb, Dumb Knight, Fair Maid of the West, Fortune by Land and Sea, Humor Out of Breath, If It Be Not Good, Night Walker, Ram Alley, Two Maids of More Clacke, Wit at Several Weapons, Woman is a Weathercock*, and *Woman's Prize*.

2. Like most of the Roman plays, the remainder of this non-Roman group of thirty-six are in basically sober genres. These include tragical histories (Webster's *White Devil*, Chapman's *Byron* and *Revenge of Bussy*, Daborne's *Christian Turned Turk*); less historical tragedies (*The Atheist's Tragedy, Match Me in London*, the Spanish tales of *Philaster* and *The Insatiate Countess*, and Sidneian romantic tragedies like *The Maid's Tragedy* and *The Second Maiden's Tragedy*); and several non-Roman tragicomedies (*Pericles, Winter's Tale, Tempest, King and No King, Faithful Shepherdess, Cupid's Revenge*).

WORKS CONSULTED

Pre-1800 Works

A[rmin?], R[obert?]. *The Valiant Welshman*. Ed. Valentin Kreb. Münchener Beitrage zur romanischen and englischen Philologie 23. Naumberg: Lippert, 1902.

Acosta, Joseph de. *The Natural and Moral History of the Indies*. Ed. Clements R. Markham. Trans. Edward Grimston. 1604. Vol. 2. Reprint of Hakluyt Society ed. New York: Burt Franklin, n.d.

Aelian [Claudius Aelianus]. *On the Characteristics of Animals*. Trans. A. F. Scholfield. 3 vols. London: Heinemann, 1959.

Aeschylus. *Aeschylus*. Trans. Herbert Weir Smyth. 2 vols. Cambridge: Harvard UP, 1952–63.

Alexander, William, Earl of Stirling. *The Tragedy of Julius Caesar*. *The Poetical Works of Sir William Alexander*. Vol. 2. Ed. L. E. Kastner and H. B. Charlton. Scottish Text Society ns 23. Edinburgh: Blackwood, 1921.

Appian [Appianos]. *Appian's Roman History*. Vol. 3. Trans. Horace White. Rev. E. Iliff Robson. London: Heinemann, 1913.

———. *An Aunciant Historie and Exquisite Chronicle of the Romanes Warres, Both Civile and Foren, with a Continuation*. Trans. W.B. London, 1578.

Aristides, Aelius. *The Roman Orator*. Qtd. in *A History of Rome, from Its origins to 529 A.D., as Told by the Roman Historians*. By Moses Hadas. Garden City: Doubleday-Anchor, 1956.

Aristotle. *Aristotles Politiques*. Trans. I.D. from the French of Loys Le Roy. London, 1598.

———. *The Poetics*. Trans. W. H. Fyfe. *Aristotle, "The Poetics"; Longinus, "On the Sublime"; Demetrius, "On Style."* London: Heinemann, 1927.

Arrian [Flavius Arrianus]. *Discourses of Epictetus*. *All the Works of Epictetus*. Trans. Elizabeth Carter. Dublin, 1759. New York: Random, 1940.

Ascham, Roger. *The Scholemaster*. Excerpted in *Elizabethan Critical Essays*. Ed. G. Gregory Smith. 2 vols. Oxford: Clarendon, 1904.

Augustine, Saint [Aurelius Augustinus]. *The City of God: John Healey's Translation with a Selection from Vives's Commentaries.* 1610. Ed. and corr. R. V. G. Tasker. 2 vols. London: Dent, 1945.

——. *The City of God Against the Pagans.* [Ed. B. Dombart and A. Kalb.] Trans. George E. McCracken. Cambridge: Harvard UP, 1957.

Aurelius, Marcus. *Meditations of Marcus Aurelius.* Trans. Meric Casaubon. 1634. London: Dent, 1906.

——. *The Meditations of Marcus Aurelius.* Trans. George Long. *Stoic and Epicurean Philosophers: The Complete Extant Writings of Epicurus, Epictetus, Lucretius, Marcus Aurelius.* Ed. Whitney J. Oates. New York: Random, 1940.

B., R. *Apius and Virginia, 1575.* Ed. R. B. McKerrow and W. W. Greg. London: Malone, 1911.

Bacon, Francis. *A Harmony of the Essays, etc.* Ed. Edward Arber. 1871. New York: AMS, 1960.

——. *The Twoo Bookes of Francis Bacon: Of the Proficience and Advancement of Learning.* 1605. Amsterdam: Da Capo, 1970.

The Bestiary: A Book of Beasts, Being a Translation from a Latin Bestiary of the Twelfth Century. Trans. T. H. White. New York: Putnam, 1954.

Bodin, J[ean]. *Method for the Easy Comprehension of History.* Trans. Beatrice Reynolds. New York: Columbia UP, 1945.

Brandon, Samuel. *The Virtuous Octavia.* 1598. Ed. R. B. McKerrow and W. W. Greg. Oxford: Malone, 1909.

Caesar's Revenge, The Tragedy of. Ed. F. S. Boas and W. W. Greg. Oxford: Malone, 1911.

Camden, William. *Britannia.* London, 1600.

——. *Remains Concerning Britain.* [1605,] 1657. New York: AMS, 1972.

Carion, John [Jean]. *The Thre Bokes of Cronicles.* [Trans. W. Lynne.] London, 1550.

C[ary, Lady] E[lizabeth]. *The Tragedy of Mariam.* 1613. [Ed. W. W. Greg.] Oxford: Malone, 1914.

Castiglione, Baldassare. *The Book of the Courtier.* Trans. Thomas Hoby. Ed. D. Henderson and E. Rhys. London: Dent, 1928.

Certaine Sermons or Homilies Appointed to Be Read in Churches in the Time of Queen Elizabeth I (1547–1571). 1623. Ed. Mary Ellen Rickey and Thomas B. Stroup. Gainesville: Scholars' Facsimiles, 1968.

Chapman, George. *Bussy D'Ambois. Elizabethan Plays.* Ed. Hazelton Spencer. Boston: Heath, 1933.

——. *Caesar and Pompey. The Plays of George Chapman: Tragedies.* Ed. T. M. Parrott. 2 vols. New York: Dutton, 1910.

---. *Revenge of Bussy D'Ambois*. *The Plays of George Chapman: Tragedies*. Ed. T. M. Parrott. New York: Dutton, 1910.
The Chester Cycle. Ed. R. M. Lumiansky and David Mills. London: Oxford UP, 1974.
Cicero, Marcus Tullius. *De officiis*. *Cicero*. Vol. 21. Trans. Walter Miller. London: Heinemann, 1913.
---. ["Dream of Scipio."] *De re publica, De legibus*. Trans. Clinton Walker Keyes. London: Heinemann, 1928.
---. *Offices*. Trans. Thomas Cockman. 1699. *"Offices" Essays, and Letters*. London: Dent, 1909.
---. *Paradoxae Stoicorum*. *Cicero*. Vol. 4. Trans. H. Rackham. Cambridge: Harvard UP, 1942.
---. [Selections from Cicero.] *Sententiae illustriores, apophthegmata item, parabolae sive similia*. Comp. Petrus Lagnerius. Paris, 1546.
Cinthio, Giovambattista Giraldi. "On the Composition of Romances." Excerpted and trans. Allan H. Gilbert. *Literary Criticism: Plato to Dryden*. New York: American Book, 1940.
Claudian [Claudius Claudianus]. *Claudian*. Vol. 1. Trans. Maurice Platnauer. London: Heinemann, 1922.
Claudius Tiberius Nero, The True Tragedy of. 1607. Ed. W. W. Greg. Oxford: Malone, 1915.
Daniel, Samuel. *Cleopatra*. *Narrative and Dramatic Sources of Shakespeare*. Vol. 5. Ed. Geoffrey Bullough. New York: Columbia UP, 1964.
D'Avenant, William. *The Cruell Brother: A Tragedy*. London, 1630.
Dekker, Thomas, and John Marston (?). *Satiromastix*. *The Dramatic Works of Thomas Dekker*. Vol. 1. Ed. Fredson Bowers. Cambridge: Cambridge UP, 1953.
--- and Philip Massinger. *The Virgin Martyr*. *The Dramatic Works of Thomas Dekker*. Vol. 3. Ed. Fredson Bowers. Cambridge: Cambridge UP, 1958.
Descartes, René. *Discours de la methode*. Leyden, 1637.
---. *A Discourse of a Method*. London, 1649.
"Dicta Catonis." *Minor Latin Poets*. Vol. 2. Trans. J. Wight Duff and Arnold Duff. London: Heinemann, 1934.
Dio, Cassius. *Dio's Roman History*. Trans. Ernest Cary and Herbert Baldwin Foster. 9 vols. 1914–27. London: Heinemann, 1954–55.
Donne, John. *John Donne's Poetry: Authoritative Texts, Criticism*. Ed. A. L. Clements. New York: Norton, 1966.
Drummond, William. "Conversations." *Ben Jonson*. Vol. 1. Ed. C. H. Herford, Percy Simpson, and Evelyn Simpson. Oxford: Clarendon, 1925. 11 vols. 1925–52.

du Bellay, Joachim. "Antiquitez de Rome." *"Les regrets," précédé de "Les antiquités de Rome" et suivi de "La défense et illustration de la langue française."* Paris: Gallimard, 1967.

Durantinus, Felicius [Costanze Felice]. [Introduction.] *Sallust: Conspiracie of Lucius Catiline*. Trans. T. Paynell. London, 1541.

Du Vair, Guillaume. *Les oeuvres*. Qtd. and trans. in *Renaissance Tragedy and the Senecan Tradition: Anger's Privilege*. By Gordon Braden. New Haven: Yale UP, 1985.

Epictetus. *The Manuell of Epictetus*. Trans. J. Sanford. London, 1567.

Erasmus, Desiderius. *The Education of a Christian Prince*. Trans. Lester K. Born. 1936. New York: Octagon, 1965.

Estienne, Charles [Carolus Stephanus]. *Dictionarium historicum, geographicum, poeticum*. 1596. New York: Garland, 1976.

The Faithful Friends. Malone Rpts. Oxford: Oxford UP, 1975.

Ferrarius [Montanus]. Qtd. in *Tragedies of Tyrants: Political Thought and Theater in the English Renaissance*. By Rebecca Weld Bushnell. Ithaca: Cornell UP, 1990.

Fisher, Jasper. *Fuimus Troes. A Select Collection of Old English Plays*. Vol. 12. Ed. Robert Dodsley and W. Carew Hazlitt. 4th ed. 1874. New York: Blom, 1964.

Fletcher, John. *Bonduca*. Ed. Cyrus Hoy. *The Dramatic Works in the Beaumont and Fletcher Canon*. Vol. 4. Gen. ed. Fredson Bowers. Cambridge: Cambridge UP, 1974.

———. *The Tragedy of Valentinian*. Ed. Robert K. Turner, Jr. *The Dramatic Works in the Beaumont and Fletcher Canon*. Gen. ed. Fredson Bowers. Vol. 14. Cambridge: Cambridge UP, 1974.

Fletcher, John, and Philip Massinger. *The False One*. Ed. A. R. Waller. *The Works of Francis Beaumont and John Fletcher*. Vol. 3. Cambridge: Cambridge UP, 1906. 10 vols. 1905–12.

———. *The Prophetess*. Ed. A. R. Waller. *The Works of Francis Beaumont and John Fletcher*. Vol. 5. Cambridge: Cambridge UP, 1907. 10 vols. 1905–12.

Fulbecke, William. *An Historicall Collection of the Continuall Factions, Tumults, and Massacres of the Romans and Italians*. Qtd. in "Shakespeare and the Elizabethan Romans." By T. J. B. Spencer. *Shakespeare Survey* 10 (1957): 21–38.

Garnier, Robert. *Cornélie. Oeuvres complètes (théâtre et poesies) de Robert Garnier*. Ed. Lucien Pinvert. 2 vols. Paris: Garnier Frères, 1923.

———. *Marc Antoine. Two Tragedies: "Hippolyte" and "Marc Antoine."* Ed. Christine M. Hill and Mary G. Morrison. London: Athlone, 1975.

The Geneva Bible: A Facsimile of the 1560 Edition. Intro. Lloyd E. Berry. Madison: U of Wisconsin P, 1969.

Gesta Romanorum. Trans. Charles Swan. London: Routledge, [1924].

Giovio, Paulo. *The Worthy Tract of Paulus Jovius*. Trans. Samuel Daniel. London, 1585.

Grafton, Richard. *A Chronicle at Large and Meere History of the Affayres of England*. London, 1569.

Greene, John. *A Refutation of the Apology for Actors*. 1605. Qtd. in "Seneca and the Elizabethans: A Case-Study in 'Influence.'" By George K. Hunter. *Shakespeare Survey* 20 (1967): 23.

Grimald, Nicholas. "Marcus Tullius Ciceroes Death." *Tottel's Miscellany (1557–1587)*. Vol. 1. Ed. H. E. Rollins. 1928. Rev. ed. Cambridge: Harvard UP, 1965.

Hakluyt, Richard. *The Principal Navigations, Voyages, Traffiques & Discoveries of the English Nation*. 2nd ed. 1598–1600. Vol. 8. New York: AMS, 1965.

Hemming [alias Heminges], William. *The Jewes Tragedy*. Ed. Heinrich A. Cohn. Materialen zur Kunde des älteren englischen Dramas 40. Louvain: Uystprust, 1913.

Henslowe, Philip. *Henslowe's Diary*. Ed. R. A. Foakes and R. T. Rickert. Cambridge: Cambridge UP, 1961.

Heywood, Thomas. *The Rape of Lucrece*. Ed. Allan Holaday. Urbana: U of Illinois P, 1950.

The Holy Bible, Translated from the Later Vulgate ["Rheims"]. Ed. George Leo Haydock, F. C. Husenbeth, et al. 1812. New York: George Virtue, 1850.

Horace [Quintus Horatius Flaccus]. *Satires, Epistles, and Ars Poetica*. Rev. ed. Trans. H. Rushton Fairclough. Cambridge: Harvard UP, 1970.

James, Thomas. "Epistle Dedicatorie." *The Moral Philosophie of the Stoicks*. By Guillaume Du Vair. Trans. Thomas James. Ed. Rudolf Kirk. New Brunswick: Rutgers UP, 1951.

Jonson, Ben. *The Alchemist*. *Ben Jonson*. Vol. Ed. C. H. Herford, Percy Simpson, and Evelyn Simpson. Oxford: Clarendon.

———. *Catiline*. Ed. W. F. Bolton and Jane F. Gardner. Regents Renaissance Drama. Lincoln: U of Nebraska P, 1973.

———. *The Poetaster*. Ed. George Parfitt. Nottingham: Nottingham Drama Texts, 1979.

———. *Sejanus*. Ed. Jonas A. Barish. Yale Ben Jonson. New Haven: Yale UP, 1965.

———. *Volpone*. Ed. Alvin B. Kernan. Yale Ben Jonson. New Haven: Yale UP, 1962.

Juvenal [Decimus Iunius Iuvenalis]. *Juvenal and Persius*. [*Satires*.] Trans. G. G. Ramsay. Rev. ed. Cambridge: Harvard UP, 1940.

Kelton, Arthur. *A Chronycle with a Genealogie*. London, 1547.

Killigrew, Thomas. *The Princess; or, Love at First Sight. Comedies and Tragedies Written by Thomas Killigrew.* 1664. New York: Blom, 1967.

Kyd, Thomas. *Pompey the Great His Faire Corneliaes Tragedie. The Works of Thomas Kyd.* Ed. Frederick S. Boas. Oxford: Clarendon, 1901.

[Languet, Hubert, or Philippe de Mornay, Seigneur du Plessis-Marly?]. *Defense of Liberty Against Tyrants: A Translation of "Vindiciae contra tyrannos" by Junius Brutus.* Intro. by Harold J. Laski. 1924. New York: Franklin, 1972.

La Perriére, Guillaume, de. *La Morosophie, contenant cent emblèmes moraux illustrez de cent tétrastiques latins, réduitz en autant de quatrains françoys.* Lyons, 1553.

Las Casas, Bartolome de. *In Defense of the Indians.* Trans. Stafford Poole. De Kalb: Northern Illinois UP, 1992.

Lee, Nathaniel. *The Works of Nathaniel Lee.* Ed. Thomas B. Stroup and Arthur L. Cooke. 2 vols. New Brunswick: Scarecrow, 1954.

Lindsay, David. *The Works of David Lindsay of the Mount, 1490–1555.* Ed. Douglas Hamer. 4 vols. Edinburgh: Blackwood, 1931–36.

Lipsius, Justus [Juste Lipse]. *Two Bookes of Constancie.* Trans. John Stradling. Ed. Rudolf Kirk. Notes by Clayton M. Hall. New Brunswick: Rutgers UP, 1939.

Livy [Titus Livius]. *The Early History of Rome.* Trans. Aubrey de Sélincourt. Harmondsworth, Eng.: Penguin, 1970.

———. *Livy.* Vol. 1. Trans. B. O. Foster. London: Heinemann, 1919.

Lloyd, Lodewick. *The Consent of Time.* London, 1590.

Lodge, Thomas. *The Wounds of Civil War.* Ed. Joseph W. Houppert. Lincoln: U of Nebraska P, 1969.

Lucan [Marcus Annaeus Lucanus]. "The First Booke of Lucan." Trans. Christopher Marlowe. *The Poems.* By Christopher Marlowe. Ed. Millar MacLure. Gen. ed. Clifford Leach. London: Methuen, 1968.

———. *The Civil War (Pharsalia).* Ed. A. E. Housman. Trans. and rev. J. D. Duff. 2 vols. Cambridge: Harvard UP, 1928.

———. *Lucan's "Pharsalia"; or, The Civill Warres of Rome, betweene Pompey the Great, and Julius Caesar.* Trans. Thomas May. London, 1627.

———. *The "Pharsalia" of Lucan.* Trans. H. T. Riley. London: Bell, 1889.

Machiavelli, Niccolò. *The Discourses.* Trans. Leslie J. Walker and Brian Richardson. Ed. Bernard Crick. Harmondsworth, Eng.: Penguin, 1970.

Machin, Lewis. *Every Woman in Her Humor.* [1609.] Ed. John S. Farmer. 1913. New York: AMS, 1970.

Mantuan [us, Giovanni Battista Spagnuoli]. *The Eclogues.* Ed. Wilfred P. Mustard. Baltimore: Johns Hopkins UP, 1911.

Marcus Tullius Cicero, The Tragedy of That Famous Orator. London, 1651.

Markham, Gervase, and William Sampson. *The True Tragedy of Herod and Antipater.* London, 1622.

Marlowe, Christopher. *Doctor Faustus.* Ed. J. D. Jump. London: Methuen, 1962.

———. *Doctor Faustus, 1604–1616: Parallel Texts.* Ed. W. W. Greg. Oxford: Clarendon, 1950.

———. *Edward II. The Complete Works of Christopher Marlowe.* Ed. Fredson Bowers. 2 vols. Cambridge: Cambridge UP, 1973.

———. *Jew of Malta: Text and Major Criticism.* Ed. Irving Ribner. New York: Odyssey, 1970.

———. *Massacre at Paris.* Ed. H. S. Bennett. *The Works and Life of Christopher Marlowe.* Vol. 3. 1931. Gen. ed. R. H. Case. New York: Gordian, 1967.

———. *Tamburlaine the Great.* Ed. J. D. Jump. Lincoln: U of Nebraska P, 1967.

Marston, John. *The Wonder of Women; or, The Tragedy of Sophonisba.* Ed. William Kemp. New York: Garland, 1979.

Marvell, Andrew. *Selected Poetry.* Ed. Frank Kermode. New York: Signet, 1967.

Massinger, Philip. *Believe As You List. The Plays and Poems of Philip Massinger.* Vol. 3. Gen. eds. Philip Edwards and Colin Gibson. Oxford: Clarendon, 1976.

———. *Believe As You List.* Ed. C. J. Sisson. London: Malone, 1927.

———. *A Critical Edition of Massinger's "The Roman Actor."* Ed. William Lee Sandidge, Jr. Princeton: Princeton UP, 1929.

———. *The Maid of Honour. The Plays and Poems of Philip Massinger.* Vol. 1. Gen. eds. Philip Edwards and Colin Gibson. Oxford: Clarendon, 1976.

May, Thomas. *The Tragedy of Cleopatra, Queene of Ægypt.* Ed. Denzell Stewart Smith. 1965. New York: Garland, 1979.

———. *Tragedy of Julia Agrippina, Empresse of Rome.* Ed. P. Ernst Schmid. Materialen zur Kunde de älteren englischen Dramas 43. Louvain: Uystprust, 1914.

Medwall, Henry. *Fulgens and Lucres. The Plays of Henry Medwall: A Critical Edition.* Ed. M. E. Moeslin. New York: Garland, 1981.

Merbury, Charles. *A Briefe Discourse of Royall Monarchie.* London, 1581.

Milton, John. *Paradise Regained. Complete Poems and Major Prose.* Ed. Merritt Y. Hughes. New York: Odyssey, 1957.

Le mistère du Viel Testament. Ed. James de Rothschild. 6 vols. Paris: Société des anciens textes français. 1891.

Montaigne, Michel de. *The Essays of Montaigne.* Trans. John Florio. Ed. W. W. Henley. Intro. George Saintsbury. 3 vols. London: Nutt, 1892–93.

Nabbes, Thomas. *Hannibal and Scipio: An Historical Tragedy. The Works of Thomas Nabbes.* Ed. A. H. Bullen. 2 vols. Old English Plays n.s. 1882. New York: Benjamin Blom, 1964.

Nero, The Tragedy of. Ed. Elliott M. Hill. New York: Garland, 1979.

"A Nest of Perfidious Vipers." 21 September 1644. *The Harleian Miscellany*. Vol. 2. 1809. New York: AMS, 1965. 590–94.

Norton, Thomas, and Thomas Sackville. *Gorboduc*. *Early English Classical Tragedies*. Oxford: Clarendon, 1912.

Orosius, Paulus. *The Seven Books of History Against the Pagans*. Trans. Irving Woodworth Raymond. New York: Columbia UP, 1936.

Ovid [Publius Ovidius Naso]. *The XV Bookes Entytuled Metamorphosis*. Trans. Arthur Golding. 1567. Amsterdam: Da Capo, 1977.

——— . *Metamorphoses*. Trans. Frank Justus Miller. 2 vols. 1916. London: Heinemann, 1977.

——— . *Ovid's "Metamorphosis" Englished, Mythologized, and Represented in Figures*. Trans. George Sandys. [1632.] Ed. John Frederick Nims. New York: Macmillan, 1965.

Peacham, Henry. *Minerva Britanna*. 1612. Amsterdam: Da Capo, 1971.

Pegme, Petrus Costalius [Pierre Coustau]. *Cum narrationibus philosophicis*. Lyons, 1555.

Pembroke, Mary Sidney Herbert, Countess of. *The Tragedie of Antonie*. *Narrative and Dramatic Sources of Shakespeare*. Vol. 5. Ed. Geoffrey Bullough. London: Routledge, 1964.

Plato. *Euthyphro, Apology, Crito, Phaedo, Phaedrus*. Trans. Harold North Fowler. London: Heinemann, 1914.

——— . *The Republic*. Trans. Paul Shorey. 2 vols. London: Heinemann, 1930–35.

Pliny the Elder [Gaius Plinius Secundus]. *Natural History*. 4 vols. Cambridge: Harvard UP, 1938–63.

Plutarch [L.(?) Mestrius Plutarchus]. *The Lives of the Noble Grecians and Romans*. [1579.] Trans. Thomas North. Intro. George Wyndham. 6 vols. 1895–96. New York: AMS, 1967.

——— . *The Lives of the Noble Grecians and Romanes*. [Selections.] Trans. Thomas North. *Narrative and Dramatic Sources of Shakespeare*. Vol. 5. Ed. Geoffrey Bullough. London: Routledge, 1964.

——— . *Plutarch's Lives*. Trans. Bernadotte Perrin. 11 vols. London: Heinemann, 1914.

——— . *Plutarch's "Romane Questions."* Trans. Philemon Holland. Ed. Frank Byron Jevons. London: Nutt, 1892.

Pope, Alexander. *An Essay on Man*. Ed. Maynard Mack. The Twickenham Edition. Gen. ed. John Butt. London: Methuen, 1950.

Procopius. *History*. Excerpted and trans. Moses Hadas. *A History of Rome, from Its origins to 529 A.D. as Told by the Roman Historians*. By Moses Hadas. Garden City: Doubleday-Anchor, 1956.

Prudentius, Aurelius Clemens. *Prudence [Oeuvres]*. Ed. and trans. M. Lavarenne. 4 vols. Paris: Les Belles Lettres, 1955–63.
Purchas, Samuel. Marginalia. Qtd. in *Threshold of a Nation*. By Philip Edwards. Cambridge: Cambridge UP, 1979.
Rainolde, Richard. *The Foundacion of Rhetorike*. 1563. Amsterdam: Da Capo, 1969.
Richards, Nathaniel. *Tragedy of Messallina, the Romane Emperesse*. Ed. A. R. Skemp. Materialen zur Kunde des älteren englischen Dramas 30. Louvain: Uystprust, 1910.
Ripa, Cesare. *Iconologia, overo descrittione d'imagini*. Intro. Erna Mandowsky. [Rome,] 1603. Hildesheim: Olms, 1970.
———. *Iconologie*. Trans. J[ean] Baudoin. Paris, 1636.
———. *Iconologie*. Trans. J[ean] Baudoin. Paris, 1644.
———. *Iconologie*. Trans. J[ean] Baudoin. Amsterdam, 1698.
Rowley, William. *William Rowley, His "All's Lost by Lust," and "A Shoemaker, a Gentleman."* Ed. C. W. Stork. Philadelphia: U of Pennsylvania P, 1910.
Sallust [Gaius Sallustius Crispus]. *Jugurtha; Conspiracy of Cateline*. Trans. Thomas Heywood. London, 1609.
———. *Jugurthine War; The Conspiracy of Catiline*. Trans. S. A. Handford. Baltimore: Penguin, 1963.
Seneca, Lucius Annaeus. *Ad Lucilium*. Ed. and trans. Richard M. Gunmere. 3 vols. London: Heinemann, 1917–25.
———. *De providentia* [Providence], *De constantia [sapientis]* [Firmness of the Wise Man], *De ira* [Anger], *De clementia* [Mercy]. *Moral Essays*. Vol. 1. Ed. and trans. John W. Basare. London: Heinemann, 1928.
———. *Octavia*. *Seneca His Tenne Tragedies, translated into English*. 1581. Trans. Thomas Nuce. Ed. Thomas Newton. Intro. T. S. Eliot. 1927. Bloomington: Indiana UP, 1966. 143–90.
———. *Tragedies*. Trans. Frank Justus Miller. 2 vols. Rev. ed. London: Heinemann, 1929.
———. *The Workes of Lucius Annaeus Seneca, Both Moral and Naturall*. Trans. Thomas Lodge. London, 1614.
Seneca, Marcus Annaeus. *The Suasoriae of Seneca the Elder*. Ed. and trans. William A. Edwards. Cambridge: Cambridge UP, 1928.
Shakespeare, William. *The Riverside Shakespeare*. Gen. ed. G. Blakemore Evans. Boston: Houghton, 1974.
Shirley, James. *The Humorous Courtier: A Comedy*. London, 1640.
Sidney, Sir Philip. *The Defense of Poesie*. *Literary Criticism: Plato to Dryden*. Selected and ed. Allan H. Gilbert. New York: American Books, 1940.

Spenser, Edmund. "Ruines of Rome." *The Poetical Works of Edmund Spenser*. Ed. J. C. Smith and E. DeSelincourt. London: Oxford UP, 1912.
Suetonius [Gaius Suetonius Tranquillus]. *History of the Twelve Caesars*. Trans. Philemon Holland. London, 1606.
———. *Suetonius*. [Ed. Maximilian Ihm.] Trans. J. C. Rolfe. Rev. ed. 2 vols. Cambridge: Harvard UP, 1951.
Tacitus, Gaius Cornelius. *Agricola. The Ende of Nero and Beginning of Galba*. Trans. Henry Savile. 2nd ed. London, 1598.
———. *Annals*. Ed. John Jackson. 4 vols. London: Heinemann, 1931–37.
Textor Ravisius, Joannes [Jean Tixier de Ravisy]. *Epithetorum opus absolutissimum*. Ed. and expanded by J. Fella. Venice, 1654.
———. *Officina Joannis Textoris epitome*. Vol. 1. Lyons, 1560.
Thomas, William. *History of Italy*. 1575. Qtd. in *The Italian Renaissance in England*. By Lewis Einstein. Columbia U Studies in English and Comparative Literature. 1903. New York: Franklin, 1970.
Topsell, Edward. *The Historie of Serpents; or, The Second Booke of Living Creatures*. 1608. Amsterdam: Da Capo, 1973.
Townshend, Aurelian. *Albion's Triumph*. London, 1632.
The Two Noble Ladies. Ed. R. G. Rhoads and W. W. Greg. Oxford: Malone, 1930.
Valeriano Bolzani [Valeriano da Bolzano], Giovanni Pierio [Joannes Pierius Valerianus]. *Commentaires hiéroglyphiques ou Images des choses*. Trans. Gabriel Chappuys. 2 vols. Lyons, 1576.
———. *Hieroglyphica seu De sacris Aegyptiorum aliarumque gentium commentarii*. 2 vols. Lyons, 1586.
———. *Hieroglyphica: Lyon, 1602*. 1602. New York: Garland, 1976.
———. *Les hiéroglyphiques: Lyon 1615*. Trans. I. de Montlyard. 1615. New York: Garland, 1976.
Vergil [Publius Vergilius Maro]. *Virgil, with an English Translation*. Ed. and trans. H. Rushton Fairclough. 2 vols. 1918. Rev. ed. Cambridge: Harvard UP, 1934.
———. *The XIII Bookes of Aeneidos*. Trans. Thomas Phaer and Thomas Twyne. London, 1584.
Vives, Juan Luis [Joannes Lodovicus Vives]. *St. Augustine's "Of the City of God" with the Learned Comments of Jo. Lod. Vives*. Trans. John Healey. London, 1610.
Webster, John. *Appius and Virginia. The Complete Works of John Webster*. Vol. 3. Ed. F. L. Lucas. 1927. 4 vols. New York: Gordian, 1966.
———. *Duchess of Malfi. The Complete Works of John Webster*. Vol. 2. Ed. F. L. Lucas. 1927. New York: Gordian, 1966.
Whitney, Geoffrey. *Whitney's "Choice of Emblemes."* [1586.] Ed. Henry Green. London, 1866.

Wilmot, Robert, et al. *Gismond of Salern. Early English Classical Tragedies*. Ed. John W. Cunliffe. Oxford: Clarendon, 1912.

———. *The Tragedy of Tancred and Gismund*. Ed. W. W. Greg. Oxford: Malone, 1915.

Worthies Pageant. Coventry Leet Book, 1455. "Verses on the Nine Worthies." Ed. Roger Sherman Loomis. *Modern Philology* 15 (1917): 211–19. 218.

Wotton, Sir Henry. *Elements of Architecture*. 1624. Ed. Frederick Hard. Washington: Folger/UP of Virginia, 1968.

Other Works

Adams, J. N. *The Latin Sexual Vocabulary*. London: Duckworth, 1982.

Adelman, Janet. "'Anger's My Meat': Feeding, Dependency, and Aggression in *Coriolanus*." *Shakespeare: Pattern of Excelling Nature*. Ed. David Bevington and Jay L. Halio. Newark: U of Delaware P, 1978. 108–24.

———. *The Common Liar: An Essay on "Antony and Cleopatra."* New Haven: Yale UP, 1973.

Adler, Doris. *Philip Massinger*. Boston: Twayne, 1987.

Adler, Mortimer J. *Philosopher at Large: An Intellectual Autobiography*. New York: Macmillan, 1977.

Ahern, Mathew Joseph, Jr. "The Roman History Play, 1585–1640." Diss. Tulane U, 1963.

Ahl, Frederick M. *Lucan: An Introduction*. Ithaca: Cornell UP, 1976.

Alvis, John. "The Coherence of Shakespeare's Roman Plays." *Modern Language Quarterly* 40 (1979): 115–34.

Anderson, Ruth L. "Kingship in Renaissance Drama." *Studies in Philology* 41 (1914): 136–55.

Anson, John. "*Julius Caesar:* The Politics of the Hardened Heart." *Shakespeare Studies* 2 (1966): 11–22.

Armstrong, W. A. "The Elizabethan Conception of the Tyrant." *Review of English Studies* 22 (1946): 161–81.

———. "The Influence of Seneca and Machiavelli on the Elizabethan Tyrant." *Review of English Studies* 24 (1948): 19–35.

Auerbach, Erich. *Mimesis: The Representation of Reality in Western Literature*. Trans. Willard R. Trask. Princeton: Princeton UP, 1953.

Avery, Charles. *Florentine Renaissance Sculpture*. London: Murray, 1970.

Ayres, Philip J. "The Nature of Jonson's Roman History." *ELR* 16 (1986): 166–81.

Bakhtin, M[ikhail] M. *The Dialogic Imagination*. Trans. Caryl Michael Holquist. Austin: U of Texas P, 1981.

Baldwin, T. W. *William Shakespere's Small Latine and Lesse Greeke.* 2 vols. Urbana: U of Illinois P, 1944.

———, ed. *Troilus and Cressida.* By William Shakespeare. Variorum Shakespeare. Ed. Harold N. Hillebrand and T. W. Baldwin. Philadelphia: Lippincott, 1953.

Barroll, J. Leeds. "Shakespeare and Roman History." *Modern Language Review* 53 (1958): 327–43.

Barton, Anne. *Ben Jonson, Dramatist.* Cambridge: Cambridge UP, 1984.

———. "*Julius Caesar* and *Coriolanus:* Shakespeare's Roman World of Words." *Shakespeare's Craft: Eight Lectures.* The Tupper Lectures on Shakespeare, sponsored by the George Washington U. Ed. Philip H. Highfill, Jr. Carbondale: Southern Illinois UP, 1982. 24–47.

———. "Livy, Machiavelli, and Shakespeare's *Coriolanus.*" *Shakespeare Survey* 38 (1985): 115–29.

Bethell, S. L. *Shakespeare and the Popular Tradition.* 1944. New York: Octagon, 1970.

Bevington, David. *Tudor Drama and Politics: A Critical Approach to Topical Meaning.* Cambridge: Harvard UP, 1968.

Bianchi Bandinelli, Ranuccio. *Rome: The Center of Power, 500 B.C. to A.D. 200.* New York: Braziller, 1970.

Blissett, William. "Caesar and Satan." *Journal of the History of Ideas* 18 (1957): 221–32.

———. "Lucan's Caesar and the Elizabethan Villain." *Studies in Philology* 53 (1956): 353–75.

Booth, Stephen. *Shakespeare's Sonnets.* New Haven: Yale UP, 1977.

Booty, John F. *The Book of Common Prayer, 1559.* Washington: Folger, 1976.

Braden, Gordon. *Renaissance Tragedy and the Senecan Tradition: Anger's Privilege.* New Haven: Yale UP, 1985.

Brenton, Howard. *The Romans in Britain.* London: Methuen, 1980.

Briggs, William Dinsmore. "The Influence of Jonson on the Seventeenth Century." *Anglia* 35 (1912): 277–337.

Brockbank J. Philip. "History and Histrionics in *Cymbeline.*" *Shakespeare Survey* 11 (1958): 42–49.

———. "Shakespeare His Histories, English and Roman." *English Drama to 1710.* Ed. Christopher Ricks. History of Literature in the English Language 3. London: Sphere, 1971. 166–99.

Broude, Ronald. "Roman and Goth in *Titus Andronicus.*" *Shakespeare Survey* 6 (1970): 27–34.

Brower, Reuben. *Hero and Saint: Shakespeare and the Graeco-Roman Heroic Tradition.* New York: Oxford UP, 1971.

Bullough, Geoffrey. *Narrative and Dramatic Sources of Shakespeare.* 8 vols. London: Routledge, 1957–75.

———. "Pre-Conquest Historical Themes in Elizabethan Drama." *Medieval Literature and Civilization: Studies in Memory of G. N. Garmonsway*. Ed. D. A. Pearsall and R. A. Waldroup. London: Athlone–U of London, 1969. 289–321.

Burckhardt, Jacob. *The Civilization of the Renaissance in Italy*. Trans. S. G. C. Middlemore. 2 vols. 1929. New York: Harper, 1958.

Burckhardt, Sigurd. *Shakespearean Meanings*. Princeton: Princeton UP, 1968.

Burke, Kenneth. "The Temporizing of Essence." *A Grammar of Motives*. Cleveland: Meridian, 1962. 430–40.

Burke, Peter. *The Renaissance Sense of the Past*. London: Arnold, 1969.

Bushnell, Rebecca Weld. *Tragedies of Tyrants: Political Thought and Theater in the English Renaissance*. Ithaca: Cornell UP, 1990.

Butler, Martin. "Romans in Britain: *The Roman Actor* and the Early Stuart Classical Play." *Philip Massinger: A Critical Reassessment*. Ed. Douglas Howard. Cambridge: Cambridge UP, 1985. 139–70.

Cantor, Paul. *Shakespeare's Rome: Republic and Empire*. Ithaca: Cornell UP, 1976.

Čapek, Milič. "Time." *Dictionary of the History of Ideas*. Ed. Philip P. Wiener. Vol. 4. New York: Scribner's, 1972. 389–98.

Caputi, Albert. *John Marston, Satirist*. Ithaca: Cornell UP, 1961.

Carcopino, Jérôme. *Daily Life in Ancient Rome*. Trans. E. O. Lorimer. Ed. Henry T. Rowell. 1941. Harmondsworth: Penguin, 1956.

Carnicelli, D. D. Introduction. *Lord Morley's Tryumphes of Fraunces Petrarke: The First English Translation of the "Trionfi."* Cambridge: Harvard UP, 1971.

Cavell, Stanley. "'Who Does the Wolf Love?' *Coriolanus* and the Interpretations of Politics." *Shakespeare and the Question of Theory*. Ed. Patricia Parker and Geoffrey Hartman. New York: Methuen, 1985. 245–72.

Chambers, E. K. *The Elizabethan Stage*. 4 vols. Oxford: Clarendon, 1923.

Chambers, Frank McMinn. "Lucan and the *Antiquitez de Rome*." *PMLA* 60 (1945): 937–48.

Charlton, H. B. "Introduction." *The Poetical Works of Sir William Alexander, Earl of Stirling*. Ed. L. E. Kastner and H. B. Charlton. Vol. 1. Scottish Text Society ns 23. Edinburgh: Blackwood, 1921. 2 vols. 1: xvii–cc.

Charlton, John. *The Banqueting House, Whitehall*. 1964. London: Department of the Environment, 1983.

Charney, Maurice. *Shakespeare's Roman Plays: The Function of Imagery in the Drama*. Cambridge: Harvard UP, 1961.

Chastel, André. "French Renaissance Art in a European Context." *Sixteenth Century Journal* 12 (1981): 77–103.

Cheney, Donald. "Tarquin, Juliet, and Other *Romei*: Shakespeare's Myth of Rome." *Spenser Studies* 3 (1982): 111–24.

Cochrane, Charles Norris. *Christianity and Classical Culture: A Study of Thought and Action from Augustus to Augustine.* New York: Oxford UP, 1957.

Collingwood, R. G. *Essays in the Philosophy of History.* Ed. William Debbins. Austin: U of Texas P, 1965.

———. *The Idea of History.* New York: Oxford UP, 1956.

Cruickshank, Alfred H. *Philip Massinger.* Oxford: Clarendon, 1920.

Dean, Paul. "Tudor Humanism and the Roman Past: A Background to Shakespeare." *Renaissance Quarterly* 41 (1988): 84–111.

DeLuna, B. N. *Jonson's Romish Plot: A Study of "Catiline" in Its Historical Context.* Oxford: Clarendon, 1967.

Derrida, Jacques. *Of Grammatology.* Trans. Gayatri Chakravorty Spivak. Baltimore: Johns Hopkins UP, 1976.

Dollimore, Jonathan. *Radical Tragedy: Religion, Ideology and Power in the Drama of Shakespeare and His Contemporaries.* Brighton, Eng.: Harvester, 1984.

Donaldson, Ian. *The Rapes of Lucretia: A Myth and Its Transformations.* Oxford: Clarendon, 1982.

Dublin, Louis I., and Bessie Bunzel. *To Be or Not to Be: A Study of Suicide.* New York: H. Smith and R. Haas, 1933.

DuBon, David. *Tapestries from the Samuel H. Kress Collection at the Philadelphia Museum of Art: "The History of Constantine the Great," Designed by Peter Paul Rubens and Pietro da Cortona.* Philadelphia: Phaidon, 1964.

Duffy, Ellen M. T. "Ben Jonson's Debt to Renaissance Scholarship in *Sejanus* and *Catiline*." *Modern Language Review* 42 (1947): 24–30.

Dunkle, J. Roger. "The Greek Tyrant and Roman Political Invective of the Late Republic." *Transactions of the American Philological Association* 98 (1967): 151–71.

Dutton, A. R. "'What Ministers Men Must, for Practice, Use': Ben Jonson's Cicero." *English Studies* 59 (1978): 324–35.

Dyce, Alexander, ed. *The Faithful Friends. The Works of Beaumont & Fletcher.* Vol 4. 1844. London: Moxon, 1855.

Edwards, Philip. "The Royal Pretenders in Massinger and Ford." *Essays and Studies* 27 (1974): 18–36.

———. *Threshold of a Nation.* Cambridge: Cambridge UP, 1979.

Ehrmann, Jean. *Antoine Caron: Peintre des fêtes et des massacres.* Centre National des Lettres. Paris: Flammarion, 1986.

Einstein, Lewis. *The Italian Renaissance in England.* Columbia U Studies in English and Comparative Literature. 1903. New York: Franklin, 1970.

Eliot, T. S. *Complete Poems and Plays of T. S. Eliot.* London: Faber, 1969.

Empson, William. *Seven Types of Ambiguity.* 2nd ed. Norwalk: New Directions, 1949.

———. *The Structure of Complex Words*. 1951. Ann Arbor: U of Michigan P, 1967.
Evett, David. "Mammon's Grotto: Sixteenth-Century Visual Grotesquerie and Some Features of Spenser's *Faerie Queene*." *English Literary Renaissance* 12 (1982): 180–209.
Ewbanks, Inga-Stina. "Webster, Tourneur, and Ford." *English Drama (Excluding Shakespeare): Select Bibliographical Guides*. Ed. Stanley Wells. London: Oxford UP, 1975. 113–33.
Farnham, Willard F. *The Medieval Heritage of Elizabethan Tragedy*. Berkeley and Los Angeles: U of California P, 1936.
Farrell, Kirby. "Prophetic Behavior in Shakespeare's Histories." *Shakespeare Studies* 19 (1987): 17–40.
Fichter, Andrew. "*Antony and Cleopatra:* The Time of Universal Peace." *Shakespeare Survey* 33 (1980): 99–111.
FitzHerbert, Margaret. "High and Low." Rev. of *Rome: The Biography of a City*, by Christopher Hibbert. *Times Literary Supplement* 12 July 1985. 769.
Foucault, Michel. *The Foucault Reader*. Ed. Paul Rabinow. New York: Pantheon, 1984.
Fowler, Warde. *The Roman Festivals of the Period of the Republic*. London: Macmillan, 1916.
Freccero, John. "Dante's Firm Foot and the Journey Without a Guide." *Harvard Theological Review* 52 (1959): 245–81.
Frye, Richard Nelso. "Parthia." *Encyclopedia Britannica*. 1973.
Fumerton, Patricia. *Cultural Aesthetics: Renaissance Literature and the Practice of Social Ornament*. Chicago: U of Chicago P, 1991.
Galinsky, G. Karl. *Ovid's "Metamorphoses": An Introduction to the Basic Aspects*. Berkeley and Los Angeles: U of California P, 1975.
Garber, Marjorie. *Shakespeare's Ghost Writers: Literature as Uncanny Causality*. New York: Methuen, 1987.
Gauthier, Maximilien. *The Louvre: Paintings*. Trans. Kenneth Martin Leake. New York: Appleton-Century, 1964.
Gentili, Vanna. "Thomas Lodge's *Wounds of Civil War:* An Assessment of Context, Sources, and Structure." *REAL: The Yearbook of Research in English and American Literature* 2 (1984): 119–64.
Gill, Roma. "'Necessitie of State': Massinger's *Believe As You List*." *English Studies* 46 (1965): 407–16.
Gillies, John. *Shakespeare and the Geography of Difference*. Cambridge: Cambridge UP, 1994.
Girard, René. *Violence and the Sacred*. Trans. Patrick Gregory. Baltimore: Johns Hopkins UP, 1977.

Glasser, Marvin. "Spenser as Mannerist Poet: The 'Antique Image' in Book IV of *The Faerie Queene*." *SEL* 31 (1991): 25–50.

Goldberg, Jonathan. *James I and the Politics of Literature*. Baltimore: Johns Hopkins UP, 1983.

Green, David C. *"Julius Caesar" and Its Source*. Salzburg: Institut für Englische Sprache und Literatur, 1974.

———. *Plutarch Revisited: A Study of Shakespeare's Last Roman Tragedies and Their Source*. Salzburg: Institut für Anglistik und Amerikanistik Literatur, 1979.

Greenblatt, Stephen. "Invisible Bullets: Renaissance Authority and Its Subversion." *Glyph: Johns Hopkins Textual Studies* 8. Baltimore: Johns Hopkins UP, 1981. 40–61.

Greene, Thomas M. *The Light in Troy: Imitation and Discovery in Renaissance Poetry*. New Haven: Yale UP, 1982.

Greenough, J. B., G. L. Kittredge, and Thornton Jenkins. *Virgil and Other Latin Poets*. Rev. ed. Boston: Ginn, 1930.

Gross, Allen. "Contemporary Politics in Massinger." *Studies in English Literature, 1500–1900* 6 (1966): 279–90.

Hadas, Moses. *A History of Rome, from Its origins to 529 AD, as Told by the Roman Historians*. Garden City: Doubleday-Anchor, 1956.

———. "Roman Allusion in Rabbinic Literature." *Philological Quarterly* 8 (1929): 369–87.

Halstead, William P. *Shakespeare as Spoken: A Collation of Five Thousand Acting Editions and Prompt Books of Shakespeare*. Vol. 9. Ann Arbor: UMI, 1978.

Hamilton, Edith. *The Roman Way to Western Civilization*. New York: Norton, 1932.

Hanfmann, George. "Giants." *The Oxford Classical Dictionary*. 2nd ed. 1970.

Hanford, James Holly. "Suicide in the Plays of Shakespeare." *PMLA* 27 (1912): 380–97.

Hankins, John E. "Suicide in Shakespeare." *The Character of Hamlet and Other Essays*. Chapel Hill: U of North Carolina P, 1941. 222–39.

Harbage, Alfred. *Annals of English Drama, 975–1700*. Rev. S. Schoenbaum. Philadelphia: U of Pennsylvania P, 1964.

Hard, Frederick, ed. *Elements of Architecture*. By Sir Henry Wotton. 1624. Washington: Folger/UP of Virginia, 1968.

Harris, Lynn Harold. *Ben Jonson's "Catiline His Conspiracy."* Yale Studies in English 53. New Haven: Yale UP, 1916.

Haskell, Francis, and Nicholas Penny. *Taste and the Antique: The Lure of Classical Sculpture, 1500–1900*. New Haven: Yale UP, 1981.

Haywood, Richard M. "Shakespeare and the Old Roman." *College English* 16 (1954): 98–101, 151.

Henkel, Arthur, and Albrecht Schöne. *Emblemata: Handbuch zur Sinnbildkunst des xvi. und xvii. Jahrhunderts.* Stuttgart: Metzler, 1967.

Herford, C. H., Percy Simpson, and Evelyn Simpson, eds. *Ben Jonson.* By Ben Jonson. 11 vols. Oxford: Clarendon, 1925–52.

Heuer, Hermann. "Lebensgefühl und Wertwelt in Shakespeares Römerdramen." *Zeitschrift für neusprachlichen Unterricht* 37 (1938): 65–90.

Hicks, Cora Eiland. "Suicide in English Tragedy, 1587–1622." Diss. U of Texas, Austin, 1968.

Highet, Gilbert. *The Classical Tradition: Greek and Roman Influences on Western Literature.* New York: Oxford UP, 1949.

Hill, Geoffrey. "The World's Proportion: Jonson's Dramatic Poetry in *Sejanus* and *Catiline*." *Jacobean Theatre.* Stratford-upon-Avon Studies 1. New York: St. Martin's, 1960. 113–31.

Hillman, Richard. "'Not Amurath an Amurath Succeeds': Playing Doubles in Shakespeare's *Henriad*." *ELR* 21 (1991): 161–89.

Hind, Arthur M. *Engraving in England in the Sixteenth and Seventeenth Centuries.* 2 vols. Cambridge: Cambridge UP, 1952.

Hogan, A. D. "Massinger as a Tragedian: *Believe As You List*." *Texas Studies in Language and Literature* 13 (1971): 407–19.

Holt, Leigh. *From Man to Dragon: A Study of Shakespeare's "Coriolanus."* Salzburg: Institut für englische Sprache und Literatur, 1976.

Howard, Douglas, ed. *Philip Massinger: A Critical Reassessment.* Cambridge: Cambridge UP, 1985.

Hunter, George K. "A Roman Thought: Renaissance Attitudes to History Exemplified in Shakespeare and Jonson." *An English Miscellany Presented to W. S. Mackie.* Ed. Brian S. Lee. Cape Town: Oxford UP, 1977. 93–118.

———. "Seneca and the Elizabethans: A Case-Study in 'Influence.'" *Shakespeare Survey* 20 (1967): 17–26.

Jenkins, Harold, ed. *Hamlet.* By William Shakespeare. London: Methuen, 1982.

Johnson, Francis R., ed. *The Foundacion of Rhetorike.* By Richard Rainolde. New York: Scholar's Facsimiles, 1945.

Johnson, Samuel. "Preface to Shakespeare." *Rasselas, Poems, and Selected Prose.* Ed. Bertrand H. Bronson. New York: Rinehart, 1952.

Johnston, Harold Whetstone. *The Private Life of the Romans.* Rev. Mary Johnston. Chicago: Scott, Foresman, 1932.

Jones, Emrys. *The Origins of Shakespeare.* Oxford: Clarendon, 1977.

———. "Stuart *Cymbeline.*" *Essays in Criticism* 11 (1961): 84–99.

Kaufmann, R. J., and Clifford J. Ronan. "Shakespeare's *Julius Caesar:* An Apollonian and Comparative Reading." *Comparative Drama* 4 (1970–71): 18–51.

Kliger, Samuel. *The Goths in England: A Study in Seventeenth and Eighteenth-Century Thought*. Cambridge: Harvard UP, 1952.
Knappe, Karl-Adolf. *Dürer: The Complete Engravings, Etchings, and Woodcuts*. London: Thames, 1965.
Knight, G. Wilson. *The Crown of Life: Essays in Interpretation of Shakespeare's Final Plays*. 1947. New York: Barnes and Noble, 1966.
——— . *The Imperial Theme: Further Interpretations of Shakespeare's Tragedies Including the Roman Plays*. 1931. 3rd ed. London: Barnes and Noble, 1965.
Knoll, Robert E. *Christopher Marlowe*. New York: Twayne, 1969.
Kranz, David L. "Shakespeare's New Idea of Rome." *Rome in the Renaissance: The City and the Myth*. Ed. Paul Ramsey. Binghamton: CEMERS, 1982. 371–80.
——— . "Clocks, Capitols, and Catos: How Anachronisms and Historical Allusions Influence the Tragic Drama of Shakespeare's Rome." Shakespeare Association of America Convention. Cambridge, Mass., 1984.
Lathrop, Henry Burroughs. *Translations from the Classics into English, from Caxton to Chapman, 1477–1620*. 1933. New York: Octagon, 1967.
Leech, Clifford. *The John Fletcher Plays*. Cambridge: Harvard UP, 1962.
Leggatt, Alexander. *Shakespeare's Political Drama: The History Plays and the Roman Plays*. London: Routledge, 1988.
Leinwand, Theodore B. "Negotiation and New Historicism." *PMLA* 105 (1990): 477–90.
Lever, J. W. *The Tragedy of State*. London: Methuen, 1971.
Levin, Harry. *The Overreacher: A Study of Christopher Marlowe*. 1952. Boston: Beacon, 1964.
——— . "Shakespeare's Nomenclature." *Essays on Shakespeare*. Ed. Gerald V. Chapman. Princeton: Princeton UP, 1965. 49–90.
Lewis, Charlton T., and Charles Short. *A Latin Dictionary*. Oxford: Clarendon, 1879.
Liddell, Henry George, et al. *A Greek-English Lexicon*. Oxford: Clarendon, 1968.
Lindenberger, Herbert. *The Historical Drama*. Chicago: U of Chicago P, 1975.
Lloyd, Michael. "The Roman Tongue." *SQ* 10 (1959): 461–68.
Long, A. A. *Hellenistic Philosophy: Stoics, Epicureans, Sceptics*. New York: Scribner's, 1974.
Lucas, F. L. *Seneca and Elizabethan Tragedy*. 1922. New York: Haskell, 1969.
——— , ed. *The Complete Works of John Webster*. London: Chatto and Windus, 1927.
Lucie-Smith, Edward. *Eroticism in Western Art*. New York: Praeger, 1972.
Macadam, Alta [and Stuart Rossiter], eds. *Rome and Environs*. London: Benn, 1956.
MacCallum, M. W. *Shakespeare's Roman Plays and Their Background*. Foreword by T. J. B. Spencer. 1910. London: Macmillan, 1967.

McDonald, Russ. "High Seriousness and Popular Form: The Case of *The Maid of Honour.*" *Philip Massinger: A Critical Reassessment.* Ed. Douglas Howard. Cambridge: Cambridge UP, 1985. 83–116.

Mahoney, Bo-Albertus. *Vergil in the Works of Prudentius.* Catholic University of America Patristic Studies 39. Washington: Catholic U of America, 1934.

Maltby, William S. *The Black Legend in England: The Development of Anti-Spanish Sentiment, 1558–1660.* Durham: Duke UP, 1971.

Marcus, Leah S. "*Cymbeline* and the Unease of Topicality." *The Historical Renaissance: New Essays on Tudor and Stuart Literature and Culture.* Ed. Heather Dubrow and Richard Strier. Chicago: U of Chicago P, 1988. 134–68.

Martindale, Charles, and Michelle Martindale. *Shakespeare and the Uses of Antiquity: An Introductory Essay.* London: Routledge, 1990.

Maxwell, J. C. "Animal Imagery in *Coriolanus.*" *Modern Language Review* 42 (1947): 417–21.

Merchant, W. S. "Classical Costume in Shakespearian Productions." *Shakespeare Survey* 10 (1957): 71–76.

Miles, Gary. "How Roman Are Shakespeare's 'Romans'?" *SQ* 40 (1988): 257–83.

Miola, Robert S. "Aeneas and Hamlet." *Classical and Modern Literature* 8 (1988): 275–90.

———. *Shakespeare's Rome.* Cambridge: Cambridge UP, 1983.

Montgomerie, William. "More an Antique Roman than a Dane." *Hibbert Journal* 59 (1960): 67–77.

Moretti, Franco. "'A Huge Eclipse': Tragic Form and the Deconsecration of Sovereignty." Rpt. from *Genre* in *The Power of Forms in the English Renaissance.* Ed. Stephen Greenblatt. Norman: Pilgrim, 1982. 7–40.

Muir, Kenneth. *The Sources of Shakespeare's Plays.* New Haven: Yale UP, 1978.

———. "Shakespeare's Roman World." *The Literary Half-Yearly* 15.2 (1974): 45–63.

Muller, Herbert J. *The Uses of the Past: Profiles of Former Societies.* New York: Mentor, 1952.

Murray, Linda. *The Late Renaissance and Mannerism.* New York: Praeger, 1967.

Nicoll, Allardyce. *British Drama: An Historical Survey from the Beginnings to the Present Time.* New York: Barnes, 1947.

Nietzsche, Friedrich. *The Complete Works of Friedrich Nietzsche.* Ed. Oscar Levy. 18 vols. 1909–11. New York: Russell, 1964.

Ong, Walter J. *Ramus: Method and the Decay of Dialogue, from the Art of Discourse to the Art of Reason.* 1958. Cambridge: Harvard UP, 1983.

Orgel, Stephen. "Counterfeit Presentments: The Economics of Shakespearean Representation." Shakespeare Association of America Convention. Austin, Tex., 1989.

———. *The Illusion of Power: Political Theater in the English Renaissance.* Berkeley and Los Angeles: U of California P, 1975.

———, ed. *The Tempest.* By William Shakespeare. Oxford Shakespeare. Oxford: Clarendon, 1987.

Oxford English Dictionary. 2nd ed. 1989.

Paradise, N. Burton. *Thomas Lodge: The History of an Elizabethan.* New Haven: Yale UP, 1931.

Partridge, Eric. *Shakespeare's Bawdy: A Literary and Psychological Essay and a Comprehensive Glossary.* London: Routledge and Kegan Paul, 1955.

Paster, Gail Kern. *The Idea of the City in the Age of Shakespeare.* Athens: U of Georgia P, 1985.

Patterson, Annabel. *Censorship and Interpretation: The Conditions of Writing and Reading in Early Modern England.* Madison: U of Wisconsin P, 1984.

Paulin, Bernard. *Du couteau à la plume: Le suicide dans la littérature anglaise de la renaissance (1580–1625).* Lyon: Editions l'Hermès, 1977.

Paulys Real-Encyclopädie der classischen Altertumswissenschaft. Ed. C. Wissowa et al. 1883–.

Payne, Michael. *Irony in Shakespeare's Roman Plays.* Salzburg: Institut für Englische Sprache und Literatur, 1974.

Payne, Robert. *The Roman Triumph.* London: Abelard-Schuman, 1962.

Peterson, Richard Gustaf. Abstract. "The Roman Image in English Literature from 1660 to 1780." *DA* 25 (1964): 2518A. U of Minnesota.

Phillips, James Emerson, Jr. *The State in Shakespeare's Greek and Roman Plays.* Columbia U Studies in English and Comparative Literature 149. New York: Columbia UP, 1940.

Pigman, G. W., III. "Du Bellay's Ambivalence Towards Rome in the *Antiquitez*." *Rome in the Renaissance: The City and the Myth.* Ed. Paul Ramsey. Binghamton: CEMERS, 1982. 321–32.

Platt, Michael. *Rome and Romans According to Shakespeare.* Salzburg: Institut für Englische Sprache und Literatur, 1976.

Pocock, J. G. A. *Politics, Language, and Time: Essays in Political Thought and History.* New York: Atheneum, 1971.

Praz, Mario. *The Flaming Heart: Essays on Crashaw, Machiavelli, and Other Stories in the Relations Between Italian and English from Chaucer to T. S. Eliot.* Garden City: Doubleday-Anchor, 1958.

———. *Studies in Seventeenth Century Imagery.* Vol. 1. 2nd ed. Sussidi Eruditi 16. Rome: Edizioni di Storia e Letteratura, 1964.

Quiñones, Ricardo. *Renaissance Discovery of Time.* Cambridge: Harvard UP, 1972.

Rabkin, Norman. *Shakespeare and the Common Understanding*. London: Collier-Macmillan, 1967.

Rackin, Phyllis. *Stages of History: Shakespeare's English Chronicles*. Ithaca: Cornell UP, 1990.

———. "Temporality, Anachronism, and Presence in Shakespeare's English Histories." *Renaissance Drama* ns 17 (1986): 103–23.

Ramsey, Paul, ed. *Rome in the Renaissance: The City and the Myth*. Medieval and Early Renaissance Texts and Studies 18. Binghamton, N.Y.: Center for Medieval and Early Renaissance Studies, 1982.

Reeves, Marjorie. *The Influence of Prophecy in the Later Middle Ages: A Study in Joachinism*. Oxford: Clarendon, 1969.

Ricks, Christopher. "The Tragedies of Webster, Tourneur, and Middleton: Symbols, Imagery, and Conventions." *English Drama to 1710*. History of Literature in the English Language 3. Ed. Christopher Ricks. London: Sphere, 1971. 306–53.

Ronan, Clifford J. "*Caesar's Revenge* and the Roman Thoughts in *Antony and Cleopatra*." *Shakespeare Studies* 19 (1987): 171–82.

———. "Daniel, Rainolde, Demosthenes, and the Degree Speech of Shakespeare's Ulysses." *Renaissance and Reformation* ns 9 (1985): 111–18.

———. "*Homo Multiplex* and the 'Man' Equivocation in *Hamlet*." *Hamlet Studies* 4 (1982): 33–53.

———. "Lucan and the Self-Incised Voids of *Julius Caesar*." *Drama and the Classical Heritage: Comparative and Critical Essays*. Ed. Clifford Davidson, Rand Johnson, and John H. Stroupe. AMS Series in Ancient and Classical Cultures 1. New York: AMS, 1992. 132–43.

———. "The Lucanic Omens in *Julius Caesar*." *Comparative Drama* 22 (1988): 138–44.

———. "The Onomastics of Shakespeare's Works with Classical Settings." *Names in Literature: Essays from "Literary Onomastic Studies.*" Ed. Grace Alvarez-Altman and Frederick M. Burelbach. Lanham: University Press of America, 1987. 53–68.

———. "*Pharsalia* 1.373–78: Roman Parricide and Marlowe's Editors." *Classical and Modern Literature* 6 (1986): 305–9.

———. "'Pompey's Blood': *Julius Caesar* I.i.51." *Explicator* 42 (1983): 11–12.

———. "Sallust's Beasts That 'Sleep and Feed,' and *Hamlet* 5.2." *Hamlet Studies* 8 (1985): 72–80.

———. "Snakes in *Catiline*." *Medieval and Renaissance Drama in England* 3 (1986): 149–63.

Rose, Mark. "Conjuring Caesar: Ceremony, History, and Authority in 1599." *ELR* 19 (1989): 291–304.

Ross, Lawrence J. "Wingless Victory: Michelangelo, Shakespeare, and the 'Old Man.'" *Literary Monographs* 2 (1969): 3–56.

———. "Symbol and Structure in the *Secunda Pastorum*." In *Medieval English Drama: Essays Critical and Contextual*. Ed. Jerome Taylor and Alan H. Nelson. Chicago: U of Chicago P, 1972. 177–211.

Rothery, Guy Cadogan. *The Heraldry of Shakespeare*. London: Moreland, 1930.

Rowland, Beryl. *Animals with Human Faces: A Guide to Animal Symbolism*. Knoxville: U of Tennessee P, 1973.

Rye, William Brenchley. *England As Seen by Foreigners in the Days of Elizabeth and James the First*. 1865. New York: Bloom, 1967.

Sandidge, William Lee. "Introduction." *A Critical Edition of Massinger's "The Roman Actor."* Princeton: Princeton UP, 1929.

Scaillérez, Cécile. *Antoine Caron: France XVIe siécle*. Paris: Louvre, 1989.

Schelling, Felix E. *Elizabethan Drama, 1558–1642*. 2 vols. 2nd ed. Boston: Houghton, 1911.

———, ed. *Ben Jonson's Plays*. 2 vols. London: Dent, 1910.

Schoenbaum, S. "Marston, Middleton, and Massinger." *English Drama (Excluding Shakespeare): Select Bibliographical Guides*. Ed. Stanley Wells. London: Oxford UP, 1975. 69–99.

Seaton, Ethel. "*Antony and Cleopatra* and the *Book of Revelation*." *RES* 22 (1946): 219–24.

Sharpe, J. A. "The History of Crime in Late Medieval and Early Modern England: A Review of the Field." *Social History* 7 (1982): 187–203.

Simmons, J. L. *Shakespeare's Pagan World: The Roman Tragedies*. Charlottesville: UP of Virginia, 1973.

Simonds, Peggy Muñoz. "*Coriolanus* and the Myth of Juno and Mars." *Mosaic* 18.2 (1985): 33–50.

Sommers, Alan. "'Wilderness of Tigers': Structure and Symbolism in *Titus Andronicus*." *Essays in Criticism* 10 (1960): 275–89.

Spencer, T. J. B. "Shakespeare and the Elizabethan Romans." *Shakespeare Survey* 10 (1957): 27–38.

Spencer, Theodore. *Death and Elizabethan Tragedy: A Study of Convention and Opinion in the Elizabethan Drama*. Cambridge: Harvard UP, 1936.

Spevack, Marvin. *The Harvard Concordance to Shakespeare*. Cambridge: Belknap-Harvard UP, 1973.

Sprott, Samuel E. *The Elizabethan Debate on Suicide from Donne to Hume*. Lasalle: Open Court, 1961.

Stampfer, Judah. *The Tragic Engagement: A Study of Shakespeare's Classical Tragedies*. New York: Funk and Wagnalls, 1968.

Stapfer, Paul. *Shakespeare and Classical Antiquity: Greek and Latin Antiquity as Presented in Shakespeare's Plays.* Trans. Emily J. Carey. London: Kegan Paul, 1880.

Steiner, George. "Introduction." *The Origins of German Tragic Drama.* By Walter Benjamin. Trans. John Osborne. London: NLB, 1977.

Stirling, Brents. *Unity in Shakespearian Tragedy.* 1956. New York: Gordian, 1966.

Sugden, Edward H. *A Topographical Dictionary to the Works of Shakespeare and His Fellow Dramatists.* Manchester: Manchester UP, 1925.

Taylor, Michael. "Beaumont and Fletcher, Heywood and Dekker." *English Drama (Excluding Shakespeare): Select Bibliographical Guides.* Ed. Stanley Wells. London: Oxford UP, 1975. 100–112.

Tennenhouse, Leonard. *Power on Display: The Politics of Shakespeare's Genres.* London: Methuen, 1986.

Tervarent, Guy de. *Attributs et symboles dans l'art profane, 1450–1600: Dictionnaire d'un langage perdu.* Travaux d' Humanisme et Renaissance 29. Geneva: Droz, 1958.

Thomson, J. A. K. *The Classical Background of English Literature.* London: Allen and Unwin, 1948.

Traversi, Derek. *Shakespeare: The Roman Plays.* Stanford, Calif.: Stanford UP, 1963.

Tricomi, Albert H. "The Aesthetics of Mutilation in *Titus Andronicus*." *Shakespeare Survey* 27 (1974): 11–20.

———. "The Mutilated Garden in *Titus Andronicus*." *Shakespeare Studies* 9 (1976): 89–105.

———. "The Dates of the Plays of George Chapman." *English Literary Renaissance* 12 (1982): 242–.

Trompi, G. W. *The Idea of Historical Recurrence in Western Thought: From Antiquity to the Reformation.* Berkeley and Los Angeles: U of California P, 1979.

Tupper, Frederick. "The Shakespearean Mob." *PMLA* 27 (1912): 482–523.

Ure, Peter. "John Marston's *Sophonisba*: A Reconsideration." *Durham University Journal* 40, ns 10 (1949–50): 81–90.

———. "On Some Differences Between Senecan and Elizabethan Tragedy." *Durham University Journal* 41 (1948–49): 17–23.

———, ed. *King Richard II.* By William Shakespeare. Cambridge: Harvard UP, 1956.

Vawter, Marvin L. "'After Their Fashion': Cicero and Brutus in *Julius Caesar*." *Shakespeare Studies* 9 (1976): 205–20.

———. "'Division 'Tween Our Souls': Shakespeare's Stoic Brutus." *Shakespeare Studies* 7 (1974): 173–95.

———. "*Julius Caesar*: Rupture in the Bond." *Journal of English and Germanic Philology* 72 (1973): 311–28.

Velz, John W. "The Ancient World in Shakespeare: Authenticity or Anachronism? A Retrospect." *Shakespeare Survey* 31 (1978): 1–12.

———. "Clemency, Will, and Just Cause in *Julius Caesar*." *Shakespeare Survey* 22 (1969): 109–18.

———. "*Orator* and *Imperator* in *Julius Caesar*: Style and the Process of Roman History." *Shakespeare Studies* 15 (1982): 55–75.

———. *Shakespeare and the Classical Tradition: A Critical Guide to Commentary, 1660–1960*. Minneapolis: U of Minnesota P, 1968.

———. "Two Emblems in Brutus' Orchard." *Renaissance Quarterly* 25 (1972): 307–15.

———. "Undular Structure in *Julius Caesar*." *Modern Language Review* 66 (1971): 21–30.

Versnel, H. S. *Triumphus: An Inquiry into the Origin, Development, and Meaning of the Roman Triumph*. Leiden: Brill, 1972.

Waith, Eugene. *The Herculean Hero in Marlowe, Chapman, Shakespeare, and Dryden*. London: Chatto and Windus, 1962.

———. "The Metamorphosis of Violence in *Titus Andronicus*." *Shakespeare Survey* 10 (1957): 39–49.

Walker, Roy. "The Northern Star: An Essay on the Roman Plays." *Shakespeare Quarterly* 2 (1951): 287–93.

Warren, Michael J. "Ben Jonson's *Catiline*: The Problem of Cicero." *Yearbook of English Studies* 3 (1973): 55–73.

Weinberger, Martin. *Michelangelo the Sculptor*. 2 vols. London: Routledge, 1967.

Whinney, Margaret. *Sculpture in Britain, 1530–1830*. Harmondsworth, Eng.: Penguin, 1964.

Whitaker, Virgil K. *Shakespeare's Use of Learning: An Inquiry into the Growth of His Mind and Art*. San Marino: Huntington Library, 1973.

White, Hayden. *The Uses of History: Essays in Intellectual and Social History*. Detroit: Wayne State UP, 1968.

Whitworth, Charles W. "*The Wounds of Civil War* and *Tamburlaine*: Lodge's Alleged Imitation." *Notes and Queries* 220 (June 1975): 245–47.

Wickham, Glynne. "Riddle and Emblem: A Study in the Dramatic Structure of *Cymbeline*." *English Renaissance Studies: Presented to Dame Helen Gardner in Honour of Her Seventieth Birthday*. Ed. John Carey. Oxford: Clarendon, 1980. 94–116.

Wikander, Matthew H. *The Play of Truth and State: Historical Drama from Shakespeare to Brecht*. Baltimore: Johns Hopkins UP, 1986.

Wilkinson, L. P. *The Roman Experience*. New York: Knopf, 1974.

William, Arnold. *The Characterization of Pilate in the Towneley Plays*. East Lansing: Michigan State College P, 1950.

Wilson, John Dover. "Ben Jonson and *Julius Caesar*." *Shakespeare Survey* 2 (1949): 36–43.

———. "*Titus Andronicus* on the Stage in 1595." *Shakespeare Survey* 1 (1948): 17–22.

———, ed. *Antony and Cleopatra*. By William Shakespeare. Cambridge: Cambridge UP, 1951.

Wilson, Lillian M. *The Roman Toga*. Johns Hopkins U Studies in Archeology 1. Baltimore: Johns Hopkins UP, 1924.

Wright, George T. "Hendiadys and *Hamlet*." *PMLA* 96 (1981): 168–93.

Wymer, Rowland. *Suicide and Despair in Jacobean Drama*. Brighton: Harvester, 1985.

Yachnin, Paul. "The Powerless Theater." *ELR* 21 (1991): 49–74.

Yates, Frances. *Astraea: The Imperial Theme in the Sixteenth Century*. London: Routledge, 1975.

Yoder, R. A. "History and the Histories in *Julius Caesar*." *Shakespeare Quarterly* 24 (1973): 309–27.

Zeevold, W. Gordon. "*Coriolanus* and Jacobean Politics." *Modern Language Review* 57 (1962): 321–34.

INDEX

Acosta, José de, 39
Addison, Joseph: *Cato*, 1
Adelman, Janet, 19, 140, 187, 188
Adler, Doris, 188
Adler, Mortimer, 155
Aelianus, 137
Aeneas, 1, 17, 19, 27, 34, 136
Aeschylus, 16–17
Aetna, 100, 105, 107, 195
Agrippina, 27, 165
Agrippina (May), 6, 22, 53, 68, 70–71, 80–81, 133, 135, 141, 165, 189, 196
Ahern, Mathew Joseph, Jr., 171, 172
Ahl, Frederick M., 142
Alexander, William: *Julius Caesar*, 35, 51, 80, 85, 93, 112, 133, 135, 141, 165, 192
Alexander the Great, 31, 43, 47, 53, 84, 102, 158
Alvis, John, 187
Ammannati, Bartolomeo, 116
Anachronism, 11–35, 152; and nondramatic art, 11–13, 20, 66; and intertextuality, 12–13, 16–35; and prolepsis/prophecy, 13, 18–21, 24–35, 61; and politico-religious topicality, 13 (cf. fig. 2), 18–20, 29–31, 54–61, 125–26; misapprehended by critics, 13–14, 20, 24–25, 27–35, 61; and alienation/identification, 14, 23, 61; classical/Medieval background of, 16–17; for verisimilitude, 20–24, 31, 52

Anson, John, 72, 87, 91, 100, 104, 188
Antiochus the Great, 165
Antique/antic quibble, 3–7, 38, 49, 90, 121, 155, 163, 188 (n. 3)
Antonie/Antonius (Garnier, trans. Pembroke), 53, 133, 148, 155, 165
Antonius, Marcus, 12, 24, 52, 83, 91, 102, 165, 166, 167, 173
Antony and Cleopatra (Shakespeare), 2, 5, 19, 24–25, 26–27, 38, 42, 43, 52, 53, 66, 67, 70, 72, 76, 80, 81–83, 85, 89–91, 92, 93, 98, 102, 104, 116, 119, 125, 131, 134, 153, 165, 172, 189
Apius and Virginia (R. B.), 41, 165, 192
Appian, 22, 33, 45, 46, 79, 93, 94, 114, 131
Appius (decemvir), 52, 143
Appius and Virginia (Webster), 23, 33, 51, 53, 76, 78, 80, 82, 85, 97, 125, 134–38, 155, 165, 189, 190, 193, 195
Aristides, Aelius, 46–47
Aristotle, 28, 30, 31, 86, 152
Armin, Robert: *Valiant Welshman*, 5, 29, 43, 53, 55–58, 80, 110, 129, 169, 174, 189
Arrian, 96
Ascham, Roger, 68
Auerbach, Erich, 17
Augustine, Saint, 41, 47, 78, 83, 88, 125, 130, 132, 144, 152, 191
Augustus/Octavius, 17, 26, 45, 47, 66, 69, 83, 119, 131, 158, 163, 165, 166, 167, 168, 195
Aurelius, Marcus, 96

Index

Avery, Charles, 116
Ayres, Philip J., 14

Bacon, Francis, 32, 39, 51, 68, 74, 79, 84, 113
Bakhtin, Mikhail, 5, 16, 61
Baldwin, T. W., 117, 138, 188
Barish, Jonas, 187, 188
Barroll, J. Leeds, 1, 45, 53, 188
Barton, Anne, 3, 49, 127, 187
Believe As You List (Massinger), 50, 59–61, 71, 82, 85, 93, 95–96, 112, 165, 173, 189, 192
Benjamin, Walter, 122
Berenice, 33
Bethell, S., 19
Bevington, David, 33
Bible: Mark, 3; Revelation, 14, 19, 45, 48, 66, 77, 126; Gospels, 19, 46; Genesis, 19, 46, 78; Luke, 20, 46, 55; Matthew, 20, 192; Romans, 45; 1 Samuel, 46; 1 Maccabees, 48; Daniel, 48, 55, 99, 132, 192; Epistles of Paul, 80; Exodus, 94; Psalms, 192. *See also* Jesus Christ
Bible, Geneva, 14, 77, 126
Bodin, Jean, 138, 172
Bolton, Whitney, and Jane Gardner, 187, 188
Bolzani Valeriano, G., 100, 103, 112, 116, 136, 137, 188
Bonduca (Fletcher), 22, 44, 58, 84, 92, 98, 110, 137–38, 165, 189, 190
Book of Common Prayer, 56
Booth, Stephen, 188
Booty, John F., 56
Braden, Gordon, 2, 39, 72, 87, 100, 188, 191
Bradshaw, John, 51
Brandon, Samuel: *Virtuous Octavia*, 71, 85, 93, 135, 167
Brecht, Bertold, 2, 23, 61
Briggs, William Dinsmore, 22, 187, 188
Brockbank, Philip, 188
Broude, Ronald, 26
Broughton, Hugh, 66, 126
Brower, Reuben, 187

Brutus, Lucius Junius, 28–29, 34–35, 51, 89, 110, 130, 146, 161, 167, 196
Brutus, Marcus Junius, 28, 29, 34, 35, 89, 142, 159, 165, 166
Bullough, Geoffrey, 172, 188
Bunzel, Bessie, 88
Burckhardt, Jacob, 113
Burckhardt, Sigurd, 14
Burke, Kenneth, 14
Burke, Peter, 48, 172
Bushnell, Rebecca Weld, 130, 187
Bussy D'Ambois (Chapman), 156, 159
Bussy D'Ambois, Revenge of (Chapman), 92, 156, 159
Butler, Martin, 22, 51, 114, 155, 171, 187, 188

Caesar, Julius, 18–39 passim, 47, 51, 52, 66, 68, 70, 78, 83, 84, 88, 110, 113, 117, 119, 125, 139, 141, 146, 149, 157, 159, 162, 165, 166, 167, 172
Caesar and Pompey (Chapman), 6, 29, 53, 73, 94, 104–6, 133, 135, 137, 161, 165, 189, 196
Caesar's Revenge, 42, 53, 71–75, 92–94, 110–13, 135–36, 148, 165, 189, 192, 195
Caligula, 38, 168
Calvin, John, 48
Camden, William, 39, 43
Campion, Edmund, 1
Cantor, Paul, 187
Caputi, Albert, 105, 106, 188
Carcopino, Jérôme, 103, 131
Carion, Jean, 45
Carnicelli, D. D., 114
Caron, Antoine, 11–13, 64, 69, 105, 160
Cary, Elizabeth: *Mariam*, 173
Castiglione, Baldassare, 69
Catiline (Jonson), 6, 22, 26, 31, 33, 43, 49, 50, 52, 53, 68, 78, 80, 82, 93, 112, 118, 128–29, 134, 136, 138, 141, 142, 147–50, 153, 161, 166, 174, 189–90, 192, 195
Catilinus, Lucius, 135, 166, 195
Cato (Addison), 1

Cato, Marcus Uticensis, 28, 31, 38, 86, 88, 89, 93, 96, 128, 142, 165, 166
Catonis, Dicta, 73, 125
Cavell, Stanley, 187
Certaine Sermons, 124
Chapman, George, 84; *Caesar and Pompey*, 6, 29, 53, 73, 94, 104–6, 133, 135, 137, 161, 165, 189, 196; *Bussy D'Ambois, The Revenge of*, 92, 159; *Bussy D'Ambois*, 159
Charles I, 23, 50, 59–61, 113–14
Charney, Maurice, 2, 100, 187, 188
Cheney, Donald, 162
Cicero, 53, 67, 134, 135, 138, 141, 166, 191, 194
Cicero, Marcus Tullius, 20, 68, 77, 83, 86, 91, 97, 131, 134, 158, 159, 162, 166; *Stoic Paradoxes*, 3; in Caron's *Massacres*, 12; in Garnier/Kyd's, *Cornélie*, 19; *De officiis*, 19, 20; in Whitney's *Emblems*, 68; "Dream of Scipio," 272
Cinthio, Geraldi, 21, 23
Claudian, 131
Claudius, 27, 70, 141, 165, 167, 169, 196
Cleopatra, 26, 33, 149, 165, 166
Cleopatra (Daniel), 26, 53, 110, 155, 166
Cleopatra (May), 6, 53, 54, 85, 97, 118, 166
Cochrane, Charles Norris, 152
Colosseum, 4, 12, 13
Comedy of Errors (Shakespeare), 111
Conrad, Joseph, 40
Coriolanus (Shakespeare), 2, 3, 5–7, 22, 23, 27, 31, 33, 35, 41, 42, 51, 52, 53, 67, 72, 73, 79, 80, 82, 85, 103, 112, 119, 121, 122, 129, 130, 133, 134–36, 138, 139–42, 147–48, 150, 152, 153, 155, 166, 172, 174, 189, 191, 194–95, 196
Cornélie (Garnier), 192; and *Cornelia* (trans. Kyd), 19–20, 30, 35, 42, 53, 67, 93, 102, 103, 110, 140, 146, 152, 155, 166
Cruel Brother (D'Avenant), 191
Cruickshank, Alfred H., 61
Cymbeline (Shakespeare), 3, 5, 23, 30, 31, 53, 58, 81–82, 89, 105, 112, 117–19, 139, 166, 172, 174, 189, 190, 191

Daniel, Samuel, 38; *Cleopatra*, 26, 53, 110, 155, 166
D'Avenant, William: *Cruel Brother*, 191
Davies, John, 39
Dean, Paul, 171
Dekker, Thomas, and John Marston: *Satiromastix*, 168, 173. See also Marston, John
Dekker, Thomas, and Philip Massinger: *Virgin Martyr*, 68, 78, 85, 93, 168, 189, 190, 192, 195
De l'Orme, Philippe, 12
DeLuna, Barbara, 50
Descartes, René, 44–45
Dio, Cassius, 131
Donaldson, Ian, 34, 88
Donatello, 116
Donne, John, 43, 100
Drayton, Michael, 1
Drummond, William, 88
du Bellay, Joachim, 6, 40, 43, 48, 135, 145
Dublin, Louis I., 88
Dubois d'Amiens, François, 13
DuBon, David, 116
Duchess of Malfi (Webster), 50, 130, 172
Duffy, Ellen M. T., 135, 188
Dunkle, J. Roger, 125
Durantinus, Felicius, 135
Dürer, Albrecht, 66
Du Vair, Guillaume, 38
Dyce, Alexander, 155

Edward II (Marlowe), 115, 145, 157–59, 172
Edwards, Philip, 39, 59, 60, 61
Edwards, Philip, 39, 188
Ehrmann, Jean, 12
Eisenstein, Sergei, 51
Eliot, T. S., 40
Elizabeth I, 25, 56, 59, 79, 160
Elizabethan vs. Jacobean drama, 22, 91, 93, 171–74, 192 (n. 5)
Elyot, Thomas, 123
Empson, William, 188

Epictetus, 96
Erasmus, Desiderius, 104, 112, 130, 191
Essex, Robert Devereux, earl of, 47, 79
Estienne, Charles, 153
Euripides, 131
Every Woman in Her Humour (Machin), 45, 87, 123, 155, 166, 173
Evett, David, 6

Faction/civil war, 3–4, 12, 30–35, 44–45, 48, 51–53, 140–50, 152–53; customary among "fellow kings," 78–80; from ingratitude, 80–83, 86, 130, 190 (n. 2). See also *Majestas*; *Superbia*
Faithful Friends, 53, 78, 84, 93, 98, 110, 147, 155, 166, 192
False One (Fletcher and Massinger), 53–54, 59, 72, 80, 92, 93, 98, 118, 134, 135, 138, 141, 148, 166, 173, 192 (n. 4), 193 (n. 1)
Farrell, Kirby, 24
Ferrarius Montanus, 125, 130
Fichter, Andrew, 19
Fisher, Jasper: *Fuimus Troes*, 45, 53, 78, 110, 138, 166, 190, 194
Fletcher, John, 43, 155; *Valentinian*, 5, 27, 32, 33, 34; *Bonduca*, 22, 44, 58, 84, 92, 98, 110, 137–38, 165, 189, 190
Fletcher, John, and Philip Massinger: *The Prophetess*, 43, 70, 82, 87, 114, 127, 133, 168, 173, 189, 196; *False One*, 53, 59, 72, 80, 92, 93, 98, 118, 134, 135, 138, 141, 148, 166, 173, 192, 194
Ford, John, 163
Foucault, Michel, 77
Fowler, Warde, 194, 195
Freccero, John, 194
Frederick, duke of Wirtemburg, 76
Fuimus Troes (Fisher), 45, 53, 78, 110, 138, 166, 190, 193
Fulbecke, William, 45
Fulgens and Lucres (Medwall), 33, 41, 73, 166

Galinsky, G. Karl, 5
Game at Chess (Middleton), 60
Garber, Marjorie, 35
Garnier, Robert, 1, 36; *Cornélie* (trans. Kyd), 19, 20, 30, 35, 42, 53, 67, 93, 102, 103, 110, 140, 146, 152, 155, 166, 192; *Marc Antoine*, 53, 133, 148, 155, 165
Geneva Bible, 14, 77, 126
Gentili, Vanna, 171
Gesta Romanorum, 36
Gibson, Colin, 39, 188
Gilbert, Allen H., 21
Gillies, John, 42, 43
Giovio, Paulo, 69
Girard, René, 141
Glasser, Marvin, 6
Goethe, Johann Wolfgang, 23
Goldberg, Jonathan, 55, 84, 155, 187, 191
Gorboduc (Norton and Sackville), 56, 113, 156
Greene, John, 122
Greene, Thomas, 14, 21, 23, 32
Greville, Fulke, 1
Grimald, Nicholas, 77
Gross, Allen, 59

Hadas, Moses, 32, 46, 48
Hakluyt, Richard, 135
Halstead, William P., 121
Hamlet (Shakespeare), 3, 6, 89, 92, 109, 110, 134, 156, 162–63
Hanford, James Holly, 191
Hankins, John E., 191
Hannibal, 60, 165, 167, 189
Hannibal and Scipio (Nabbes), 53, 82, 93, 110, 167, 191, 192
Harbage, Alfred, 173
Hariot, Thomas, 39
Harris, Bernard, 188
Haskell, Francis, and Nicholas Penny, 137
Haywood, Richard M., 49
Hemming, William: *Jews' Tragedy*, 93, 167, 173, 193

Henkel, Arthur, 100, 188
Henry IV, Part 1 (Shakespeare), 119, 156, 161–62
Henry IV, Part 2 (Shakespeare), 119, 135, 143, 161–62
Henry V (Shakespeare), 27, 37, 42, 43, 47, 67, 84, 119, 123, 156, 161–62
Henry VI, 18, 27, 117
Henry VI, Part 1 (Shakespeare), 117, 156
Henry VI, Part 2 (Shakespeare), 131, 134–35, 156, 158–59
Henry VIII, 30, 47, 57, 144
Henslowe, Philip, 69
Herford, C. H., 31, 43, 187, 188
Herod and Antipater (Markham and Sampson), 126, 136, 167
Herods (the Great and/or Antipater), 13, 17, 19, 22, 29, 122, 143, 162, 167
Heuer, Hermann, 69
Heywood, Thomas: *Rape of Lucrece*, 6, 30, 33, 52, 57, 80, 93, 97, 118, 147, 155, 167, 189, 190, 192, 195
Hicks, Cora Eiland, 191
Highet, Gilbert, 188
Hill, Geoffrey, 58, 187
Hillman, Richard, 14, 143
Hind, Arthur M., 66, 100
History play: implicit sequel for, 16, 19, 24–29; classical/Medieval background of, 16–18, 122; multiple chronotopes in, 16–35. *See also* Anachronism, Roman play: cyclical return in
Hobbes, Thomas, 47
Hogan, A. D., 187
Homer, 21, 131
Horace, 14, 15, 37, 48, 128, 154
Houppert, Joseph W., 28
Howard, Douglas, 187, 188
Hughes, Thomas: *The Misfortunes of Arthur*, 156
Huguenots, 3, 13, 29, 30, 126, 157
Humorous Courtier (Shirley), 191

Hunter, George K., 1, 24, 171–72, 187, 188, 189
Hydra, 52, 126, 145

James I, 23, 30, 47, 50, 56–58, 74, 84, 112, 113, 155
Jenkins, Harold, 6
Jesus Christ, 18–20, 27, 36, 45, 46, 55, 60–61, 83, 113, 140, 166. *See also* Bible
Jew of Malta (Marlowe), 132, 156
Jews' Tragedy (Hemming), 93, 167, 173, 194
Joachim of Fiore, 18
Johnson, Samuel, 13
Johnston, Harold Whetstone, 77
Jones, Emrys, 47, 156, 162
Jonson, Ben, 43, 50, 56, 58, 61, 88, 155, 168, 172; *Sejanus*, 3, 6, 14, 22, 26, 31, 32, 33, 34, 50, 52, 53, 55, 68, 70, 71, 73, 76, 80, 81, 85, 92–93, 98, 103, 104, 106–7, 113, 118, 128, 138, 140, 142, 147, 168, 172, 189, 195; *Catiline*, 6, 22, 26, 31, 33, 43, 49, 50, 52, 53, 67, 68, 78, 80, 82, 93, 112, 113, 118, 128–29, 134, 136, 138, 141, 142, 147–50, 153, 161, 166, 173, 189–90, 192, 195; *Poetaster*, 6, 50, 53, 68, 78, 122, 147, 167–68, 173, 195; *Volpone*, 92
Julius Caesar (Alexander), 35, 51, 80, 85, 93, 112, 133, 135, 141, 165, 192
Julius Caesar (Shakespeare), 2, 3, 5–6, 24–26, 30–35, 40, 41–42, 44, 52, 53, 55, 66, 68, 70, 73, 75–76, 78, 79, 80, 81, 83, 85, 92–95, 103, 104, 112, 119, 136, 138, 139, 140, 142, 146, 147–50, 155, 161, 165, 189, 191, 195
Jupiter, 17, 77, 96, 115, 157, 159, 172, 189, 194
Juvenal, 5, 43, 127, 160, 162

Kaufmann, R. J., 104
Kelton, Arthur, 144
Killigrew, Thomas: *The Princess*, 167, 173
King John (Shakespeare), 44, 81, 119, 143, 148, 162

King Lear (Shakespeare), 28, 81, 83, 136, 145, 172
Kliger, Samuel, 26, 193
Knoll, Robert E., 156
Kranz, David L., 32
Kyd, Thomas: *Cornélie/Cornelia*, 19, 20, 30, 35, 42, 53, 67, 93, 102, 103, 110, 140, 146, 152, 155, 166, 192

Laelius, 141, 142, 149
Languet, Hubert, 146
La Perrière, Guillaume de, 3–4, 145
Las Casas, Bartolome de, 135
Lee, Nathaniel, 133
Leech, Clifford, 188
Legenda aurea, 36
Leinwand, Theodore B., 51, 187
Lever, J. W., 171, 187
Levin, Harry, 188
Lindenberger, Herbert, 1
Lindsay, David, 99
Lipsius, Justus, 192
Livy, Titus, 49, 88, 91, 101, 126, 127, 137, 171, 172
Lloyd, Michael, 49
Lodge, Thomas: *The Wounds of Civil War*, 5–7, 26, 28–30, 33, 34, 41–42, 53, 54–56, 67, 70, 71, 73–75, 78, 80–82, 84, 92, 93, 96–97, 102–3, 104, 105, 109, 112, 114, 133, 137, 138, 145, 155, 161, 169, 172, 173, 189, 193
Long, A. A., 105
Love's Labor's Lost (Shakespeare), 28, 36, 108, 115
Lucan, 5, 131, 163, 167; *Pharsalia*, 32, 34, 40, 43, 48, 52, 54, 79, 88, 131, 132, 139, 142, 144, 145–50, 157–58, 161, 162, 163; Caesar in, 43, 131, 141–42, 156; Laelius in, 141, 142, 149
Lucas, F. L., 6, 23, 188
Lucie-Smith, Edward, 116, 192
Lucretia (wife of Collatinus), 22, 33–35, 52, 71, 75, 88, 89, 91, 102, 119, 120, 130, 143, 161, 162, 167

Macbeth (Shakespeare), 6, 81, 89, 92, 108, 119, 135, 156, 163
MacCallum, M. W., 7, 27, 28, 30, 102, 187, 188
Machiavelli, Niccolò, 5, 27, 52, 57, 58, 59, 60, 81, 86, 124, 172, 191
Machin, Lewis: *Every Woman in Her Humour*, 45, 87, 123, 155, 166, 173
Mahoney, Bo-Albertus, 117, 193
Maid of Honour (Massinger), 86, 113
Majestas, 44, 65–86; in self-mastery, 2–3, 91–92; in monumental and verbal art, 4, 11–12, 21, 37, 65–71, 94–99; in soldiers and governors, 36–39, 41, 47, 67–68, 71–80, 92, 108–13; in clemency, 83–86, 191 (nn. 3, 4). *See also* Stoic *Constantia*
Maltby, William S., 60
Mantegna, Andrea, 113
Mantuan, Baptista, 67
Marc Antoine (Garnier), 53, 133, 148, 155, 165
Marcus, Leah S., 23
Mariam (Cary), 173
Marius, 26, 28, 33, 71, 112, 157, 169, 188
Markham, Gervase, and William Sampson: *Herod and Antipater*, 126, 136, 167
Marlowe, Christopher, 52, 57, 78, 79, 122, 132, 145, 156; *Tamburlaine*, 38, 70, 74, 109, 115, 118, 156–57, 162; *Edward II*, 115, 145, 157–59, 172; *Jew of Malta*, 132, 156; *Massacre at Paris*, 157
Mars, 4, 19, 103
Marston, John [and Thomas Dekker?]: *Sophonisba*, 33, 53, 93, 105, 106, 114, 133, 155. *See also* Dekker, Thomas, and John Marston
Martindale, Charles, 187
Martindale, Michelle, 187
Marvell, Andrew, 140
Massacre at Paris (Marlowe), 157
Massacre of Saint Bartholomew, 1572 (Dubois), 13
Massacres du Triumvirat (Caron), 12, 13, 69, 105, 160

Massinger, Philip, 50, 59–61, 113, 155; *Roman Actor*, 6, 22, 41, 50, 53, 68, 70, 80, 82, 93, 95–96, 114, 138–39, 168, 172, 189, 190, 192, 193, 196; *The King and the Subject* (lost), 50; *Believe As You List*, 50, 59–61, 71, 82, 85, 93, 95–96, 112, 165, 173, 189, 192; *Maid of Honour*, 86, 113. See also *False One*; *Prophetess*; *Virgin Martyr*
May, Thomas: *Agrippina*, 6, 22, 53, 68, 70–71, 80–81, 133, 135, 141, 165, 189, 195; *Cleopatra*, 6, 53, 54, 85, 97, 118, 166
McDonald, Russ, 113
Measure for Measure (Shakespeare), 28, 84, 108, 115
Medwall, Thomas: *Fulgens and Lucres*, 33, 41, 73, 166
Merbury, Charles, 67
Merchant of Venice (Shakespeare), 85, 162
Messalina, 127, 138, 167, 195
Messallina (Richards), 6, 22, 27, 52, 53, 76, 79, 80, 93, 110, 126, 129, 135, 167, 189, 192, 195
Middleton, Thomas: *Game at Chess*, 60; *Revenger's Tragedy*, 156, 160–61
Miles, Gary, 14
Milton, John, 51, 110, 113
Miola, Robert S., 152, 162, 187
Misfortunes of Arthur (Hughes), 156
Montaigne, Michel de, 37, 40, 74, 76, 83, 88, 128, 135
Moretti, Franco, 123
Mornay, Philippe de, Seigneur du Plessis-Marly, 146
Muir, Kenneth, 188
Muller, Herbert J., 43, 191
Munday, Anthony, 1
Murray, Linda, 13

Nabbes, Thomas: *Hannibal and Scipio*, 53, 82, 93, 110, 167, 191, 192
Nashe, Thomas, 1
Nero, 4, 7, 14, 17, 27, 38, 109, 123, 129, 132, 134, 165, 166, 167, 195

Nero, 33, 54, 68, 70, 133, 134, 155, 167, 195
Nicoll, Allardyce, 1
Nietzsche, Friedrich, 130, 163

Octavia (pseudo-Seneca), 7, 41, 52, 128, 132–34, 167, 192
Octavia (wife of Emperor Nero), 167
Octavia (wife/sister of triumvirs), 167
"Octavyan" (Chester Cycle), 17, 36
Orgel, Stephen, 22, 39
Orosius, Paulus, 130–31, 143
Ortelius, 42
Othello (Shakespeare), 92, 119–21, 136, 138, 156, 162
Ovid, 5, 13, 22, 37, 43, 48, 113, 119, 131, 167, 172

Palindrome of *Roma/Amor*, 36
Parricide, 3, 44, 79, 128–50, 190 (n. 2), 195 (n. 3)
Parrott, T. M., 188
Partridge, Eric, 188
Paster, Gail Kern, 37, 49, 69, 81, 187, 195
Patterson, Annabel, 50, 51, 187
Paulin, Bernard, 89, 93, 191
Payne, Robert, 116, 131
Peacham, Henry, 20
Pembroke, Mary Sidney Herbert, countess of: *Antonie*, 53, 133, 148, 155, 165
Peterson, Richard, 123
Phillips, James Emerson, Jr., 80, 187
Pigman, G. W., III, 14
Plato, 52, 88, 102, 111, 130
Platt, Michael, 187
Plautus, 40
Pliny the Elder, 38, 127
Plutarch, 2, 32, 34, 35, 43, 49, 53, 71, 83, 91, 102, 115, 128, 131, 137, 140, 141, 149, 171, 172
Poetaster (Jonson), 6, 50, 53, 68, 78, 122, 147, 167–68, 173, 195
Political drama focused on prudent generalities, 50–59; and providential historiography, 18, 45, 47; and imperial thieving/

230   Index

Political drama (*continued*)
civilizing imperialism, 19–20, 36, 39, 47, 50–58; and class struggle, 23, 51–52, 135; and radical transition to/from centralized tyranny, 33, 51–55, 121–25; and Machiavellian manipulation, 51–58, 86, 124. *See also* Faction/civil war
Pollaiuolo, Antonio del, 137
Pompey the Great, 28–40 passim, 59, 67, 69, 70, 79, 80, 119, 132, 139, 142, 143, 149, 159, 165, 166
Pope, Alexander, 6, 108
Praz, Mario, 29, 126
Princess (T. Killigrew), 167, 173
Procopius, 32
Prophetess (Fletcher and Massinger), 43, 53, 70, 82, 87, 114, 127, 133, 168, 173, 189, 196
Prudentius, 117, 131, 192, 193
Purchas, Samuel, 39
Puttenham, George, 114, 123

Quibbles on "Rome," 15, 42–45, 49; and the Ancient vs. papal regime, 14, 29–30, 57, 125–26
Quiñones, Ricardo, 32

R. B.: *Apius and Virginia*, 41, 165, 192
Rabkin, Norman, 187
Rackin, Phyllis, 14, 16, 23, 27, 38, 172
Rainolde, Richard, 66
Ralegh, Walter, 88, 131
"Rape of Lucrece" (Shakespeare), 52, 102, 119, 120, 162
Rape of Lucrece (T. Heywood), 6, 30, 52, 53, 71, 75, 80, 82, 92, 97, 118, 147, 155, 167, 189, 192, 195
Reeves, Marjorie, 18
Regulus, 89
Revenger's Tragedy (Middleton), 156, 160–61
Richard II (Shakespeare), 54, 111, 143

Richard III (Shakespeare), 143
Richards, Nathaniel: *Messallina*, 6, 22, 27, 52, 53, 76, 79, 80, 93, 110, 126, 129, 135, 167, 189, 192, 195
Ricks, Christopher, 160
Ripa, Cesare, 85, 100, 112, 136, 188
Rogers, William, 65, 66
Roman Actor (Massinger), 6, 22, 41, 50, 53, 68, 70, 80, 82, 93, 95–96, 114, 138–39, 168, 172, 189, 190, 192, 193, 196
Romanitas: overview of, 2–7, 11–12, 19, 28, 125, 151–56, 163; ambivalence toward, 3, 11–12, 14, 35, 40–41, 44–49, 65–66, 71–72, 86–91, 108–12, 123, 136–37, 151–55; as type/antitype of power, 3, 14–15, 17–18, 36–49, 52–54, 65–99, 125, 127, 150–55; hollowness in, 3, 40–41, 148–50; in tension with (Protestant) Christianity, 14, 26, 29–31, 36, 39, 41, 44–45, 54–61, 65–66, 88–89, 113, 135–50; intertwined with *Britannitas*, 18, 25, 33, 37–40, 47, 54–59, 88–89, 111–12, 119, 161–62. *See also* Faction/civil war; *Majestas*; *Saevitia*; Suicide; *Superbia*; Triumph
Romanized plays/pseudo-Roman plays, 81, 92, 114–16, 118–19, 120–21, 156–63
Roman play: seriousness and historicity of, 1, 13, 165–69, 177–79, 196 (nn. 1, 2); nature and history of, 1–2, 91–99, 152–56, 171–74, 177–85, 192 (n. 5), 196 (nn. 1, 2); gender stereotyping in, 2, 41, 49, 52, 66, 71, 90, 109, 120, 123; classical/Medieval background of, 4–7, 16–18, 32–34; "noble"/hierarchical honorifics in, 13, 67–78, 83–92 passim; cyclical return in, 14–15, 28–29, 32–35, 58, 89; omens, augury, magic, and the occult in, 17, 31, 52, 115, 125–26, 131–37, 188 (n. 3); non-Roman ethnicity in, 27–28, 29–30, 58, 81–82, 190 (n. 2); rape and sexual conquest in, 33, 52, 189 (n. 2); "Rome"/nationality marker in, 41–42, 89, 92; "faction" in, 79–90; "ingratitude" in,

81–82, 190 (n. 2); "constancy" and "resolution" in, 89–92, 192 (n. 4); "pride" in, 110–11, 113
Romeo and Juliet (Shakespeare), 89, 162
Romulus, 14, 32, 35, 76, 78, 126–48 passim, 158, 166, 193
Ronan, Clifford, 3, 30, 42, 49, 74, 104, 109, 142, 147, 161, 162
Ross, Lawrence J., 17, 193
Rowland, Beryl, 136, 137
Rowley, William: *Shoemaker, a Gentleman*, 6, 35, 53, 87, 110, 112, 118, 126, 131, 133, 134, 135, 168, 173, 174, 190
Rubens, Peter Paul, 113, 116
Rutilius, 43

Saevitia, 106, 109–12, 115, 121, 126–50, 151–53; (voluptuous) bloodlust in, 94, 117–21, 127–29, 192 (n. 1); autodestruction and the cancer/lupus symbol in, 139–40, 145–50. *See also* Parricide; Roman play: omens, augury, magic, and the occult in
Sallust, 71, 83, 146, 162
Sandidge, William Lee, 195
Sandys, George, 77
Satiromastix (Dekker and Marston), 168, 173
Scaevola, Mutius, 89, 101
Scailléirez, Cécile, 12
Scaliger, Julius Caesar, 123
Schelling, Felix E., 27, 50, 69, 171
Schöne, Albrecht, 100, 188
Scipio Africanus, 38, 114, 151, 154, 167, 168
Sebastian, Don (pretender to the Portuguese throne), 59, 60–61, 165
Sejanus (Jonson), 3, 6, 14, 22, 26, 31, 32, 33, 34, 50, 52, 53, 55, 68, 70, 71, 73, 76, 80, 81, 85, 92–93, 98, 103, 104, 106–7, 113, 118, 128, 138, 140, 142, 147, 168, 172, 189, 195
Seneca, Lucius Annaeus, 2, 7, 17, 22, 38, 40, 79, 80, 83, 87, 88, 89, 91, 94, 96, 103, 105, 123, 127, 128–29, 131, 141, 150, 156, 159, 160, 162, 163, 167, 189, 191; pseudo-Senecan *Octavia*, 7, 41, 52, 128, 132, 134, 167, 192; *Thyestes*, 17, 161
Seneca, Marcus Annaeus, Rhetoricus (Seneca the Elder), 43, 91
Sforza, Francesco, Duke, 113
Shakespeare, William: *Julius Caesar*, 2, 3, 5–6, 24–26, 30–35, 40, 41–42, 44, 52, 53, 55, 66, 68, 70, 73, 75–76, 78, 79, 80, 81, 83, 85, 92–95, 103, 104, 112, 119, 136, 138, 139, 140, 142, 146, 147–50, 155, 161, 165, 189, 191, 195; *Coriolanus*, 2, 3, 5–7, 22, 23, 27, 31, 33, 35, 41, 42, 51, 52, 53, 67, 72, 73, 79, 80, 82, 85, 103, 112, 119, 121, 122, 129, 130, 133, 134–36, 138, 139–42, 147–48, 150, 152, 153, 155, 166, 172, 174, 189, 191, 194–95, 196; *Antony and Cleopatra*, 2, 5, 19, 24–25, 26–27, 38, 42, 43, 52, 53, 66, 67, 70, 72, 76, 80, 81–83, 85, 89–91, 92, 93, 98, 102, 104, 116, 119, 125, 131, 134, 153, 165, 172, 189; *Cymbeline*, 3, 5, 23, 30, 31, 53, 58, 81–82, 89, 105, 112, 117–19, 139, 166, 172, 174, 189, 190, 191; *Hamlet*, 3, 6, 89, 92, 109, 110, 134, 156, 162–63; *Sonnets*, 4, 15, 44, 121; *Titus Andronicus*, 6, 20–22, 24, 26, 30, 33–34, 42, 52, 53, 67, 70, 72, 80, 82, 85, 92, 103, 105–6, 115, 118–20, 125, 131–34, 137, 140, 148, 168, 171, 172, 173, 189, 190–91, 192, 195; *Henry V*, 27, 37, 42, 43, 47, 67, 84, 119, 123, 161–62; *Troilus and Cressida*, 28, 30, 42, 138–39; *Love's Labor's Lost*, 28, 36, 108, 115; *King Lear*, 28, 81, 83, 136, 145; *Measure for Measure*, 28, 84, 108, 115; *Richard III*, 37, 143; *Tempest*, 39, 53, 84; *King John*, 44, 81, 119, 143, 162; "Rape of Lucrece," 52, 102, 119, 120, 162; *Twelfth Night*, 52, 119; *Richard II*, 54, 111, 143; *Timon of Athens*, 81, 163; *Merchant of Venice*, 85, 162; *Romeo and Juliet*, 89, 162; *Othello*, 92, 119, 120, 136, 138, 156, 162; *Comedy of Errors*, 111; *Henry IV, Part 1*, 117, 119, 156, 161–62; *Henry IV, Part 2*, 119, 135, 143, 161–62; *Henry VI, Part 2*, 131, 134–35, 156, 158–59; *Henry VI, Part 1*, 156

232 Index

Sharpe, J. A., 143
Shirley, James: *Humorous Courtier*, 191
Shoemaker, a Gentleman (W. Rowley), 6, 35, 53, 87, 110, 112, 118, 126, 131, 133, 134, 135, 168, 173, 174, 190
Sidney, Philip, 88, 123, 154
Simmons, J. L., 48
Simonds, Peggy Muñoz, 103
Simpson, Evelyn, 31, 43, 187, 188
Simpson, Percy, 31, 43, 187, 188
Sophocles, 16, 25, 41
Sophonisba (Marston and Dekker[?]), 33, 53, 93, 105, 106, 114, 133, 155
Spanuoli, Giovianni Battista, Mantuanus, 67
Sparta, 94, 139–40
Spencer, T. J. B., 1, 34, 45, 52, 79, 171, 172, 188
Spencer, Theodore, 191
Spenser, Edmund, 39, 40, 43, 48
Sprott, Samuel E., 191
Stanyhurst, Richard, 52
Stapfer, Paul, 31
Steiner, George, 122
Stoic *Constantia*, 2–3, 33, 39–40, 44, 65, 71–72, 101, 89–92, 192 (n. 4); self-mastery in, 65, 73–74; self-hollowing in, 65, 139–40. *See also* Suicide
Suetonius, 5, 38, 49, 109, 116, 149, 195
Sugden, Edward H., 191
Suicide: ambivalent displays of, 34, 44, 87–99, 192 (n. 5)
Sulla, 5, 28, 82, 129, 131–32, 134, 157, 158, 169
Superbia, 41, 66, 108–24; sullying consumption in, 49, 71; overness and royal/superhuman aspiration in, 70–83 passim, 108–24, 151, 192 (nn. 1, 2, 3). *See also* Faction/civil war; Triumph
Symbolism, 2–3, 153; totemic horse, 3, 101–3, 153; totemic eagle, 3, 109–12, 153, 189 (n. 1); totemic wolf/canine, 3, 130–39, 153, 193 (n. 1), 194 (n. 2); majestic city, statues, buildings, 32, 68–70; staging, 32, 69–70, 74–78, 80, 89–99, 112, 114, 189–90, (nn. 1,

2); scarlet (blood-red/purple) and gold, 74–78; hard, cold objects vs. (Stoic) fire, 89–90, 99–101, 102–7; bestiary, 130, 132, 144–47, 195; bowel-piercing and intestine strife, 144–50

Tacitus, 4, 22, 47, 171
Tamburlaine (Marlowe), 38, 70, 74, 109, 115, 118, 156–57, 162
Tarquins (Sextus and/or Superbus), 33, 35, 52, 102, 120, 126, 129, 135, 161, 166, 190
Tate, Nahum, 191
Taylor, Michael, 188
Tempest (Shakespeare), 39, 53, 84
Tertullian, 43
Tervarent, Guy de, 100, 102, 112, 137, 188
Theatrical records: Sir Henry Herbert's censorship, 59; Bereblock Diary, 69; Henslowe's Diary, 69; Revels Accounts for 1581, 69; Admiral's Company, 69, 70, 78, 189; King's Men/Lord Chamberlain's Men, 70, 78, 189–90; Beeston's Boys, 78; Queen's Chapel, Children of the, 78; Magdalen College/Hall at Oxford, 78, 190; Red Bull Theater, 78, 190; Little Missenden mural, 122; Trinity College at Oxford, 189; Queen's Revels, 190
Thomas, William, 65–66, 162
Thompson, J. A. K., 188
Thyestes (Seneca), 17, 22, 161, 189
Tiberius, 14, 17, 26, 50, 93, 99, 123, 127, 168
Tiberius, 80, 110, 123, 134–35, 168, 191, 194, 195
Timon of Athens (Shakespeare), 81, 163, 172
Titus Andronicus (Shakespeare), 6, 20–22, 24, 26, 30, 33–34, 42, 52, 53, 67, 70, 72, 80, 82, 85, 92, 103, 105–6, 115, 118–20, 125, 131–34, 137, 140, 148, 168, 171, 172, 173, 189, 190–91, 192, 195
Tixier, Jean/Textor Ravisius, 67, 91
Townshend, Aurelian, 114
Traversi, Derek, 187, 188
Tricomi, Albert H., 159, 187

Triumph, 3, 54–56, 65, 110–21, 192 (nn. 1, 2, 3)
Troilus and Cressida (Shakespeare), 28, 30, 42, 138–39
Trompi, G. W., 15, 32
Tupper, Frederick, 52
Twelfth Night (Shakespeare), 52, 119
Two Noble Ladies, 53, 67, 87, 168, 173, 190

Ure, Peter, 61, 155

Valentinian (Fletcher), 5, 27, 32, 33–34, 53, 59
Valeriano. *See* Bolzani Valeriano, G.
Valerius Maximus, 131
Valiant Welshman (Armin), 5, 29, 43, 53, 55–58, 80, 110, 129, 169, 174, 189
Velz, John W., 31, 33, 68, 81, 128, 146, 187
Vergil, 16, 21, 46, 47, 48, 83, 88, 109–10, 130, 131, 136, 137, 145, 162, 192, 194
Vespasian, emperor of Rome, 12, 160, 167
Virgin Martyr (Dekker and Massinger), 53, 68, 78, 85, 93, 135, 168, 189, 190, 192, 195
Virtuous Octavia (Brandon), 71, 85, 93, 135, 167
Vives, Juan Luis, 132
Volpone (Jonson), 92

Waith, Eugene, 187
Walker, Roy, 105, 188
Webster, John, 163; *Appius and Virginia*, 23, 33, 51, 53, 76, 78, 80, 82, 85, 97, 125, 134–38, 155, 165, 189, 190, 193, 195; *Duchess of Malfi*, 50, 130, 172
Weinberger, Martin, 193
Whinney, Margaret, 100
Whitney, Geoffrey, 68, 77, 100
Whitworth, Charles W., 156
Whore of Babylon, 66, 77, 126
Wickham, Glynne, 187
Wikander, Matthew, 14, 26
Wilkinson, L. P., 131
William, Arnold, 17
Wilson, John Dover, 116
Wilson, Lillian, 77
Wilson Knight, George, 2, 100, 102, 119, 187, 188
Worthies Pageant (Coventry 1455), 18, 156
Wotton, Henry, 69
Wounds of Civil War (Lodge), 5–7, 26, 28–30, 33, 34, 41–42, 53, 54–56, 67, 70, 71, 73–75, 78, 80–82, 84, 92, 93, 96–97, 102–3, 104, 105, 109, 112, 114, 133, 137, 138, 145, 155, 161, 169, 172, 173, 189, 194
Wright, George T., 162
Wymer, Rowland, 88, 93, 191, 192

Yachnin, Paul, 187
Yoder, R. A., 188

Zeevold, W. Gordon, 51
Zonaras, Joannes, 131